NICHOLAS WRIGHT

Five Plays

introduced by the author

Treetops

One Fine Day

The Custom of the Country

The Desert Air

Mrs. Klein

NICK HERN BOOKS

London

www.nickhernbooks.co.uk

A Nick Hern Book

Wright: Five Plays first published in Great Britain in 2000
as a paperback original by Nick Hern Books Limited,
14 Larden Road, London W3 7ST.

This collection copyright © 2000 Nicholas Wright
Treetops copyright © 2000 by Nicholas Wright
One Fine Day copyright © 2000 by Nicholas Wright
The Custom of the Country copyright © 1983, 2000 by Nicholas Wright
The Desert Air copyright © 1984, 2000 by Nicholas Wright
Mrs. Klein copyright © 1988, 2000 by Nicholas Wright

Introduction to *Wright: Five Plays* copyright © 2000 by Nicholas Wright

The Custom of the Country and *The Desert Air* are published
by arrangement with Methuen Publishing Ltd

Nicholas Wright has asserted his rights to be identified as
author of this work

Front cover photo: Nicholas Wright by James Hunkin
Typeset by Country Setting, Kingsdown, Kent CT14 8ES
Printed and bound in Great Britain by Athenaeum Press Limited,
Gateshead, Tyne and Wear

A CIP catalogue record for this book is available from
the British Library

ISBN 1 85459 473 7

NICHOLAS WRIGHT

Nicholas Wright trained as an actor. He joined the Royal
Court Theatre as Casting Director and became the first
Director of the Royal Court's Theatre Upstairs, where he
presented an influential programme of new and first-time
writing. From 1975 to 1977 he was joint Artistic Director of
the Royal Court. He joined the Royal National Theatre in
1984 as Literary Manager, and was an Associate Director
of the National until 1998.

His plays include *Treetops* and *One Fine Day* (Riverside
Studios), *The Gorky Brigade* (Royal Court), *The Crimes of
Vautrin* (Joint Stock), *The Custom of the Country* and *The
Desert Air* (both Royal Shakespeare Company), *Mrs. Klein*
(Royal National Theatre) and *Cressida* (Almeida Theatre at
the Albery).

His version of Ibsen's *John Gabriel Borkman* was produced
at the National Theatre in 1996 and his version of Pirandello's
Naked was presented in 1998 at the Almeida Theatre.

His screenplays include adaptations of novels by Patrick
Hamilton, Doris Lessing, Josef Skvorecky and Ford Madox
Ford. In 1998 he received an Emmy nomination for
'Outstanding Writing for a Miniseries or Movie' for his
screenplay of Armistead Maupin's *More Tales of the City*.

His writing about the theatre includes *Ninety-Nine Plays*,
a personal view of playwriting from Aeschylus to the present
day (1992), and *The Art of the Play*, a week-by-week introduction to dramaturgy which appeared in the *Independent
on Sunday* in 1993–1994.

Other titles in this series

Contents

Introduction

I wrote my first play in order to prove that I was interesting
enough to be given a job at the Royal Court. The scheme paid
off, and I worked there for the next ten years, first as Casting
Director, then running the Theatre Upstairs and finally as co-
Artistic Director.

When I wrote my second play, *Treetops*, I'd just left the Court.
I was 37, out of a job and without the faintest idea of what to
do with my life. Writing was what was left: it was the tin of
sardines at the back of the larder.

Everything I knew about writing plays till then came from my
experience as a director and producer, so I knew both quite a
lot and nothing at all. Writing *Treetops* was my first experience
of the eerie, tickling sensation which occurs when a sleeping
part of the brain is teased awake by the act of writing. Most
dramatic was the stirring of sense-memory: the weight of my
heavy old Hercules bike, the sound of bugles, the smell of
grass on a hot day, the clever, assertive voices of my father's
political friends. So writing the play was more than just an
achievement at a time when I badly needed one: it was a
greeting to a part of my life which I'd tried to forget about.

I had left the country of my birth, South Africa, almost twenty
years before, since when I'd seldom thought about it. These
were the apartheid years, so it never crossed my mind to
wonder why I had cut myself off so completely. There were
sound political reasons, and no further explanation seemed
required. The truth was that my political revulsion – real
though it was – was masking my need to escape.

I was born in Cape Town in 1940 – just after the fall of France,
my mother was fond of saying. My father was away in the
Army. His stand-in at home was his mother-in-law, my
grandmother, a proud and forceful figure. In the morning she
went off to work as a book-keeper for the Old Mutual Life

Insurance Society; in the evenings, she taught me to read with the aid of Smarties and Scrabble letters. My two brothers, twelve and thirteen years older than me, had a dashing but seldom-seen existence, sometimes glimpsed while passing milk-bars, poised over their bicycles and chatting up girls. Aged sixteen, the elder then joined the Navy, not to be seen again till the end of the war, when his sailor-hat and curiously-creased white trousers ('the Seven Seas') made a lasting impression. My mother sang at amateur concerts, went to parties and looked after me.

This existence was unimprovable as far as I could see. There was clearly no need for an extra male, and it never occurred to me that the father I heard so much about had any more solid existence than the photograph on the mantelpiece which I used to kiss before going to bed. So his arrival at the end of the War, when I was five, was a lasting shock.

Even when waiting with my mother at Cape Town station, I still hadn't quite worked out that the father we were there to meet was someone with whom I had any prior connection. So when the train arrived, it presented a bewildering choice, being full of potential fathers, all in khaki and leaning cheerfully out of the windows. Other mothers and children began to collect them at alarming speed. It reminded me of a Church Jumble Sale which my mother had helped arrange, when a crowd of Coloured and Black domestic servants had rushed in the moment the doors were opened and stripped the stalls in seconds.

My worry was that exactly the same thing seemed to be happening here. No sooner would I see some suitable candidate than a perfectly strange woman would swoop on him and carry him off. My mother, meanwhile, seemed paralysed by indecision, walking anxiously up and down the length of the train, peering first at one window, then at another, then shaking her head and moving on to another carriage. It was like those interminable waitings-around in shops while she tried on first one pair of gloves and then another, then the first again. But dithering over a pair of gloves now seemed a minor crime compared with taking so long to choose my father that all the best ones got taken.

I thought the father we finally ended up with was more or less what you would expect under the circumstances. This was nothing compared with my feelings when he appeared the following morning, clearly having spent the night in the house and wearing a suit. The difference between soldiers and men in suits was something I knew all about. Soldiers came for tea and went back to England. Men in suits hung around: you met them in their shops or at church, week after week: they were indelible. I'm not on the whole very good at speaking my mind, but this was an emergency. 'Either that man goes, or I go,' I announced at breakfast: the start of a long campaign.

I fought my Oedipal war in a house like Rusty's 'Treetops': single-storied, tin-roofed, striking when I see it now for its gloom and pokiness. Cape Town was then both an English colonial outpost and a Coloured city. White Afrikaans was seldom heard, and black South Africans were few compared to the unique community which suffused the life around us. 'Coloured' seems an awkward, patronising word; during the apartheid years, people who spoke it would do little rabbits-ears quotation-marks in the air to add a note of irony. But the word has stuck for the simple reason that nothing better has replaced it. It describes a community made up of pure-bred Malays, able to trace their genealogies back to the seventeenth century; descendants of the Hottentots who lived in the Cape before either black or white arrived; and people of mixed race, all united by marriage, language, cuisine, culture and (when speaking English) an Afrikaans/Indonesian accent found, for obvious reasons, nowhere else.

Aesthetically, Cape Town was spun around the mountain: that vast, gorgeous, ever-changing hulk, sometimes bleached, sometimes mauve, often iced with cloud. The mountain defined everything: the weather, what school you went to, the social meaning of where you lived. But the soul of the city was Coloured. It was a Malay call to prayer which filled the evening skies from the tops of the minarets; it was Malay funerals which stopped the heart as they walked through the streets bearing a coffin; there was nothing so delicious as Malay food, nothing so sensational as Malay magic: the haunted houses, the poltergeists, the amazing rituals with flashing swords, walking-on-fire and knives stuck into eyeballs. It was a Coloured fish-cart which clop-clopped down the road, the driver wearing a woven conical hat and blowing a trumpet; a Coloured janitor at school who gave up his time to talk to you about world affairs with a gravity which nobody else seemed capable of; a Coloured tailor who made your first suit with the air of a Nobel prize-winner called upon to solve some small arithmetical problem, a bevy of Coloured moffies – ethnic drag artistes, you'd call them now – sashaying down the Main Road, loudly hailing each other as Alice (Faye) and Dorothy (Lamour), who first suggested a world of sexual adventure. Cape Town, like all old sea-ports, has a long transvestite tradition.

Things changed fast after 1948 when the Nationalist government was voted into power. Soon the visible signs appeared. The rattle-trap train which crosses the Peninsula was 'segregated': a new and ominous word. Petty apartheid grew: park benches, bus shelters, railway waiting rooms. Then Coloured people were expunged from the electoral roll. In the 1960s, they would be expelled from the city, to be dumped on the windswept plains inland.

The job which had been patriotically kept open for my father during the War turned out not in fact to exist, so he became a commercial traveller, a job for which he was completely un-suited on account of his shyness. But he plugged on, carting his suitcase of samples from shop to shop, meanwhile working within the Trade Union movement to protect liberal values. He was, as even I could see, a man of complete integrity, constitu-tionally incapable of judging anyone on the basis of class or colour.

Treetops is set in 1952, by which time the Cold War had given legitimacy to the persecution of Communists: a useful policy in South Africa, where hardline Communists were the spearhead of the opposition. Once the Party had gone under cover, it looked around for support among liberal organisations. Writing the play, I remembered how my father was wooed to give his energies to the cause.

South African Communism was very much old-style: inextric-ably linked with Moscow thinking and obsessed with theory.

My father must have worked this out for himself, because his brush with the Communist movement didn't last long. What's odd is that he put it behind him so quickly, while for me the attraction of these clever, brave, rash, working-class intellectuals – often commercial travellers, like my father – has never faded.

'I hope you don't marry a Jewish girl,' my mother would say, 'because then your children might be persecuted and put into concentration camps.' Nearly all of the leading white South African politicos were Jewish – characteristically, Jewish refugees from Lithuania – and they struck me as the feistiest, brightest people to be. So Jewish girls would have been a very considerable attraction, were I that way inclined. Jewish boys were more to the point. A crucial moment was the marriage of Arthur Miller and Marilyn Monroe: a comical misalliance between an undesirable person and a sexy one, or so it said in the papers. Seeing the photos, I felt the same, only the other way round: what did he *see* in her?

Father, apartheid, heterosexuality: everything around me seemed worthy only of rejection. Thus grew my megalomaniacal conceit. In defiance, I became a trousered moffie. I grew my hair, I played sports so badly that no team would have me, I wrote essays in green ink. At school, I minced about the playground challenging other boys to throw rocks at me, which they happily did. I refused to learn that beautiful language, Afrikaans, and hated rugby, which was the only thing my school was notable for.

That's my *Treetops* kit. For many years the play was, at least in memory, my favourite thing of anything I'd written. But I remembered it as sweet and pastoral. Now it seems darker and more neurotic. Rupert, my younger self, seems totally mad, which perhaps is what I was.

Treetops was produced at Riverside Studios, then a thriving Arts Centre run by an old friend from my days at the Royal Court, Peter Gill; another Royal Court colleague, John Burgess, directed it. It was the first play to come out of my love-on-the-rebound affair with Africa.

Re-reading the next one, *One Fine Day*, reminded me how important politics used to be to younger playwrights, myself included. Steve's hopes of finding the Revolution alive and well in a place remote from Britain are very much of the late 1970's, when the revolutionary fantasies of 1968 had collapsed. I wanted to treat the sad reality in a cheerful way, and the result was a village comedy, hopefully like the rough, tough, sceptical improvisations I'd seen young Tanzanian actors perform when I was travelling through their country, courtesy of the British Council. Again, John Burgess directed and the designer, Alison Chitty, made something witty and beautiful out of my rather challenging stage-directions.

I wrote *The Custom of the Country* while I was spending a year with David Lan, who was doing the fieldwork for his Social Anthropology doctorate in a remote village in the Zambesi Valley. He and I had met at the Royal Court, when I was running the Theatre Upstairs. The fact that he was a writer who came from Cape Town was just one of the things which drew us together, but not a trivial one. You'd expect to get used to a relationship which has coloured every moment of your life for over thirty years, but the opposite is the case. His influence on my writing is profound, and he appears in disguised form in several of the plays, not least as Lazarus, the patient partner of the unstable, bullying Daisy.

The play is based on a romantic comedy of the same name attributed to the seventeenth-century playwriting partnership, Beaumont and Fletcher. My starting-point was a description by the contemporary gossip, John Aubrey, of their household arrangements: they 'lived together . . . both batchelors; lay together; had one Wench in the house between them, which they did so admire; the same cloathes and cloake, etc. betweene them.'

It was my own circumstances which inspired me to follow up this earlier example of two male writers living on top of each other and, though the similarity soon broke down, I quickly became fascinated by the sweep and sensationalism of seventeenth-century romantic comedy. Beaumont and Fletcher's *Custom of the Country* was one of the strangest examples, with its outrageous coincidences, snap-infatuations, sudden deaths and iconographic trio of heroines (matriarch/virgin/courtesan) straight out of a Renaissance allegorical painting. It's nominally set in Lisbon, partly I suppose because they thought of it as a bustling hive of louche behaviour. But also, Lisbon was the port from which new continents were explored and vanquished. Colonialism, I realised, was the great unacknowledged seventeenth-century theme.

Johannesburg in 1890 seemed as exact an equivalent as anyone could find of a seventeenth-century melting pot: a hectic, jerrybuilt, gold-rush town where fortunes could be made overnight, characters could disappear or change identity and chance had a hand in every encounter. 'Monomatapa' really existed, though as an ancient memory of Portuguese settlement rather than the Xanadu of Dr. Jameson's fevered imagination. Jameson existed too, of course, reviled to this day in South Africa for his hand in starting the Boer War.

The play was produced by the RSC, which then commissioned *The Desert Air*. Like the first three plays in this book, it's about the English abroad, and again it's set in Africa, sort of. Does Cairo count? The real connection lies in the fact that I found the story in a memoir of his years in the Special Operations Executive by the African historian Basil Davidson.

I wrote the play – basing it in a fictional way on Davidson's account – with a little sandalwood carving of an antelope on my work-table. My father had bought it in Cairo when he was stationed there during the war, and it was from Cairo that he sent, to the son he had never seen, air-letters filled with drawings of camels, pyramids, cockroaches. So I felt an affinity with the place. Why I was so drawn to Davidson's narrative I didn't know, or didn't want to know. This was the second time I'd worked from a found story, as opposed to a made-up one, and I was already forming a rule, which I've since stuck to, that you find out why you like it in the process of doing it. It seems to me now that I wanted to write about 'goodness', not as a hard-earned reward for daily effort, but as a state that anyone, however mad or awful, can blunder into.

I talked to a few old Secret Service hands while researching *The Desert Air*, and it amazed me how often they said they were telling me something they'd never told anyone before. More than forty years after the bitter and acrimonious episode on which the play is based, they judged it just about permissible to talk about it. Since I wrote the play, tongues have loosened, and Churchill's switch to support for the partisans is now even more controversial than it was at the time. Modern right-wing historians see it as a classic act of betrayal, engineered by Communists in S.O.E. To others, it was a simple victory for commonsense.

None of this quite rules out the notion that a key role might have been played by a Brigadier seeking merely to make the notoriously difficult jump to Major-General. But I'm not insisting that this is what happened. The Hippo's stamping-ground is hearsay, and his story is viable rumour, part of the anecdotal theatre which, in wartime, takes the place of fact. It was Enoch Powell, who had worked in Cairo for the original Hippo, who gave me this theme. 'Do you know what it's like,' he said, 'when you think you know something, and then you realise that it's only something somebody told you? And when you're not even sure it was that?'

The Desert Air opened at The Other Place in Stratford-on-Avon in the depths of winter. The architecture of the theatre was so contrived that the actors had to make a lot of their entrances directly from out-of-doors, which led to the interesting sight of sweating, sunburned men in khaki with snowflakes on their shoulders. The production then moved to London where, on the final night, I sat watching an early scene (now cut) between the Hippo and Carp. Geoffrey Hutchings and Gary Oldman, who had taken over the part of Carp in London, were playing it as beautifully as could be imagined. But I knew that no sooner would these two characters establish themselves in the audience's interest, than they'd be whisked off-stage and a new lot of actors would start the upward climb. The Hippo, of course, would return, and he would have scope aplenty. But Carp's appearances would be few, and if he ever achieved the illusion of depth it would be thanks to Gary Oldman, not me. It suddenly seemed incredibly wasteful to create a whole character and then not make the most of him or her. What would happen, I wondered, if the scenes were longer, so that a character who arrived, then stayed? What if I kept the outer story very simple, but made the characters' inner lives as packed and detailed as I could?

This led me to read about psycho-analysis, the science, so-called, of inner lives. I knew almost nothing about it, nor had I undergone it. Peter Gill and I used to play a game in which we analysed mundane events at ludicrous length in spoof Viennese accents, and that was about the size of it. Reading a review of Phyllis Grosskurth's biography of the great psycho-analyst Melanie Klein gave me the kernel of a story, but it was at least a year before I started work, in a tentative way, by meeting some of Klein's disciples and reading her books.

Klein's theories are intricate, but what they're based on is very straightforward: it's her recognition of the inner violence of infancy and childhood. Key to her thinking is the phenomenon of projection: the way in which we shoot our hatred and fury on to the figure closest to us, only to have it come cannoning back in distorted or amplified form. It's in the fusillade of emotions and counter-emotions whizzing to and fro between the infant and the mother that the pattern is formed for emotional life in adulthood.

I read, made notes and thought about all this, and soon began to have terrible nightmares. What I had done, without really meaning to, was embark on a process of amateur self-analysis. This wasn't, for psycho-analysts of Klein's generation, a particularly bad thing to do: there weren't that many first-generation analysts around in those days, so a spot of D.I.Y. now and then was unavoidable. But it was hard. I had adored my mother, given her up with uttermost resentment and then abandoned her in petulant fury. Now in my dreams she came knocking at my door. Once again I saw her lost prettiness, her rare but devastating rages – amazing in somebody barely five foot tall – and her vivacious energy, like the energy of a rather brilliant actress never off-stage. I heard her sweet soprano singing voice, long silenced by the death of my father. My grandmother stood beside her, as firm a moral force as ever. My father never appeared.

Psycho-analysis, as its enemies often point out, is a closed system: objections are treated as though they came from within, which makes them easier to absorb and neutralise. Writing the play, it made sense to set it inside the theatre's own closed system: the form of Aristotle where unities of time and place are either observed or perceived to be observed. This led me to make the play a naturalistic one. At its core, for me, was Paula's journey from near-stranger to surrogate daughter: her slow invasion of Mrs. Klein's drawing-room mirrored my own.

The play was produced at the National Theatre, in a beautifully crisp and suave production by Peter Gill, and it was subsequently done all over the world. In Latin-American countries it went down a storm. Off-Broadway, it was illumined by the marvellous Uta Hagen. I had high hopes of Germany, but the translator's decision to direct the play herself, perform the title role and cast her own daughter as the rivalrous Melitta was perhaps stretching it.

By now, my life had changed. I'd taken a job at the National, first promoting new writing there and later, when Richard Eyre took over, advising on the programme overall. I was pushing, arguing, listening and debating about just what it was that we ought to be doing. I loved the work and I was proud of what we achieved. Besides, I passionately believe in a National Theatre: I believe, as some doctors do about the National Health Service, that part of the nation would die if we didn't have it.

But looking at plays from the outside isn't the same as writing them yourself. It doesn't even help you do so. It's a sensible, objective process. Plays go deeper. Ten years passed, during which time I wrote all kinds of other things: books, articles about the theatre, adaptations. But I didn't write an original play. And then I left the National. And then I did: *Cressida* is due to open in the Spring of 2000.

For this collection, I've revised the first four plays. Except in the case of *Treetops*, my main aim was to make each play more like I remembered it. A lesser aim was concerned with moments which I never thought worked in performance and where I knew the fault was mine. Here I tried to make the play *less* like I remembered it.

Nicholas Wright

TREETOPS

Treetops was first presented at Riverside Studios on 15 June 1978. The cast, in order of appearance, was:

RUSTY	Bill Paterson
LEO	John Bluthal
EDITH	Gillian Barge
RUPERT	Joff Wild
MARK	David Sassieni
ANNIE	Judith Harte
MAY	Lila Kaye
MRS. MATLALA	Jumoke Debayo

Director   John Burgess
Designer   Pamela Howard
Lighting Designer   Andy Phillips

Characters

RUSTY
EDITH
LEO
MAY
RUPERT
MARK
ANNIE
MRS. MATLALA

The play is set in Cape Town in 1952.

*Rupert and Mark are thirteen. All the others are in their late
thirties or early forties, except for Annie who is fifty-five.*

*Rusty and Edith are from England, Leo and May from
Lithuania. All the others are South African. Annie is Cape
Coloured and Mrs. Matlala is black.*

ACT ONE

Scene One

Debris of a meeting. A baize-covered table and chairs at the end of a hall. Above, a banner: GOD SAVE THE QUEEN, the word QUEEN stuck over another. To each side, cardboard cut-out torches shaped like ice-cream cones.

RUSTY is up a ladder untying one end of the banner. LEO comes in with two bottles of Castle lager, one already opened.

LEO. Quite a party in the Red Lion.

RUSTY. Meeting adjourned to catch last orders.

LEO. I can believe it.

RUSTY. First sensible decision all night.

LEO. I believe that too.

RUSTY. I thought I'd stay and clear up a bit, if you're not too pushed, that is.

LEO. No rush. My son's asleep in the car. I brought you a beer if that's of interest. You coming down?

RUSTY. In a minute.

LEO sits on the edge of the platform. Opens the bottle with the opener on his pen-knife.

LEO. I had an uncle who used to open bottles with his teeth.

RUSTY fiddles with a knot. LEO drinks, looks around, then up at the QUEEN sign.

'The Day the King Died.' You remember that? Some so-called comic monologue. By . . . no I forget.

He's looking at a sheaf of paper next to him.

This your speech?

RUSTY. Take a look if you like.

LEO (*reads*). 'We ex-servicemen see South Africa threatened
    by all the things we fought against and losing the freedom
    for which our comrades died.' Terrific.

RUSTY. Thanks.

LEO. Nothing like a rousing passage of hard-hitting waffle.

RUSTY. Come on, Leo.

LEO. Address these words to a sea of snow-white faces, it is
    waffle, Rusty, pure and simple. Were there any dusky,
    brown or beige ex-servicemen here tonight?

RUSTY. They've all resigned.

LEO. What about blacks? They fought too in the war.

RUSTY. Yes of course they ought to be here. That's what I said
    in my speech. Read to the end.

LEO. I have. I glanced at it. I'm looking.

He skims on.

Mm hm.

Skims over the page.

Oh yes, you spoke up nicely. May I ask, with what result?

RUSTY *starts coming down the ladder, carrying the loose
end with him.*

RUSTY. Not much.

LEO. Exactly. I'm sorry, Rusty, you can start a movement with
    the best intentions, but if there's no class basis, no correct
    analysis, pfft, forget it, don't get me on my hobby-horse.

RUSTY. What should I do?

LEO. When did you last listen to my advice? Forget it, I'll give
    you some anyway. You're wasting your time with these
    shits. They don't want your opinion. They want you to sit
    on the platform wearing your famous medals and snoring
    from time to show that you're still alive. You should resign.

No old boy rubbish, you get my meaning, nothing diplomatic. Send them a telegram, nice and short, state your case, it'll do them good. Your beer's getting cold.

He gives RUSTY *the beer.*

Cheers.

RUSTY. Cheers.

RUSTY sits. They drink. RUSTY lights a cigarette.

They'd be a decent bunch back home. They would. They'd be the normal sort of Englishman you'd meet in a pub. Or play a round of golf with. Something seems to alter people when they come to another country.

LEO. Travel rots the mind.

A voice is heard calling 'Oo – oo!'

Was that a ghost?

RUSTY. It's Edith.

He hands LEO *his bottle of beer.* EDITH *comes in. To* RUSTY*:*

EDITH. I knew it was you the moment I saw the light on. Hello, Leo. I've made up a bed for Mark.

RUSTY. Where's he sleeping?

EDITH. Rupert's room. Mark can have the bottom bunk and Rupy on top for once.

RUSTY. He'll fall out. Break his neck.

EDITH. Rusty, not even in fun. Oh I am glad I caught you. Are we going now?

RUSTY. I thought I'd better clear up.

EDITH. Don't do that. Leave it for the janitor, he'll know the proper place for everything.

She goes out.

LEO. Have I told you Mark's definition of a pullover? It's something he has to put on when his mother feels cold.

Pause.

Edith's a good woman. Pretty in her way. May likes her too.

RUSTY (*irritated*). All right.

EDITH *is heard calling 'Oo-oo!'* RUSTY *finishes his beer.*

Thanks for the advice. About resigning. I don't think I'll take it, though. Don't feel I can rock the boat.

As they go:

We're taking the boys to the beach tomorrow. Did I tell you that?

End of scene.

Scene Two

RUSTY*'s car.* RUSTY *is driving,* MARK *is beside him.* ANNIE *the maid is in the back on the left,* RUPERT *on the right. All are singing:*

> 'We're off to see the wizard,
> The wonderful wizard of Oz,
> We hear he is a wiz of a wiz
> If ever a wiz there was . . . ' etc.

MARK. Which route, Mr. Walker?

RUSTY. Main Road.

RUPERT. That's the long way, that's the long way. Can't we go past Spotty Dog?

MARK. Ag, that's to hell and gone out of the way. Pardon my French, Mr. Walker. What I mean is, my dad takes the Main Road too, unless the traffic's heavy or we want to stop by Spotty Dog for a cool drink.

They drive on. RUPERT *is still singing 'off to see the wizard,' etc.*

RUSTY. Rupy, don't you know another song?

ANNIE. The young master's giving me a migraine in my ear with his doleful chant.

RUSTY. Now, when we get to the Indian shop I'm going to turn left, and I want you to stick your hand out, Mark, because the indicator's not a hundred-per-cent reliable.

RUPERT. I'll do it, I'll do it.

He climbs over ANNIE.

ANNIE. Mind yourself hey.

RUPERT. Annie thinks I'm getting fresh, ha ha ha!

RUSTY. What's going on back there?

ANNIE. I nearly spilled the cool drink. Shame on you, Master Rupert, and on such a sad day. Can't you think for one minute who's given you a long weekend so's you can go for a swim?

RUSTY. Tell the boys how you saw the King in '47.

MARK. Did you really, Annie?

ANNIE. Yes, master Mark. My brother took me up to Stuttaford's corner so's we could stand and cheer.

RUPERT. Was he in a coach or in a car?

ANNIE. He was very dignified, quite small and his face was pinkish.

RUPERT. Unlike *some* people I could mention.

RUSTY. Rupert, if it wasn't for Annie and our guest I would stop and drive straight back. Now will you act your age or do I have to drop you off at the bus-stop? Go on, Annie.

ANNIE. Well on his right was his madam the Queen Elizabeth dressed all in light blue with a big ostrich-feather hat, and sitting behind was the two young madams. The oldest girl was smiling nicely, but young Princess Margaret Rose looked very cross, and later when they's being given a bunch of flowers each, she frowns and says 'Sies, there's some sticky stuff on these flowers, now I must wash my frock.' Then the King turns round and says, 'Now you've really had your chips, when we get home you will go straight to bed and have nothing to eat but Weetabix with no milk or sugar till the end of the week.'

RUSTY. Ready, Mark?

MARK *puts his hand out.*

That's right.

They turn left. A car passes close.

Damn fool.

ANNIE. May I ask, master, what's to become of the old madam now that the King's passed on?

MARK. She'll get a pension and a palace to live in and all the peasants in the cottages for miles around will have to work to support her.

ANNIE. Shame, Master Mark, who'd begrudge her a home for the rest of her days?

RUPERT. Rather slave away for her than our rotten lot.

RUSTY. To be fair, Mark, she has her position to keep up. Your father and I might not see eye to eye on this.

RUPERT. Well three cheers to King George the Sixth for dying and giving us all the day off. Hip hip. Come on Mark.

MARK. Well since it's only thanks for the holiday.

RUPERT. Hip hip –

ALL. Hooray!

RUPERT. Hip hip –

ALL. Hooray!

RUPERT. Hip hip –

ALL. Hooray!

All sing: 'Why was he born so beautiful, why was he born at all?', etc.

RUPERT. Hey, look what's coming up now!

MARK. Groote Schuur!

RUPERT. Know what that is, Annie? Where the Prime
Minister hangs out.

*Both boys blow raspberries at the Prime Minister's
mansion.*

RUSTY. Drop it, boys, shall we? Let's talk about something
we understand.

MARK. Sorry Mr. Walker.

RUPERT *makes quiet slurping noises by way of comment
on* MARK's *politeness. They drive on.*

ANNIE (*sings*).
'Mona Lisa, Mona Lisa, men have named you,
You're so like that lady with the mystic smile,' etc.

RUSTY. Maybe we can take in Spotty Dog after all.

RUPERT. Yay yay! I bags a milk-shake.

RUSTY. Guests first. What'll you have, Mark?

MARK. I like Seven-Up, Mr. Walker, if that's agreeable. My
mom said I was to use my own money though.

RUSTY. Well we'll see. Let's say the first one can be on the
house. And it's next on the left.

MARK. Can I do the gear-stick, Mr. Walker?

RUSTY. Have you driven a Packard, Mark?

MARK. Oh sure. My ambition is when I'm fourteen to be
able to drive fourteen different makes of car. Right now
I can drive seven, that's a Morris Minor, a Chevvie, a
Studie, an Austin 7, a Volksy, a Packard and my uncle's
red MG.

RUSTY. Clutch down.

MARK *does the gear.*

Well done.

RUPERT *sings. The others join in:*

'Cape Town, that is the place for me,
Cape Town, beside the sea.
Kimberley is very nice, you know,
Jo'burg is pretty, and so is Durban City,
But it's Cape Town, that is the place for me,
Its sunny climate suits me to a T,
Bloemfontein and Mafeking
Are just as nice as anything,
But Cape Town's the place for me!'

End of scene.

Scene Three

ANNIE *looks out over the sea. She wears her green overall and has put on wellington boots and an oilskin hat and carries a basket and a fishing-rod.*

ANNIE. Here's a good place to stop and bait my hook.

She sits cross-legged, rod based on the ground behind her and over her shoulder so that the hook hangs down in front.

Some eyes will pop to see this sight. Nobody's seen a coloured woman fishing before, not in this part of the world. Stay at home to gut and bone the monsters, now that's another matter.

My father's boat was his own. He left it to his oldest son, but the boy turned his nose up at it. You fool, I said, the sea's good for coloured people. Long before those black heathens arrived, our grandmas were picking shells off the beach and making hay with the Boers off their wooden ships.

She looks at the sand.

There's the deep funnels the boats made this morning. There's two . . . let's see . . . three, four, five. Where've they got to?

She looks.

Oh ja. Far's the eye can see, two yellow sails. That's the life, hey? Sit in the sun with your hand on a net, tell rude jokes and pass the bottle round. Live your life away, boys. Two more years, so make the most of it. Some cold morning not too far away, there'll be a boot through your door and a form too quick to read flashed in your face. You won't look so big then! Explain to your kids why they're being piled along with the three-piece suite into the government truck. Explain to your granny how times have changed. She wore a short dress when she first saw the boats ride out. Now they're waving her good-bye.

She has baited her hook.

All present and correct. I'll climb up those steep rocks and try my luck. Maybe on my way back I'll pay a call on those crayfish pots.

She walks off to the right. We're on the beach. The sun is high. MARK *comes on left, wet from swimming. He sits and leans his head back, panting. We see* RUSTY *lying asleep, wearing only a pair of baggy green swimming-shorts.*

ANNIE (*out of sight*). Hey there master Rupert.

RUPERT (*out of sight*). Crikey what a sight!

ANNIE (*out of sight*). You're not so brilliant either, master.

MARK (*to himself*). I'm a physical wreck.

He puts his head between his knees. RUPERT *comes on. He wears a hat, a shirt, a towel round his neck, long shorts, socks pulled up to meet them, sandals, a hankie under his hat hanging down the back of his neck and a tie holding up his pants. He carries a book. He looks at* MARK.

RUPERT. Count to a hundred.

MARK. What for? If you're passing out, you want to get your breath *back*, not waste it counting to a stupid hundred, that's the last thing you want.

RUPERT. Oh yes that's hiccups.

MARK. You're a fool, you know that?

RUPERT. I love to faint.

He turns away from MARK, jumps up and down flapping his straight arms up and down at his side.

MARK. What's going on now?

RUPERT. Physical jerks.

MARK. Well stop it, you're making my head spin. My God, I could have gone rock-climbing. There's a whole team of boys going up today with old whatsy.

RUPERT. Yes and get your bum pinched in the forester's hut.

MARK. What you dressed up like that for?

RUPERT. I burn easily. You know I burn easily. It's because of my red hair.

MARK. People with red hair burn easily?

RUPERT. Yup.

MARK. Everyone with red hair?

RUPERT. Yup.

MARK. You'd better tell your old man then.

RUPERT. Why?

MARK. Take a look.

They look at RUSTY.

Out for the count.

RUPERT. Last year he went to a cricket match and the next day all the skin peeled off the front of his face like tissue-paper. He was delirious, too.

MARK. Hadn't you better wake him?

RUPERT. S'pose I should.

Pause.

Do you want me to read to you?

MARK. What you reading?

RUPERT. Poetry.

MARK. I can see that, who's it by?

RUPERT *hands him the book.* MARK *looks at it.*

There must be one million wonderful poets. You could read
Shelley or Byron. If you prefer modern poems, you could
read T. S. Eliot or W. H. Auden. There's even South African
poets you could read. But no, it must be Algernon
Swinburne. You're really under the impression you're
something special. Wake your dad.

RUPERT. He's all right now. Look, it's cloudy. What you
doing this weekend?

MARK. Mucking about I reckon.

RUPERT. Can you stay on at my place?

MARK. I already asked but they said no they want me home
Friday night as usual, then Saturday morning I must go to
shul.

RUPERT. You can bunk shul, you always used to bunk shul.

MARK. Not any more.

RUPERT. Why not?

MARK. Because I'm studying for my barmitzvah, that's why.

RUPERT. Will you get a lot of money?

MARK. Just because we're Jews doesn't mean we're rich. I
might get a couple of hundred maybe.

RUPERT. What'll you do with it?

MARK. It has to go into the Post Office till I go to Varsity.

RUPERT. My brain will be worn out by the time I'm
seventeen.

MARK. You're fairly brainy.

RUPERT. No, you're the brainy one round here. I have to make up for it by being artistic.

MARK. You don't *do* anything artistic. You just look artistic and talk lah-di-dah. I don't know why you go round making such an arse of yourself. It's me has to stick up for you.

RUPERT. I can't help it. I'm not doing it on purpose. I don't even like it particularly. It's what I'm stuck with.

MARK. Sit. I've got something to tell you.

RUPERT *sits.*

RUPERT. Well?

MARK. Anyone can change what they are just by behaving differently. In Russia even criminals get reformed. They've even made a different kind of wheat in Russia, just by teaching it how to change. Scientists all over the world tried to prove it was impossible. But Dr. Lysenko stuck to his guns and they doubled the harvest.

Pause.

So what do you think?

The sun comes out. RUPERT *lies back on the sand.*

Hey?

RUPERT *answers lazily.*

RUPERT. You really think the sun shines out of Uncle Joe Stalin's arse. Don't you?

MARK *stretches out on the sand.*

MARK. Is it true what Murison says?

RUPERT. Don't know, do I?

MARK. He says last year he went round to your house to find you. And your mom came to the door and said 'He can't come out to play, he's washing his hair.' And she had her sleeves rolled up and her arms full of soap-suds. So Murison reckons she's washing your hair for you in the bath.

RUPERT. Hell no, what do you think.

MARK. Why don't you have a haircut?

RUPERT. Next term I'm doing a play.

MARK. You'll let it grow till next term? Hell, you're a braver
man than me. I'll tell you what.

RUPERT. What?

MARK. No, tell you what.

RUPERT. *What?*

MARK. What's the date today?

RUPERT. February the 7th.

MARK. In twenty-five years it'll be what?

RUPERT. February the 7th 1977. Oh, what about leap year?

MARK. It makes no difference. On that date, wherever I am,
Cape Town or Jo'burg or Pretoria or overseas even, I'll
come here. I'll come in the morning and wait all day. And
you come too. We'll meet and say 'Hello, old maat,' and
compare what's happened with our lives.

RUPERT. I'll see you before then.

MARK. If we're still maats we'll come here anyway. Have a
beer or a Pepsi or whatever we like to do. OK?

RUPERT. OK.

MARK. Let's shake on it then.

RUPERT. All right.

They shake hands.

Do you want to mix blood or anything?

MARK. I've got nothing to cut our arms with.

RUPERT *looks round vaguely.*

RUPERT. There might be a bit of glass or something.

MARK. Isn't it good enough just to shake?

RUPERT. Besides we might get lockjaw.

He holds his hand out.

All right, let's shake.

MARK. We just did.

RUPERT. Oh I forgot.

MARK. OK, let's shake again.

They shake hands. RUPERT *looks at* RUSTY.

You going for a dog-paddle?

RUPERT. After lunch.

MARK. That's the worst possible time to choose. Nine out of ten people who drown, it's because they've gone for a swim immediately after lunch. First they get cramp. And then they panic. And the next thing is, they've had their chips.

RUPERT *looks at* RUSTY.

RUPERT. Look out.

MARK. What?

RUPERT. I think he moved. No, false alarm. Let's go.

MARK. What about him?

RUPERT. You can't teach him anything. He'll just have to burn I'm afraid.

They go. RUSTY *lies where he is, in the sun.*

End of scene.

Scene Four

RUPERT's *bedroom: it's a separate cubicle in the back garden, built originally for a live-in maid.*

RUPERT *and* MARK *are sitting.* MARK *baleful,* RUPERT *reading with an air of insouciance.*

MARK. Now we've done it. Now we've *really* had our chips.

RUSTY. Shut up. I'm reading.

EDITH *bursts in with a tray on which are two glasses of milk and an apple. Also a bottle of white calamine lotion. Her manner is dangerously bright and highly-charged.*

EDITH. Here you are boys. Grub to fill you up. Not undressed yet? Chop chop.

They start getting into their pyjamas.

I'm cutting Mark's apple in half, Ru, so you can help yourself if he's not too hungry. I don't suppose, Mark, you've slept in a bunk before. Bounce, bounce.

RUPERT. Mark wants the top bunk, don't you Mark?

EDITH. Just as he likes. Do you have a bunk at home?

RUPERT. Ag ma, he just sleeps in a bed.

EDITH. That's enough, Ru, how would you know. Don't put your pie-jam top on, I'm going to do your back with calamine lotion.

RUPERT. I don't need it, honest, do I Mark?

MARK. He never went in the sun, not once.

EDITH. What a tale, what a tale. Let's have a look. Take that silly towel off.

She makes a grab at him. He dodges her.

What modesty in front of Mark. Mark doesn't mind, do you Mark? Sit down.

RUPERT. Oh all right.

He sits. EDITH *plasters his back with calamine lotion.*

EDITH. Dear oh dear what a fuss. (*To* MARK.) I don't suppose your mother does your back for you when you've been in the sun. You probably don't need it with your colouring.

RUPERT. It's cold.

EDITH. It's meant to be cold, it takes the sting away. You wouldn't believe, Mark, the times Ru has howled and screamed because the sunburn was stinging and I've had to go into his room in the middle of the night and cover him with lovely cool calamine lotion. Don't you like your milk? Would you like me to put an egg in it?

MARK. An *egg*?

EDITH. Didn't you know you could put an egg in milk? Ru loves an egg in his milk, don't you Ru?

RUPERT. Not any more, ma.

EDITH. You know what that's called, don't you Mark? It's called an egg flip. When it's cold in winter I break an egg into a glass of hot milk and swizzle it round and give it to Ru with his hottie. He's a real egg flip person. (*To* RUPERT.) Now your chest.

RUPERT *grabs the bottle.*

RUPERT. I'll do it myself, look.

EDITH *snatches it back.*

EDITH. Nonsense. What is it, Mark?

MARK. Can I go brush my teeth?

EDITH. Go *and* brush your teeth, yes of course you can go *and* brush your teeth, but I think you'll find Mr. Walker's still in the bath. Why don't you knock on the bathroom door, then he can get out of the bath and let you in, you're a big boy after all, just so long as it's only to brush your teeth.

RUPERT. Mark and me are going to brush our teeth together.

EDITH (*to* MARK). Do as I say and knock on the door, there's a good boy.

MARK *goes.*

See how keen Mark is to brush his teeth. That's why his teeth are so strong and white. Isn't it funny, he's a plain boy in other ways. Now leggies.

RUPERT. Leave it, ma.

EDITH. Will you stop it? Anyone would think I'd never seen your legs.

She throws him his pyjama jacket and he puts it on. Then he rolls his pyjama trousers up a little.

EDITH. Really, Ru, take them off.

RUPERT. I don't want to. Mark will be back in a minute.

EDITH. Heavens above, child, Mark won't mind your legs. Do you want me to get annoyed?

He takes off his pyjama trousers. She slaps lotion on his legs.

I'm sure Mark's mummy doesn't have to put lotion on his legs. Mark's mummy would probably have a great deal to say if he'd done what you did today.

RUPERT. I said I was sorry.

EDITH. Well we won't talk about it. Lucky you have a friend to stay. Mark, that was quick.

MARK *is standing in the doorway.*

You have to close your eyes, Ru doesn't want anyone to see his legs. Is Mr. Walker still in the bathroom?

MARK. Yes Mrs. Walker.

EDITH. Have you brushed your teeth?

MARK. Not exactly.

EDITH. Did you knock?

MARK. I didn't want to disturb him.

EDITH. Well go back and bang on the door.

MARK *goes.*

At least *you* don't have to be told everything twice. I don't think he's your kind of chum at all. You wouldn't have done it if you'd been on your own. Tell me you wouldn't. How did it happen?

RUPERT. We were sort of talking and Mark said let's go for a walk.

EDITH. Didn't you tell him you had to wake your father?

RUPERT. Yes I did.

EDITH. And then you wandered off and left him *roasting*. Never will I let you go to the beach again. Certainly not with that big lout Mark.

RUPERT. We'd still be stuck there if Mark hadn't driven us home.

EDITH. Not one more word about that! Not one. It makes me physically sick just to think about it. How you didn't all get killed in a car crash I cannot imagine. Don't wriggle!

RUPERT. Are you still angry?

EDITH. Angry, I'm *furious*. You don't think of a damn thing except yourself. I told you to keep an eye on him. I might have known you'd go sauntering off with your new friend. Stupid selfish pest. I could kill you.

RUPERT *cries.*

Oh what a dreadful thing to say. Don't cry. You silly silly fool.

She hugs him.

I'm finished now. Drink your milk.

She gets up.

RUPERT. Don't go.

EDITH. Don't tell me what to do and what not to do. I'm going to see what's happened to Mark.

RUPERT *pulls his trousers up and climbs into the bottom bunk, snuffling.*

Don't you say prayers any more?

RUPERT. I'll say them lying down.

EDITH. Of course you don't want Mark to see you. I suppose he doesn't say prayers at school?

RUPERT. He goes out with the other Jewish boys.

EDITH. Well, God won't mind if you miss a day. Drink your milk.

RUPERT. I can't.

EDITH. Heavens above, what's wrong with it?

RUPERT. I feel sick.

EDITH. Give it to me.

She takes the glass and throws it out of the window.

And just think of all those poor little African children.

MARK *comes in.*

All right, Mark?

MARK. Yes, Mrs. Walker, he's out of the bath now.

EDITH. What's he doing?

MARK. He's getting dressed. He says he's going for a walk.

EDITH. He didn't. Oh he didn't. Oh what utter madness. Get into bed, Mark. You can read if you like for twenty minutes, then it's lights out.

RUPERT. I haven't brushed my teeth.

EDITH. You'll just have to do until the morning. I can't have the whole house dashing about in their bare feet. Twenty minutes, and no torches under the sheets. I'm going to find your father.

She dashes out. MARK *gets into the top bunk.*

RUPERT. What kept you?

MARK. He wanted to talk.

RUPERT. Is he all right now?

MARK. Not really. He was trying to tell me about a dream he'd had, but he couldn't remember any of it. Then he fell over and banged his head.

RUPERT. Was he badly hurt?

MARK. He went on talking, if that's any comfort to you.

RUPERT. What did he say?

MARK. It was all nonsense, man.

RUPERT. Oh hell. Put the light out. I feel too ill to read.

MARK. You reckon he's flipped his lid for good?

RUPERT. You know whose fault it is if he has.

Brief silence.

MARK. I'm sorry, but I can't talk to your ma when she's like that.

RUPERT. She's upset.

MARK. I don't care. I'm upset now 'cause of her.

RUPERT. She doesn't like you.

MARK. Why doesn't she say so?

RUPERT. She's being polite.

MARK. Well I've got news for her. If she doesn't like me she can put it where the monkey put the nuts. *Why* doesn't she like me?

RUPERT. I don't know. She's like that.

MARK. Why'd she invite me here? Shit, now I'm really angry. What's that rubbish she put all over you? Taking your pants down. Egg flip. You ought to be ashamed.

RUPERT. I've just remembered, it wasn't you she said she didn't like. It was somebody else.

MARK. Oh yeah? Well I don't like *her*. Old granny.

He switches the light off.

RUPERT. What's your worst fear?

MARK. You first.

RUPERT. No, you.

MARK. I'd hate to die, knowing I'd wasted my life.

RUPERT. 'So much to do, so little done.'

MARK. Who said that?

RUPERT. Cecil John Rhodes.

MARK. You don't know a damn thing. Rhodes was vile and wicked. I hope he died with the screams of the Africans he'd massacred ringing in his ears.

RUPERT. My ma says we'll all get out throats cut in the end, liberals, the lot.

MARK. Rubbish. It may sound very exciting to you, the idea of being shot by a lot of Africans. But they've got too much sense. They've got to prepare the ground.

RUPERT. *Before* they shoot us?

MARK. Are you being deliberately obtuse?

RUPERT. No. I don't think I'm cut out for this kind of conversation.

MARK. What's *your* worst fear?

RUPERT. Well, do you think a man can turn into a woman?

MARK. Yes, but only once.

RUPERT. You mean you can cut it off but you can't stick it on again?

MARK. No you idiot. I mean only one person's done it. That okie who went to Denmark.

RUPERT. Do you think it could happen in Cape Town?

MARK. You getting worried? It'd certainly cause a stir at school. Might not be such a bad idea, I could prob'ly quite reckon you.

RUPERT. I'm going to sleep.

Silence. Then the sound of whispering.

MARK. What?

RUPERT. Nothing.

MARK. You said something.

RUPERT. No I didn't.

MARK. You got your fingers crossed?

RUPERT (*lies*). No.

MARK. Well just you watch it.

Pause. More whispering.

You being funny?

RUPERT. I was asleep.

MARK. Like hell. Do it again and I'll really beat you up.

Silence. Whispering.

MARK. OK, that's it. You've had your chips now. You've got
till five to own up. One, two, three . . .

RUPERT. Pax pax I'll tell you.

MARK. Get on with it then. Four, four and a half, four and
three quarters . . .

RUPERT. I was saying my prayers if you really want to know.

MARK. Why didn't you say so?

RUPERT. Dunno. Now I've got to go back to the beginning.

Pause.

MARK (*sepulchral voice*). 'Our Father who shouts in Heaven,
Hello what's your name?'

RUPERT. Ssh!

MARK *giggles.*

No, shut up and listen.

Footsteps are heard coming down the path outside.

It's my old man. Did you know we lived next to Niagara Falls?

MARK. Hey?

RUPERT. He's stopped for a swazz in the canna lilies. 5, 4, 3, 2, 1, bombs away!

Sound of RUSTY *peeing on leaves. The boys stifle their giggles.*

MARK. It's like an elephant!

RUPERT. Did you see it in the bath?

MARK. Ja, of course.

RUPERT. What's it like?

MARK. Pretty big. Haven't you seen it?

RUPERT. He'll shake it now.

They try to listen, but giggle too much to hear.

Now he'll go back to the house.

The door opens. RUSTY *is silhouetted in the moonlight.*

RUSTY. Rupy? Are you awake?

RUPERT. Yes dad.

RUSTY. Just thought I'd say good night.

RUPERT. 'Night, dad.

RUSTY. Mark asleep?

RUPERT. It sounds like it.

RUSTY. I'm coming in.

He does.

Where are you?

RUPERT. Here.

RUSTY sits on the end of the bunk.

Ow.

RUSTY. That your foot?

He moves.

How's that?

RUPERT. OK.

RUSTY. It's been a good day. Didn't you have a good day?

RUPERT. Yes it was . . . interesting. Are you feeling all right now?

RUSTY. I've never felt better in my life.

RUPERT. I'm sorry we didn't wake you up.

RUSTY. We needn't talk about that now. Have you seen the moon tonight?

RUPERT. Yes?

RUSTY. A full moon. I've been out in the garden looking at it. There are times when you have to think seriously about your life. I care very much about what's happening in this country. You know that, don't you?

RUPERT. Yes?

RUSTY *stands up. Paces about. Meanwhile:*

RUSTY. You know, Rupy, there was once a very great man who, every night, after a hard day's work, work which affected the destinies of thousands of people, would walk out into his garden and look at the stars. He'd count as many as he could. Then when he could count no more . . .

There's a loud thud: RUSTY *has walked into the wall.*

Oh crumbs.

RUPERT. What happened?

RUSTY. I hit my head.

RUPERT. Are you all right?

RUSTY. I've never felt better in my life. Where are you?

RUPERT. Here.

RUSTY. Everything went black for a moment. What was I saying?

RUPERT. He'd count the stars.

RUSTY. He'd count them one by one. Then he'd say to himself, 'In one single galaxy there are fifty million . . . ' I think I'm bleeding.

RUPERT. Ma's got some Elastoplast in the house.

RUSTY. Ah. Let's just the two of us talk, Rupy, just for once. Have you got a hankie?

RUPERT. No.

RUSTY. Don't worry, it's stopped. Better sit down. Yes. And there are five million galaxies visible from Mount Palomar Observatory alone. I'm a bit dizzy actually. Where are you?

RUPERT. Here.

RUSTY *sits.*

Ow!

RUSTY. That your foot again? Sorry, chum.

He moves off RUPERT*'s foot.*

I'd like to take you to the beach again. We should spend more time together. I know you're not a rugger fan, but what do you think of tennis? It's always a social asset. You'd be surprised, but sometimes I'm as shy of you as you are of me. I wish you'd known me in the Army. Well you've seen the photos. We'd have hit it off. When you're older you'll see there are faults on all sides. Other personalities involved. Your mother, now, she's a wonderful woman. She's in continual discomfort as you know. If anything happens to me I want you to look after her. Are you listening, Rupy?

RUPERT. Yes.

RUSTY. You might not see me for a bit. I've got things to do. Things one just can't do with a woman around. You remember your mother's birthday, don't you? It's July the fifth. If I'm not here . . . if we lose touch . . .

He cries. Sobs and sobs.

. . . I want you to give her a dozen red roses . . .

Through his sobs:

. . . I'll get the money to you somehow. And the present of course.

He slowly stops crying.

Thanks for listening, Rupy. Where are you?

RUPERT. Here.

RUSTY. Good night, son.

He kisses RUPERT.

What's that smell?

RUPERT. It's calamine lotion.

RUSTY. She tried to put some on me. I know she means well. You sure you're not wearing scent?

RUPERT. No it's calamine lotion.

RUSTY. Never trust a man who wears scent. You're a good pal, Rupy.

He stands up and bangs his head on the bottom of the top bunk.

Ow. Ow. Oh God. No it's going now. Oh that was a shock. Good night.

Walks into the middle of the room.

RUPERT. 'Night Dad.

RUSTY. The secret of a woman is her . . .

Pause.

RUPERT. Are you all right?

He panics.

Dad?

RUSTY *crashes to the ground.*

RUSTY. Where are you?

RUPERT. Here.

RUSTY. You've moved.

RUPERT. No you fell over.

RUSTY. I'll tell you something I've never told anyone. Since I
    met your mother . . . Oh my God. Oh my God. Everything's
    spinning round.

He utters a terrible groan. RUPERT *gets out of the bunk.*

RUPERT. Dad? Dad? Hey Mark!

MARK. What's he done now?

RUPERT. Were you awake?

MARK. You bet, was I supposed to sleep through that?

RUPERT. Wasn't it awful.

MARK. I've never been so embarrassed in my life.

RUPERT. What shall we do with him?

MARK. Put him in the bunk.

RUPERT. Shouldn't I tell my ma he's here?

MARK. Up to you, he's *your* father.

RUPERT. Where will *I* go?

MARK. Up there with me.

RUPERT. Let's put him in the bunk.

MARK *climbs down.*

MARK. I'll take the heavy end. A one and a two and a 'up'!

They lift RUSTY, *struggle over to the bottom bunk and lay
him in it.* EDITH *is heard calling* 'RUSTY!'

Shut the door!

RUPERT *rushes over to close the door, then climbs up into
the top bunk.*

Grab my hand. That's it. Ssh.

Footsteps outside. The door opens. EDITH *is in the doorway.*

EDITH. Boys? Hello boys? Are you awake?

RUPERT *snores quietly.*

MARK. Is that you, Mrs. Walker?

EDITH. Mark?

MARK. You won't put the light on, will you Mrs. Walker? We've both got terrible headaches from the sun and Rupert's just gone to sleep. Have you come to take our tray?

EDITH. Not at this time of night, child. It's nothing. Sleep well.

MARK. Thanks Mrs. Walker.

EDITH. Oh, by the way Mark, Mr. Walker didn't say, did he, what time he'd be back?

MARK. No Mrs. Walker.

EDITH. Did you see which way he went?

MARK. Well he could have gone up to the station as though he was going to school, or the other way over the bridge. When I last saw him, he was standing at the front gate trying to decide.

EDITH. Thanks, Mark, it doesn't matter.

She goes, closing the door behind her. Footsteps, then silence.

RUPERT. Phew.

MARK. How was that?

RUPERT. Pretty damn good. Move over.

They re-arrange themselves.

Isn't it difficult with the middle arms?

RUSTY *mumbles in his sleep.*

MARK. Ssh!

They listen.

What did he say?

RUSTY. Heliograph.

RUPERT. He wants a heliograph.

MARK. What's that?

RUPERT. Something in the Army.

RUSTY. Send the catering corps down to the river.

MARK. Do you reckon he'll go on all night?

RUPERT. I don't know.

Pause.

He's stopped.

Pause.

Mark, listen. I'm too happy to sleep. We could have a quiz. Or tell each other jokes. Play noughts and crosses in the air. Or mental battleships.

Pause.

Mark?

Silence. MARK *is asleep.* EDITH *is heard in the distance calling: 'Rusty!'*

RUPERT. Mark?

End of scene.

Scene Five

LEO*'s office.* LEO *behind his desk,* RUSTY *is taking a sandwich out of his briefcase and unwrapping it. His face is red and bits of skin are hanging off it.*

LEO. I'm flattered. No, I mean it. That you should come to me for advice. That would be what, a cheese and tomato?

RUSTY. Have some.

LEO. I'll show you something while I'm thinking.

He takes RUSTY*'s sandwich and puts it in a Jaffle Iron: this looks like a pair of saucers clipped together to form a cup by means of two foot-long handles.*

You should have called me at the weekend. Yesterday I caught up on the garden. Saturday night the film society. *The Childhood of Maxim Gorky.* I tell you, Rusty, that is one heck of a film. Every time I see it, I find something new to admire. One scene brings tears to my eyes.

He points to his eyes.

Look, that's just from thinking about it. Suddenly, in the kitchen, his grandmother does this little dance. From the old days, a wedding ceremony or some such, I don't know, traditional. Beautiful, sheer magic. I'm sorry, go on.

RUSTY. I want to do something . . . constructive. Only every time I get an idea, I immediately think of fifty reasons why not. Whereas you're so practical. So . . .

Pause.

Is that thing working?

LEO. Can't be rushed. Pop-up toasters the same problem, which by the way I can't supply fast enough. They're no damn use but they're cheap, they look good and they take people's minds off their troubles. Now ask why I'm so cheerful about it. What does Edith think you ought to be doing?

RUSTY. I've not talked to her at all. Fact of the matter, I've moved out.

LEO. Ah. Time's up.

He opens the Jaffle Iron, revealing that it has toasted RUSTY*'s sandwich. Places it before* RUSTY.

And Edith, she's happy with this?

RUSTY. I wasn't there when she got my note. My guess is that her immediate reaction would be rather mixed.

He takes a bite of the sandwich.

LEO. What's it like?

RUSTY. Tastes good. I can't eat hotel stuff, it makes me nervous. Sleep's another problem. The first night out, I'd forgotten the alarm. I tried the old trick of banging my head on the pillow, seven bangs for up at seven, but I was so worried I'd balls it up that I kept getting out of bed to check. Last night I couldn't get off at all. And work, well I copped a fair quota of embarrassment today. Word travels, everyone's heard about me and Edith, so they look at me in a funny way. I can take all this in my stride, question of self-control. No, the thing is there's something else. I can't grasp it, it's like grabbing a bar of soap. Something to do with travelling light. I could climb off next stop if I wanted to, stay a day or two, disappear into the landscape, learn the local customs, talk sign language. I've not gone potty have I? There's nothing in the family. No, the worry is that when the temporary thing wears off, I'll find myself pointing in the wrong direction. Or two directions at once. One thing's settled.

LEO. Good, good.

RUSTY. I'm taking your advice about the Torch Commando.

LEO. Ah.

RUSTY. Resigning.

LEO (*remembers*). Yes.

RUSTY. I've drafted a telegram. But I can't get it right. Either it gets completely stuffy or it sounds as though I've gone off the deep end. Can I read it to you?

LEO. Sure.

RUSTY. Here goes.

He takes out a sheet of paper and reads.

'Accept resignation in default open door policy all ex-
servicemen irrespective colour for protest against
unconstitutional laws signed George quote Rusty unquote
Walker 11th Field Company South African Engineering
Corps 1939–45.'

Well?

LEO. It's good, you know, good. One or two things . . .

Fingers splayed he rocks his hand to and fro.

. . . I might have put a little differently, but no, this is you
talking.

Pause.

Let me look at it.

RUSTY *hands it over.* LEO *puts on his glasses.* RUSTY
waits.

Are you very fond of 'open door policy'.

RUSTY. What's wrong with it?

LEO. It's perhaps a little abstract. Surely people must first
confer, so that the policy is coherent?

RUSTY. What do we say then? 'Conference'?

LEO. You need a forceful word, a word a soldier might use.

RUSTY. 'Alliance'?

LEO. Good.

RUSTY. 'Regrouping'?

LEO. We'll use them both.

RUSTY. They won't pay a blind bit of notice.

LEO. But the idea is planted.

RUSTY. Which is what?

LEO. I'll tell you. I'm beginning to warm to this. There are
dozens of organisations like yours, liberal-minded middle-
class groups, all admirable in intention but incoherent and

therefore inept. If they were to link forces under dynamic leadership, policy would be clarified and their work would be more effective.

He stands. Puts two sheets of paper plus carbon in the typewriter and types. Meanwhile:

I'll do a draft.

MAY *comes in.*

MAY. Rusty, what a pleasure. Long time no see.

LEO. Where's Mark?

MAY. He's choosing books still.

LEO. What did he buy?

MAY. 'Crime and Punishment'.

LEO. We've got it on the shelves.

MAY. But he'll appreciate it more if he buys it himself. Rusty, I was heart-broken to hear your news. Have you somewhere nice to stay?

RUSTY. It's all right.

MAY. You must come over soon. We can have a long talk and here's a big soft shoulder if you're looking for one to cry on.

LEO. May, you're embarrassing him.

MAY (*to* RUSTY). What does he know? How's business?

RUSTY. Booming. Times are good.

LEO. Rusty says there's been a small revolution in ladies footwear.

MAY. And all the time I never knew.

RUSTY. Reinforced stilettos.

LEO (*to* RUSTY). May and fashion don't see eye to eye.

MAY. What're you typing?

LEO. It's for Rusty.

He takes the paper out of the machine.

RUSTY (*to* MAY). I've some samples I don't need. I'll dig them out for you. They're just your style.

LEO. They must be enchanting. Here.

LEO *gives him the top copy.* RUSTY *looks at it.*

Thank you, Leo. I'll send it now.

Gets his briefcase. To MAY:

I'll see you soon.

MAY. Make it a promise.

LEO. You're holding him up.

RUSTY *goes.* MAY *sits.* LEO *starts clearing up prior to leaving.*

MAY. The Petersen girl's getting her compensation after all.

LEO. How much?

MAY. Three months she's been off work and the mean-fisted buggers have offered her twenty pounds.

LEO. You should fight it.

MAY. Let her fight it herself. I haven't the time.

LEO. You don't mean that.

MAY. My girls have got their heads screwed on. I tell you, the day they find they don't need an organiser will be the happiest day of my life. I can stay home and raise cabbages. What's this?

LEO. Rusty's resignation from the Torch Commando. Read it if you like.

MAY. I'd rather not. It's nothing to me one way or the other. He's a nice man but politically he's irrelevant. There isn't some girl we never knew about?

LEO. I don't think so.

MAY. Well, it happens. Phoo, I'm hot and sticky. I wish Mark would hurry up. What's this?

LEO. A Jaffle Iron.

MAY. Toasted sandwich maker?

LEO. More or less.

MAY holds it.

MAY. And I stand like a fool holding it? Forget it.

LEO. Yes?

MAY. Don't touch it. Trust the Yanks to come up with just such a white elephant. You should be ashamed.

LEO. Maybe.

MAY. You boys never learn. There's the slump of all time round the corner.

LEO. How long have you been saying that?

MAY. How often have I been right? Rusty with his boom talk.

LEO. How can he walk out on his wife like *that*?

He snaps his fingers.

I don't understand it. Do you?

MAY. Maybe.

She lights a cigarette.

I saw old Mannie Mannheim today. He crossed the street to pay his respects, two sticks he carries now. 'Your name slips my mind,' he said, 'but I remember you and your husband as good people.' He had a raid last week, he couldn't wait to tell me.

LEO. He's done nothing for years.

MAY. I think if they'd left him alone any longer he'd have complained to the Special Branch. I almost forgave him on the spot.

LEO. Don't drag it up, May.

MAY. I couldn't believe that he was the man who stood at the back of my night-school class, inspecting every word I spoke for theoretical errors. That draughty hut was the centre of my life. Never mind that, what do you think it meant to the workers we taught to read and write? Mannie it was who stood up next evening at the Political Bureau to close it down.

LEO. He had his reasons. Party discipline was a mess. Everyone knew you were doing a good job, but there were too many individual schemes flying around. We couldn't co-ordinate them.

MAY. So you said at the time. I could have walked out on you then. Just like *that*.

She snaps her fingers.

LEO. But you didn't.

MAY. I walked out on the Party instead. I don't regret it. I've got my life. And I still have you.

She looks at the carbon-copy of RUSTY*'s telegram.*

This thing I dread before I've even read it.

She reads:

Blar blar blar, 'regrouping and alliance of democratic groupings nationwide committed to the defeat of fascism.' Rusty wrote this, huh?

LEO. It was a collaborative effort.

MAY. Oh sure. Like the rabbit-and-horse-meat pie. Fifty-fifty, one horse, one rabbit. I don't like it.

LEO. I didn't think you would.

MAY. Pray God times are never so bad that the Party must try to co-ordinate these nobodies. I couldn't work with them.

LEO. I'm trying to picture you working with anyone. You work as an individual. That's why you're effective. The Party doesn't have that choice. It's banned. It's a crime to work for it.

MAY. So you're in an undercover phase. It isn't the first time in the world. What I don't like is that this is addressed to an imperialist, paramilitary organisation. Since when is it policy to look to them for support?

LEO. I didn't say it was policy.

MAY. You mean you made it up?

LEO. It's guesswork. Maybe in a couple of years we'll be glad of the manpower. I don't know. Don't badger me.

MAY. Leo, I'm shocked. What right have you got to play such monkey-tricks?

LEO. It came out of conversation.

MAY. And you talk about discipline? My God, I'm glad it's nothing to do with me. When I resigned, orders came from the Political Bureau and you damn well carried them out.

LEO. So you said at the time. I know what I'm doing. Rusty was going to send it anyway, he simply wanted it phrased to make it generally helpful.

MAY. No-one will believe he wrote it.

LEO. He signed it.

MAY. Ha ha ha. I don't think it's very clever to make use of people with no commitment. Forget the moral aspect, how you treat your friends is your own affair. It's lousy tactics. It will blow up in your face.

LEO. May, in the eighteen years we've known each other, I have quite lost count of the times when your assessment of a situation has saved the day, but the fact remains that I'm more grateful for your opinion at some times than at others. Can we please go.

MAY. We're waiting for Mark.

LEO. Oh fuck.

MAY. Still It's nice to know I'm still effective.

LEO. You always were.

MAY. Pity you didn't say it then.

LEO. That was 1935 for God's sake!

MAY. Instead of denouncing my night-school as a social-democratic deviation.

LEO is trying to disentangle his car keys from the keys of the office.

LEO. I need a drink. Lock up the office.

MAY. I'm taking the car. Give me the keys.

She grabs at them.

LEO. Let go. Will you let go.

MAY. Rampant, rampant egoism, you deserve to walk!

They struggle over the keys. LEO grabs the Jaffle Iron, waves it at her threateningly, misses. The door flies open. RUSTY hurtles in, his hair dishevelled, jacket torn, breathing heavily.

RUSTY. Just thought I'd report 'mission completed'.

LEO. Good, well done, this is that telegram, May, I told you about.

MAY. Oh yes.

LEO. Fancy a drink? May has to wait but . . .

RUSTY. Give us a chance.

He sits.

LEO. You all right?

RUSTY. I've never felt better in my life.

MAY. Who tore your jacket?

RUSTY. Well they didn't really want to send it. Wrong counter.

LEO. Wrong in what sense?

RUSTY. Non-whites.

LEO. You sent the telegram from the non-whites counter?

RUSTY. I knew there was something missing. Then it struck me. Moral protest. Make a proper job of it.

He goes over to the window.

MAY. I think he has more to tell us.

LEO. What happened next?

RUSTY *is looking out.*

RUSTY. Somebody grabbed me, so I gave him a clout and made a run for it. There he is. He's calling a copper. Two coppers. Blimey, I've been observed.

He ducks.

LEO. This is disastrous.

RUSTY. They'll be up in a minute.

MAY (*to* LEO). We'll have to let them in. I'll do the talking.

LEO (*to* RUSTY). Don't make a statement. Ring your lawyer.

There's a loud knock at the door. RUSTY *trots up and down in boxing stance.*

RUSTY. Make it hot for them, shall we? Bit of a left hook? Swift jab to the right?

More knocking.

LEO. Button your jacket. Do up your tie.

MAY. I'm letting them in. You ready?

Loud knocking. RUSTY *reaches into his pocket and brings out a toothbrush.*

RUSTY. Bought it this morning. Must have guessed. Some kind of premonition.

More loud knocking.

Shouldn't somebody answer that?

More knocking.

End of Act One.

ACT TWO

Scene One

Wind. A washing line. ANNIE *comes on with a basket of washing.* RUPERT *cycles on and rides round her.*

ANNIE. Will the young master keep his gymnastics to himself? I'm not Tickey the clown and this isn't Boswell's Circus.

RUPERT. What if I don't?

ANNIE. Then someone's going to get a klap on his ear he won't forget in a month of Sundays.

RUSTY. Ha ha! You wouldn't say that if my dad was here.

ANNIE drops the basket and sits on it.

ANNIE. Phoo!

RUPERT. Now what's the matter?

ANNIE. If the master saw me now, he'd be a proper gentleman and give a poor old lady a lift up.

RUPERT stops cycling round, gets off his bike and pulls ANNIE up.

That's enough. I've got washing to hang while it's windy still.

She starts hanging washing.

RUSTY. It'll blow for a month now. Where's the madam?

ANNIE. She's gone into town. She's had her hair permed and tried three different hats on. So who do you think she's gone to see, hey?

RUSTY. You needn't drop hints. She's gone to see the master, we all know that. She's having tea with him in the Gardens, and I hope she puts arsenic in his sugar.

ANNIE. Sies, for shame!

RUSTY. I know I'm very wicked, but you'll just have to pray for me to be forgiven.

He starts cycling off.

See you later, alligator.

ANNIE. Get us a comic, hey?

RUSTY. What will you give me for a comic?

ANNIE. I'll let the young master watch me gut a chicken.

RUSTY. We got chicken for dinner? Boy oh boy, are we living well since a certain person left.

He cycles off. ANNIE *leaves the opposite side.*

End of scene.

Scene Two

Same day. The Gardens. A large statue of a man pointing decisively forward. The inscription reads:

Cecil John Rhodes
1853–1902
'Your hinterland is there.'

RUSTY *is sitting on a park bench. Beside him is his briefcase and a stack of tabloid-sized newspapers. He is feeding the pigeons.*

RUSTY. Fellow came up to me this morning. 'I'd like to shake you by the hand,' he said. 'A lot of people feel like you, trouble is they're afraid to stand up and be counted.' 'Thanks,' I said, 'Well I'm still on bail, if you want to see me state my case I'm in the Magistrate's Court week after next.' 'I'll think about it,' he said, then he shuffled off.

The noon gun is heard from Signal Hill. EDITH *enters,*

looking smart and well-groomed. Sound and shadows of wings.

EDITH. How they fly!

RUSTY. This one's stayed for his food.

EDITH. I can't stop long.

She sits.

RUSTY. Fancy a cuppa?

EDITH. Not now. It's twelve o'clock. The tea-room's serving lunches.

RUSTY. Stay here?

EDITH. Whatever you like. We've been reading about you.

RUSTY. They've fixed a date.

EDITH. When?

RUSTY. The nineteenth. Will you be there?

EDITH. If you'd like me to be.

RUSTY. We've heard from the Public Prosecutor. I'm charged with obstructing the business of the Post Office.

EDITH (*surprised*). That sounds quite modest.

RUSTY. It is. I'll plead guilty and they'll settle for a fine.

EDITH. Rusty darling, that's wonderful.

RUSTY. I wanted to tell you myself. I thought you'd be pleased.

EDITH. What about the rest of it?

RUSTY. They can't prosecute.

EDITH. Didn't you go to the wrong counter?

RUSTY. I didn't break the law. There's nothing in the regulations saying that different races have to be served separately.

EDITH. They always are. There are signs on the wall.

RUSTY. They're just advisory.

EDITH. Did you know that?

RUSTY. No. I'm amazed. It's like finding you can do whatever you like and get away with it.

EDITH. Once in a while, perhaps. If you won something on the tombola, you wouldn't think you could earn your living that way. What about the fine?

RUSTY. They think eighty to a hundred pounds.

EDITH. There you are.

RUSTY. I knew you'd disapprove.

EDITH. Not if it's what you wanted to do. What are those?

RUSTY. Newspapers.

EDITH. Not proper ones.

RUSTY. It's *The Sentinel*.

EDITH. I've never read it.

RUSTY. I sell it in my spare time.

EDITH. Not in the street?

RUSTY. At the station.

EDITH. That seems a very funny thing to do. Don't you bump into people you know?

She picks up a copy.

RUSTY. That'll be tuppence if you want it.

EDITH. Oh poo.

She looks at it.

Rupert sends his love.

RUSTY. How is he?

EDITH. He's doing a play at school. 'Murder on the Nile'. He tried his costume on last night. Of course he will sit with his knees apart and it looks so silly in a dress.

Pause.

It's pleasant here. It's blowing a gale in town. There are two bushmen on show, have you seen them?

RUSTY. Real ones?

EDITH. From the Kalahari. A man and a lady bushman. It can't be very nice for them being gawped at all day. I should think they're none too pleased with life. I didn't stop. People were feeding them peanuts.

RUSTY. And you're well?

EDITH. Oh yes. I'm waking early for some reason. First the milkman, then the birds, then suddenly the room is drenched with light. I wouldn't call it dawn, it's far too hasty an affair. It's like everything else in Africa. Unfinished, somehow.

Skims the paper again.

I can't say I've heard of most of these people.

RUSTY. It prints things the other papers won't touch.

EDITH. And big for tuppence. I always thought it was just a commie rag. Your cheque arrived.

RUSTY. Oh good.

EDITH. And I've opened an account.

RUSTY. I thought it was better, you know, just pop it in an envelope.

EDITH. Well I don't know the proper form. Do whatever's best. It's more than I'm used to, just for Rupy and me. Is business good?

RUSTY. For some.

EDITH. Oh dear.

RUSTY. I've lost the Natureform account. They said they didn't want their rep at the centre of controversy.

EDITH. Mean blighters. And now you've legal fees and a fine to pay.

RUSTY. I'm cutting back a bit.

EDITH. Not smoking.

RUSTY. You noticed.

EDITH. Fingers.

She moves to touch his clean smoking fingers, then withdraws her hand.

Rusty, this is ridiculous. I can't accept more than you can afford. You gave me eighty pounds. Wouldn't sixty be better?

RUSTY. Could you manage on that?

EDITH. I could if I tried. Annie might have to go.

RUSTY. I wouldn't want that.

EDITH. There's always a price to pay. I don't mind sullying my hands with honest toil.

Something has caught her eye in the paper.

Goodness me.

RUSTY. What is it?

EDITH. There's a picture of you. Wherever did they dig it up? It makes you look like a pansy.

RUSTY. Let me see it.

EDITH. In a minute.

She reads:

'Today the ruling classes celebrate three centuries of white rule. They see a vast land opened up, gold and diamonds retrieved from desert soil . . . ' Nothing about you at all.

RUSTY. Go on.

EDITH (*with an air of finality*). 'Skip skip skip, how appropriate that the African National Congress has chosen the eve of the festivities to launch its campaign of defiance at mass meetings throughout the land.' That's it.

RUSTY (*points*). 'Continued'.

EDITH *turns several pages.*

EDITH. They don't do this in real newspapers. Oh, here at the bottom.

RUSTY. What does it say?

EDITH. It's not very nice. 'It characterises the frivolous bias of the bourgeois press that it has ignored the existence of this great people's movement, while ample space has been found for the student pranks in the Post Office of Mr. R. Walker, whose ridiculous antics . . . ', you don't want to read this.

RUSTY. Waste of time.

Pause. He's upset.

EDITH. Don't worry about it. Commies are always having goes at each other. Look at poor old Trotsky.

RUSTY. Well I don't like it.

EDITH. You had to watch them even in the War when they were Allies. You should have seen me with my collecting box. 'Arms for Stalingrad'. There was a banner over my head with a hammer and sickle on one side and the Union Jack on the other. It was all the thing to do, in those days. How times change.

RUSTY. Who wrote that?

EDITH. It wasn't signed.

RUSTY. Typical.

EDITH. It was a regular column.

RUSTY. Was it?

He seizes the paper, reads:

'The Man on the Spot'!

EDITH. Do you know him?

RUSTY. It's Leo!

EDITH. Leo? It can't be. Didn't he even warn you?

RUSTY. No he didn't.

He puts the paper down in disgust.

If he wants to be clever, he can damn well do it to my face.
Bloody armchair general.

Pause.

I suppose you couldn't stay for a bite to eat?

EDITH. Perhaps just this once.

End of scene.

Scene Three

Same day. An open space. Wind. RUPERT *and* MARK *cycle
on.* MARK *stops.*

RUPERT. Why here?

MARK. You can see across the town.

RUPERT. I can't stop long.

Pause. Faintly in the distance a bugle blows a phrase.

Listen.

The bugle is heard again.

It's the cadets. They practise every day now. I'm putting my
name down for the band. No drill for me, thank you very
much.

MARK. What you doing this Christmas?

RUPERT. Why?

MARK. Sit around the Yule log and that shit?

RUPERT. My dad does the tree. Perhaps he'll be back. Cotton-
wool for snow. Turkey, mince pies, Christmas pud.

MARK. Ninety degrees in the shade and the sweat running
down your cheeks.

RUPERT. When I was a kid, my presents used to come in a proper stocking. I felt sorry for the Jewish boys not getting any.

MARK. That's all *you* know. Next Christmas I'm going away.

RUPERT. Oh ja?

MARK. For two weeks. I'm staying on a farm in the Eastern Cape. We went there once before, but Mom and Dad came too. You can ride all day on the beach and never see a house or another farm. If you want to swim you just strip off your clothes and dive in. When it's time for lunch, you can build a fire out of driftwood and cook a fish. At night you build a fire to keep the jackals away, open a bottle of wine and get drunk under the stars. A nice old couple lives there, they don't fuss, no asking when you'll be back or where you've been. Do you like the sound of it?

RUPERT. I'm thinking about it.

MARK. Would you like to come with?

RUPERT. With you?

MARK. Ja, sure.

RUPERT. At Christmas?

MARK. Yes!

RUPERT. I don't know. It's such a very long time away. December isn't the sort of thing I can apply my mind to. Wouldn't it be better if you took someone who was likely to enjoy it?

MARK (*frowns*). Ja, well I was going by myself. I reckon that's still the best idea.

RUPERT. I'm not saying it doesn't sound fun, if it's the kind of thing you're interested in.

MARK. Change the record, will you?

RUPERT. OK. As long as we don't have to talk about life or death or get too morbid. I think I liked you better when you had lots of friends and wouldn't talk to me. You had quite a gang last year, and the thing you liked most was throwing rocks at yours truly. I didn't enjoy it exactly, but it wasn't uninteresting. I almost used to look forward to the next ambush. The others were just having a good time. I could have been a flea as far as they were concerned. You were different. You hated me in a more elaborate way.

MARK. There's nothing special about throwing rocks at someone who pisses you off. And I didn't hate you. I didn't know what the word meant.

RUPERT. And now you do?

MARK. What do you think? Look around you, can't you? This is such a terrible place. There's not a decent thought in it. I could hurt myself. I mean on purpose. Stick a red-hot needle in my eyes.

RUPERT. I couldn't, I'll tell you that for free. You couldn't either. You're just feeling sorry for yourself. You talk and you think and the time flies by.

MARK. Like my dad. He says it's tactics. But if you ask me, he just wants a quiet life.

RUPERT. Most people do. But I always imagined you were more adventurous.

MARK *gets up and climbs on his bike.*

MARK. Maybe you expected too much.

RUPERT. Where are you going?

MARK. Home, where do you think?

He cycles off.

RUPERT. Don't go.

He follows on his bike.

End of scene.

Scene Four

Later that day. Wind. The washing line. ANNIE *takes down the washing and folds it into the basket.*

ANNIE (*sings*).
  'Hushed was the evening hymn,
  The temple courts were dark,
  The lamp was burning dim
  Before the sacred ark,
  When suddenly a voice divine
  Rang through the silence of the shrine.'

  Meanwhile EDITH *comes on with a cup of tea.*

EDITH. You're working late, Annie.

ANNIE. Don't like to leave things unfinished, madam.

EDITH. I thought you might like a cup of tea. I put three sugars in.

ANNIE. That's very nice of the madam.

  EDITH *gives her the tea.* ANNIE *drinks.*

  Three sugars?

EDITH. Lumps.

ANNIE. Bottle milk or condensed?

EDITH. It was ordinary milk out of a bottle.

ANNIE. That explains it. Very nice thank you.

EDITH (*of the washing*). Would you like me to finish off for you?

ANNIE. If the madam doesn't mind, I'm not so young but I mustn't find everything just where I left it last. If I catch the later bus, I don't have to listen to the other maids and their chatter, I can sit and think.

EDITH. Let me give you a hand.

  She starts taking washing down. ANNIE *protests.* EDITH *continues.*

Are things better at home? You said you had a problem with your grandson. That he'd been in trouble with the police.

ANNIE. Ag, madam knows these young boys when they must show how big they are. He got into a small fight that was happening anyway, so they locked him up all night and in the morning they hit him and sent him home. Then his mother beat him so's he couldn't sit down for a week.

EDITH. I see.

ANNIE. If the madam would mind not getting any impressions? There's never been any trouble in my family and I don't intend starting at my time of life.

EDITH. Oh, I only asked because I knew you'd been worried. Is he back at work?

ANNIE. He is.

EDITH. And the girl? Is she still with British Leyland?

ANNIE. She's in charge of her own bench now.

EDITH. So they're both in a position to help at home. I do think about you, you see.

ANNIE. It's nice of the madam to ask.

She retrieves a sheet which EDITH *has let crumple into the basket and folds it neatly.*

EDITH. Mr. Walker asked kindly after you.

ANNIE. Tch, shame.

EDITH. Was your husband a good man? I know no-one's perfect. He was lonely today but I didn't talk much. That's the art of a good listener. He asked if I could make do on less. Of course he wouldn't grasp the difficulties. I wish I could promise to keep you on. But I can't.

ANNIE *sits on the washing basket.*

ANNIE. I could work less hours.

EDITH. I can't afford it. I'm sorry, Annie. I've always thought of you as a friend.

She cries.

ANNIE. Can madam not find it in her heart to wait? This foolishness can't last.

EDITH. Do you think so?

ANNIE. Wait and see. A month. No, less.

EDITH. You've read my thoughts. He will come back, I know.

ANNIE. They always do. My Peter just the same. They're like the little boys who run away to sea.

End of scene.

Scene Five

LEO*'s garden. Same day. Light wind. A couple of garden chairs. Sound of sawing.*

RUSTY *comes on carrying two glasses of beer.*

RUSTY. Leo?

The sawing stops. LEO *calls from above:*

LEO. I'm up here.

RUSTY *looks up, shading his eyes.*

LEO. Mind yourself, huh?

RUSTY. I've got a bone to pick with you.

LEO. Is that a beer?

RUSTY. What does it look like?

LEO. Be down in a minute.

The sawing starts again. RUSTY *calls up:*

RUSTY. Look, what's the big idea about . . .

LEO. Heads!

A branch crashes down from above and thuds on the ground.

I told you to look out.

RUSTY. Was it you wrote that stuff in the *Sentinel*?

LEO. You've read it?

RUSTY. You might have told me. I've been flogging it up and down town. It makes me look a complete idiot.

LEO. You behaved like one.

RUSTY. Well I think that's a bit bloody ironic the day before the Defiance Campaign kicks off.

LEO. That's different.

RUSTY. So I see.

LEO. You set a very bad example.

RUSTY. Thanks. I damn near risked a gaol sentence. I spent a night in the cells and I'll be lucky to get off with a hundred pounds.

LEO. How many blacks do you think can afford a hundred pounds? Six months inside, more like. If people start breaking the law as and when it suits them, the Campaign won't last a week. What it needs is mass support and mobilisation. Not adventurist heroics.

Sawing starts again.

RUSTY. Well I think you might have . . .

LEO. Heads again.

Another branch crashes down.

RUSTY. Don't you want your beer?

LEO. Are you going to punch me on the nose?

RUSTY. I'm thinking about it.

LEO. I'll risk it.

RUSTY. I did *something*. Which is more than most of my pals can say. Certainly more than most commercial travellers.

And it wasn't just because I'd flipped my lid. I broke the law. Deliberately. All right?

He takes out a packet of Policansky cigarettes and lights up.

Small things count. They all add up. Whatever you say. Man with one hair on his chin. Is that a beard? Of course not. Two hairs. How about that? And so on. Skip to the end. Ninety-nine. No, that doesn't quite count. One more. Ah ha, now that is a beard and no mistake. So . . .

LEO *appears at ground level in open-neck shirt, shorts, tackies* (*i.e. canvas tennis shoes*) *and carrying a saw.*

LEO. Sorry to be rude, old chap, but really you should talk about things you know something about.

RUSTY. If everyone did what I did . . .

LEO. 'If everyone threw their porridge down the toilet, the sewerage system would collapse.' Children know better. Everyone won't. OK?

He drinks.

All you achieved was to remind the Post Office of a loophole in their regulations. Quite apart from whatever whim of strategy inspired you to make a beeline back to my office. So it got raided two days later. Help like that I can use like a rat in my stew.

He taps RUSTY's *empty glass.*

What's this? We can't have this.

He calls:

May! Bring us another beer.

He sits. To RUSTY:

How was Edith?

RUSTY. Fine.

LEO. Comes flooding back?

RUSTY. She's a wonderful woman. She didn't complain. She's quite prepared to do without the comforts. I'd forgotten how pretty she is.

LEO. Bet you miss the other thing, hey?

RUSTY. Well, you know, it was never the be-all and end-all.

LEO. Lucky for you. I couldn't do without it. Hello you
beautiful angel.

This to MAY, *who has come on with a crate of Castle lager.*

MAY. Here's the crate.

She dumps it on the ground.

I'm not running in and out of the house every time you
want a drink.

LEO. Come and sit on my lap.

She does.

Ouch.

She moves.

My God you weigh a ton.

She flicks dandruff from his shoulders.

MAY. You're sweaty like a horse.

LEO. You smell good. Run your fingers through my hair.

MAY. Like I used to.

She does.

What's this stuff on it? To make it grow back?

LEO. Put your arm round me.

She does.

Ah, that's what I like.

MAY. You've had your ration, I must go now.

She doesn't move off.

LEO. Are you on the platform tonight?

MAY. Sure, I'm introducing the speakers.

LEO. I'll drive you.

MAY. No, I must get there early.

LEO. I don't mind.

MAY. There won't be room in the car. I'm taking my girls.

LEO. It's clear to me where your affections lie. (*To* RUSTY.)
Her girls work in the fisheries. May's their union dep.

MAY. Provisional.

LEO. She's been provisional now for fifteen years.

MAY. They don't need me.

LEO. So she says. The white girls won't let the coloured girls
use the lift, the coloured girls won't share the toilet with the
Africans.

MAY. What do you expect? Those white girls have seen life at
the bottom of the rubbish heap, they don't want another
look. Rusty where's your beer?

RUSTY. I don't know.

MAY. Leo's got it.

LEO. You've got mine. You give me my glass back, Rusty take
this . . .

MAY. Leo, what has got into you that you sit with your feet up
and play musical chairs with the glasses?

RUSTY. It's too cold for beer.

LEO. Do you want to go inside?

RUSTY. It's nice out here.

MAY. I'll get you a blanket.

LEO (*to* MAY). Don't get up.

RUSTY. I'll go.

He goes into the house.

MAY. I want to stretch my legs.

She gets down off LEO's *lap. Walks a little way. Her feet hurt.*

LEO. Funny day, huh?

MAY. You're restless.

She holds one foot in her hand.

I wish you were speaking tonight.

LEO. Oh no.

MAY *sits. Takes a shoe off, rubs her feet.* LEO *watches.*

Serves you right for dressing up for a democratic meeting.

MAY. My girls expect it. Is Rusty angry with you?

LEO. Somebody had to tell the truth.

MAY. But the way you said it. It's so boring. 'Toiling masses'.

LEO. It's a scientific term. I've often used it.

He calls:

Rusty! Bring the cake-tin!

To MAY:

Cold? What's he on about. He must have been sitting in a shadow. That branch up there, that little one. Lucky I didn't put the tools away.

RUSTY *appears with a cake-tin and a blanket. To* MAY:

RUSTY. Do the shoes not fit?

MAY. I'll get used to them. Open the tin.

RUSTY *does.*

RUSTY. Apple slices.

LEO. Apfelschnitten. My mother used to make them.

MAY. So you say.

LEO. She did.

RUSTY *passes round the tin. Wraps himself in a blanket and sits on the ground. They all eat.*

May is having fun with my vocabulary. 'Toiling masses'. 'Deepening economic crisis'. Those words were magic to me once. I've seen rough country boys who couldn't sign their names, come alive up at the sound of a word that for people like us had lost whatever glamour it ever possessed.

He takes a bite.

'Committee'. They passed it along the pits. It was alluring, thrilling. 'Tonight there will be, not just a meeting, but a "*committee*" meeting.'

MAY (*to* RUSTY). My, you're wrapped up.

LEO *holds up a piece of cake.*

LEO. I remember these being laid out for a man who came to ask for my sister's hand in marriage. And she died in Lithuania, so if my mother didn't make them, who did?

RUSTY. Why are there so many Lithuanians?

LEO. It's news to me there's so many Lithuanians.

RUSTY. In South Africa.

LEO. It's nicer here. Believe me. This is a wonderful country.

He continues. Meanwhile, RUSTY *falls asleep on the ground, wrapped up.*

Lithuania wasn't our place anyway. Muddy streets, sour vegetables, hostile peasants. The day I arrived in Johannesburg, I thought my eyes were playing tricks on me. I heard a shout. A boy was running down the road, shouting in Russian. Windows flew open, old women ran out the doorways, business stopped. Six thousand miles away, the Tsar had abdicated. The revolution had arrived, not just in Russia but in Europe, the United States, wherever the international brotherhood of workers heard the news. Nobody paid the rent for weeks. I was twelve.

MAY. Don't look round. We have a friend.

LEO. Where?

MAY. Black car in the road outside.

LEO nods. Gets up. Walks about, seemingly casual, glances at the car in the road, comes back.

LEO. It's the boy who came when they searched for books. Do you want to go inside?

MAY. Not because of him.

LEO. Have a beer.

MAY. Why not.

They open beers. Drink.

LEO. One day it won't be all such fun.

MAY. We'll survive.

LEO. What if I can't earn a living? If my friends are too scared to come round? If I can't go to meetings?

MAY. What makes you think they'll pick on you?

LEO. The boot doesn't look where it treads.

MAY. Oh yes it does. You think that fascism won half the world by luck and chance? That's rubbish. If they move against you now, it would be because they're handing out medals for things that you did in the past. I'm active in a Trade Union. Has it crossed your mind it could be me they're following?

She indicates the sleeping RUSTY.

Even he's a better candidate than you are.

LEO. I'm not proud. Till they raided the office, I'd have agreed with you. I had files in there going back fifteen years.

MAY. Well I don't know about that.

LEO (*quietly, of* RUSTY). Besides, we don't know what he told them.

MAY. I think we're both a little upset. It's a nice evening. I wish we could just sit and enjoy it.

LEO. You must go, huh?

She nods. They get up.

I think my column does a little bit of good.

MAY. Sometimes it's all right. Nice and punchy.

She looks at RUSTY.

What do we do with him?

LEO. Let him sleep.

They go. It's darker. RUSTY *wakes. He sees the police car, gets slowly up.* MAY's *car is heard driving off.* RUSTY *folds the blanket, still watching.* LEO *comes back.*

RUSTY. I'm being followed.

LEO. Is that a fact?

He glances back at the road. Something catches his attention.

Hello.

RUSTY. What?

LEO. He's getting out of the car.

RUSTY. Is he coming this way?

LEO. He is.

End of scene.

Scene Six

Dark. Wind. An open space. RUPERT *rides on with his bike.* MARK *comes on after.*

MARK. What you playing at?

RUPERT. Nothing.

MARK. You're mad.

RUPERT. Go home, then.

MARK. Hell, I'm not going without you.

He moves to RUPERT, *puts a hand on him.* RUPERT *shakes it off.*

What's the matter?

RUPERT. Your hands are getting very damp. I've been noticing it lately.

MARK. Come on. I'm hungry.

RUPERT. You don't mind though, do you? I could make you miss supper and breakfast too, there'd be nothing you could do about it.

MARK. Why're you being like this?

RUPERT. You're soft. You're feeble. If I prodded you with my finger it would go in like a jelly.

MARK. Try it and see.

RUPERT. Come here then.

MARK *does.*

Thanks. I've made my point. Now I needn't bother.

MARK *thrusts his hands deep into his pockets.*

MARK. I'll kill you.

RUPERT. There's nobody here, you could if you wanted. You could bash my head with a stone. You could put your hands round my throat and squeeze till the blood squirted out of my ears. I wouldn't stop you.

MARK. I couldn't hurt you.

RUPERT. What if you hated me?

MARK. I don't.

RUPERT. What if I was someone else? What if I was that cop who arrested your maid. And he pulled her out of the toilet and threw her in the van with the piss still running down her legs. What if I was him?

MARK. I don't know.

Pause.

RUPERT. What you want to do?

MARK. Anything.

RUPERT. OK.

He sits. MARK *sits next to him.*

MARK. What is it?

RUPERT. It's a new game. Close your eyes.

MARK *does.*

Now open your mouth.

MARK *opens his mouth.* RUPERT *spits in it.* MARK *opens his eyes, hits* RUPERT *hard.* RUPERT *falls on his hands and knees.* MARK *stumbles away, spitting.*

MARK. Stupid arse. You all right?

RUPERT. I thought you couldn't hurt me.

MARK. Ja, well, you pissed me off.

RUPERT *gets up.*

RUPERT. Want to do it for real now?

MARK. Wasn't that enough?

RUPERT. You were holding back, I could feel. What if I was that policeman?

MARK. I don't know.

RUPERT. All talk, huh?

MARK *grabs him and throws him on the ground. Walks away towards his bike.*

That meant to hurt, don't make me laugh. I reckon I've seen all of you there is to see.

MARK *comes back and kicks him several times.* RUPERT *lies still.*

MARK. Want some more?

RUPERT. I think I fainted just then. Pull me up.

MARK. Get lost.

RUPERT *gets up slowly. Looks hard at* MARK, *then spits at him.* MARK *grabs him by his hair, throws him down and kicks him.* RUPERT *lies still.* MARK *gets* RUPERT'*s bike and throws it on the ground beside him.*

RUPERT. Who's that?

MARK. It's me. You OK?

RUPERT. I'm looking at the stars.

MARK. Must run in the family. Why don't you hit back?

RUPERT. I only like doing things I'm good at.

MARK. Damn girl.

RUPERT. I think I'm going to be sick.

MARK. Get it out, best thing.

RUPERT *retches.*

RUPERT. It won't come. Oh please come.

He tries sticking his fingers down his throat.

I can't. That's a pity.

MARK. Your blazer's torn, look.

RUPERT *feels.*

RUPERT. Right down the side. What'll I wear to school? Oh God.

He cries.

MARK. Let's go home, Rupy.

RUPERT. I can't. I've got to clean up and stuff.

MARK. You can do it at my place. My ma and pa's gone out. Can you ride?

RUPERT. Dunno.

He gets up.

MARK. I got an idea about the blazer. They're stupid anyway. I mean, in summer. Don't wear yours and I won't wear mine. And we'll tell them they can stick their blazers up their jacksies.

RUPERT. S'long as you do the talking.

MARK. Sure.

RUPERT. Where's my bike?

MARK. It's here.

They get on their bikes.

RUPERT. Tell you what.

MARK. What?

RUPERT. I can ride. It hurts, but I can ride.

MARK. Wanna go then?

RUPERT. Hang on.

He stops, thinks.

MARK. What?

RUPERT. Nothing important. Come, let's go.

They cycle off.

End of scene.

Scene Seven

That night. A platform on the Parade. Lights hang above it. Six or seven chairs at the back and a table. A microphone at the front. We hear a crowd, noisy and responsive.

MAY *comes on with a bottle of water and glasses. Applause and wolf whistles. She lays out the glasses, but nervously knocks over the bottle. Laughter and cheers. As she mops it up, LEO appears at the side of the platform. He gesticulates to get her attention.*

Dialogue in brackets is inaudible above the noise of the crowd.

LEO. (May! May!)

Applause and wolf-whistles from the crowd.

VOICE. Master says did merram put the supper in the oven?

Laughter. MAY *sees* LEO.

MAY. (What do you want?)

LEO. (I've got to talk to you.)

MAY. (Go away. I'm busy.)

He waves at him to join the crowd. Derisive laughter and applause. LEO *climbs up on the platform. Cheering and shouts: 'Chuck him off!' etc.*

MAY. (Leo, this is nonsense, get off at once.)

LEO. (I couldn't wait. I had to show you.)

He shows her a piece of paper. MAY *closes her eyes, strikes her forehead.*

MAY. (Oh my God, those buggers.)

LEO *puts an arm around her. Bawdy cheers and slurping noises.*

VOICE. Pas op, it's Errol Flynn in disguise!

MAY. (Go home. I'll come back as soon as I can.)

LEO. (I'll wait for you here).

MAY. (It's best if you go, you'll be seen here.)

LEO. (Don't bloody tell me what to do.)

He strikes the table.

VOICES. Hoeré!/ You tell her, master./ Don't take any cheek from the old madam./ etc.

Laughter. LEO turns to the crowd.

LEO. (I'm sorry to interrupt the proceedings but . . .)

VOICES. Speak up/ Can't hear/ Speak or shut up./ etc.

LEO points to the microphone, shakes his head pointedly, puts a finger to his lips. Cheers and laughter, on the assumption that he's clowning about. He goes to the microphone, blows into it.

LEO. Sorry . . .

The amplification screeches. LEO tries again.

Sorry . . .

The screeching stops.

. . . that's better.

Cheers and shushes. Comparative quiet.

I only wanted to say that I'm sorry to interrupt the proceedings, but I had to have an urgent word with my wife.

Some laughter, less than before.

Thanks for your patience. I'd stay if I could but I have to go.

VOICES. Why?/ Why not?/ Got a date and it just can't wait?/ etc.

LEO. This piece of paper here, as I've been telling my wife, is from the Department of Justice. Hot off the press. I won't bother you with the small print, or the spelling mistakes . . .

Laughter.

. . . including my name, no excuse for that, they've had it on their files long enough . . .

Laughter.

. . . it's what they call a 'Banning Order'. It says I cannot in future attend gatherings, except for . . .

He reads:

. . . 'recreational, sport or religious purposes.' And I can't
address meetings. Don't ask me what I'm doing here now,
I'm not addressing anyone, let's make that clear, I'm
leading the devotions.

Laughter.

My pleasure. Good night to you all. Good night to my
friends and comrades who are here tonight, some I've been
associated with for many years, there's one down there in
the front, Major Joubert, busy with his notebook, did you
get that, Major?

Much laughter.

One last comment before I go.

*He raises his fist in the African National Congress salute.
The crowd explodes with cheers.* LEO *stems it.*

Well I should have kept my big mouth shut. These people
won't rest until they've turned this country into the biggest
slum factory in the world. It's not advice they want, it's
cheap labour. But you bet your life you won't see the Prime
Minister and his gang queuing for work at the factory gates,
or covered in grease on the factory floor. Those people
experienced poverty and exploitation two generations ago,
and they fear it. It's the fear that lurks at the back of every
white man's mind. The white man in this country is in such
a state of terror he'll believe anything. He'll believe that six
out of seven of his countrymen are foreigners. Enemies.
Slaves to be ruled with all the cruelty which the modern
police state can command.

Applause.

I don't like to leave, having talked only about the
foolishness and waste of life in this country, but that's not
my decision. What I'd say . . . if I could say it . . .

Stops. Quiet.

We believe that the ultimate remedy for the evils of this
country lies in a change to a socialist system. Socialism is a

system by which the means of production are owned by the people. Production takes place, not for profit, but for the benefit of the people as a whole, in accordance with a planned economy. It is not subject to the ups and downs of a capitalist economy. It can ensure full employment at all times and will therefore abolish fear.

Think for one moment of the violence caused in this country by economic fear, and then ask yourself why I'm such a menace I can hardly be let out at night. I mean. look at me!

Laughter.

I ask myself in amazement where you and I discovered such patience in the face of daily attacks on our rights. This defiance campaign is peaceful. It's a fine tradition of this country, passive resistance, or 'satyagraha' as Dr. Gandhi called it when he taught it, in South Africa, nearly half a century ago. We believe in it still. Pray God we're right to do so. The ruling class has everything to lose. Their answer may be savage. Their reprisals those of total war. They're desperate men . . .

A voice crashes in from a rival P.A. system:

POLICE P.A. This is a police instruction. This meeting is now illegal. Will all persons disperse in an orderly manner.

Boos, shouting, bottles thrown.

LEO. What I'm defending is the purpose and content of my life. I see down there, Major Joubert's pencil striking sparks off his notepad, and I know we're both wondering the same thing: 'what's got into him to get up and say all this?' But I'm not special. I've no secret knowledge.

Loud shouting and women crying out. The platform begins to rock. The hanging lights sway and flicker. MAY takes LEO by the hand, tries to lead him off.

. . . What I'm saying is commonsense. Anyone can see it. Almost anyone. I'm not counting people too foolish and greedy to . . .

His P.A. is cut off. The police have mounted a baton charge. Screams of women. Car hooters. The platform subsides. MAY tries to drag LEO away. Crowd noise deafening. The lights black out.

End of scene.

Scene Eight

Later that night. LEO and RUSTY are sitting on the wreck of the platform. Both are dishevelled and RUSTY has a cut on his forehead. LEO is handcuffed. RUSTY is holding a woman's shoe.

Also seated, MRS. MATLALA, holding a parcel neatly wrapped in brown paper.

LEO (*sniffs*). Air's fresher now.

   RUSTY looks at the shoe.

RUSTY. Lost in the charge. You can't run in these things.

   He looks at the ground.

   There's another. When we're gone, they'll creep back to collect them.

   MAY comes on. She's carrying her shoes.

MAY. Move up, you've company for tonight. Rusty, you must have that looked at. What they want you for?

RUSTY. Questioning, they said.

MAY. Me too. Let's keep it short, huh? I've got nothing to add to such an exhibition.

LEO. You enjoyed it.

MAY. Not the baton charge, that would be macabre. My, they're bastards, those boys.

LEO. Rusty wants to return the shoes to their rightful owners.

MAY. Look, there's another.

RUSTY. I've seen it.

He goes to collect it.

MAY. Some of it, Leo, I enjoyed very much indeed.

LEO. My pleasure.

MAY (*to* RUSTY). Rusty, I thought you'd gone home. Thank you for staying.

RUSTY. That's bloody decent of you. I didn't mean to land you in it. It's just that whatever I do, I seem to balls it up.

MAY. Nonsense, I'm used to it. Once in Vienna, every man in my family was in prison. The only difference was, in those days, people took the trouble to tell if you if they were planning on getting arrested, and I could pack sandwiches.

EDITH comes on.

EDITH. Is there room for me?

LEO. Hello Edith.

MAY. Hello Edith.

They shift up. EDITH sits.

EDITH. They didn't want to let me through.

She looks at RUSTY's face.

You've been in the wars.

RUSTY. Look.

The ground is now brighter. Women's shoes lie everywhere. As the floor becomes more visible, more and more shoes are seen.

These two are a match. I could keep them together. In a box of some kind. Place an ad. They'll want them back, you don't grind down the heels like this if you own two pairs.

It's always the same. You think you know where to start.
Then it all opens up like a chasm. I can't see.

EDITH. There's blood in your eyes. Let me. I'll have to use
spit.

EDITH *spits on her handkerchief.*

MRS. MATLALA. It's a shame to spoil such a pretty
handkerchief. Would the madam like to use mine?

EDITH. Thank you.

MRS. MATLALA. I always carry two.

MAY. You were at the meeting?

MRS. MATLALA *nods.*

You've brought clothes?

MRS. MATLALA. Only sewing.

EDITH. Not clothes?

RUSTY. I don't think she understands.

EDITH. Yes she does.

MRS. MATLALA. Tonight I complete it. It is for the meeting
tomorrow at the location. But now I am under arrest, I do
not know how to get it there.

MAY. May I ask what it is?

MRS. MATLALA *unwraps the parcel. It contains a
carefully-worked banner in the colours of the A.N.C: green,
gold and black. It reads* FREEDOM FOR ALL PEOPLE.
All look at it.

MAY. Better put it back. Thank you.

EDITH. I wish I could do work like that.

MRS. MATLALA. Many women have contributed. The work
is not only mine. Just the finishing touches. I am a
seamstress, you see.

Pause.

RUSTY. Why don't you take it, Edy?

EDITH. It looks as though I'll have to, what with everyone *hors de combat* as it were.

RUSTY. There's an address on the parcel.

MAY. They won't let her in.

LEO. She could go as far as the location.

EDITH. Would that be a help, Mrs. . . . ?

MRS. MATLALA. Matlala.

EDITH. I could deliver it in the morning.

MRS. MATLALA. Madam need only take it to the gate. There will be many people there. All of them will know where the meeting is. Madam need not be fussy, she can give it to anyone. We will be grateful from our hearts.

EDITH. That's done, then.

She takes the banner from MRS. MATLALA.

It's nice to have met you. I'm glad I could help.

She stands holding the banner. To the others.

Do I look very conspicuous?

RUSTY. You do a bit.

A van is heard approaching, headlights cast across them.

LEO. This looks like us. You ready, Mrs. M?

MRS. MATLALA. Yes.

LEO. May?

MAY. If you say so.

LEO. Rusty?

RUSTY. Oh, yes.

They are all standing. To EDITH.

Good night.

EDITH. I could pass by the office in the morning, if you think it a good idea.

RUSTY. I'd like that. I doubt I'll be in before twelve.

EDITH. Oh, you've earned your lie-in. See you soon, then.

RUSTY *kisses her on the cheek.*

RUSTY. Better go.

EDITH. 'Night.

The others go. The van is heard driving off.

EDITH *checks that no-one is watching. Wraps up the banner carefully in its brown paper. Puts it under her coat. Looks round. Walks off.*

End of play.

ONE FINE DAY

One Fine Day was first presented at Riverside Studios on 9 July 1980. The cast, in order of appearance, was:

Violet	Valerie Buchanan
Nkwabi	Brian Bovell
Frank	Larrington Walker
Starford	Troy Foster
Steve	Mike Grady
Mr. Kaduma	Yemi Ajibade
Mr. Mzoga	Joe Marcell

Director   John Burgess
Designer   Alison Chitty
Lighting Designer   David Richardson

Characters
in order of appearance

VIOLET
NKWABI
FRANK
STARFORD
STEVE WINTER, *a visiting expert in audio-visual aids in education.*
MR. KADUMA, *vice-principal of a Teachers' Training College*
MR. MZOGA, *the principal*

The play is set in an African People's Republic, at about the time the play was written.

Apart from Steve, all the characters speak English as a second or third language, and they do with an East African accent. The students are in their early- to mid-twenties, certainly older than comparable students would be in the West. They should carry their hoes whenever possible.

The only scenery recommended is a row of three or four banana trees stuck into paraffin tins and lined up at the back of the stage.

Furntiture, etc., including the Rangerover, should be made up out of odd tables and chairs.

ACT ONE

Scene One

The new shamba.

*Three young men in ragged working clothes. They are
FRANK, NKWABI and STARFORD. They are breaking up
the earth with hoes. NKWABI wears his spectacles to do so. A
young woman, VIOLET, is collecting stones in a basket and
piling them up.*

*When not speaking English, they speak in KiSwahili.
Translation in brackets.*

VIOLET. Aa! Mungu wangu jamani! Mawe milioku sanya sasa
ni kama mlima. (God help us! The stones I've collected are
piled up high as a mountain.)

NKWABI. English! English!

VIOLET. Aa! Si kizungu mi jumatano? (What? English on a
Wednesday?)

NKWABI. From today. New rule for people hoeing in the
shamba.

VIOLET. Kwa amri ya nani? (Says who?)

NKWABI. The boss have made this rule for us. English on
Monday, English on Thursday, now we must speak English
on Wednesday too.

VIOLET. U uzungi mwingi. (There's too much Englishness
going on.)

She moves away, her basket of stones balanced on her head.

FRANK. Anasema nini? (What's he talking about?)

STARFORD. Anasema bullshit. (He's talking bullshit)

NKWABI (*angry*). Yatosha! Yatosha! Kama mikisikia mtu
anasema Kiswahili ataona cha mtema kuni! (Enough!

Enough! The next person to be caught speaking Swahili is in big trouble!)

The boys laugh. VIOLET *returns with her basket empty.*

VIOLET. It is not a problem. In English then. For what reason do the boss buy this shamba?

NKWABI. He buy the shamba because Mr. Chatterjee sell it to him so cheap.

STARFORD. But why the boss so keen to buy?

NKWABI. The more shambas the better.

STARFORD. Bullshit. How can we grow coffee in a shamba so full of stones?

NKWABI. The boss have a use for them.

FRANK. What is that use?

NKWABI. We keep them, and when it is enough we build a wall around the shamba.

STARFORD *and* FRANK *groan.*

STARFORD. That is too much work!

VIOLET. You are all complaints,

STARFORD. It is a fact! I am sick of this dust. I am sick of this hot sun. I am fed up with this hard shamba work. When did we once get any benefit from all our shambas?

FRANK. Never.

NKWABI. Then who get the benefit?

STARFORD. Who have the stomach? Who have the big black suit? Who sit all day behind his desk? The boss.

FRANK. He get all these things and do no work for us.

NKWABI. He have administrative duties.

STARFORD. What?

NKWABI. He buy the shamba.

STARFORD. We get the shamba work! Stones to pick up. Tree stumps to pull out. Coffee-beans to pick.

FRANK. It is true. The boss do nothing.

NKWABI. He sell the coffee.

STARFORD. That is a fact. He sign the chiti and he take the cash. We do not see that cash. We do not even drink that coffee. Bullshit. I stop.

He throws down his hoe and walks away.

FRANK (*surprised*). What you stop?

STARFORD. I stop to work.

NKWABI. You stop to work, that leave more work for the rest of us.

STARFORD. Still I will consider it.

NKWABI. You tell the boss you stop to work?

STARFORD. Wait and see.

VIOLET. He will get hot with you.

STARFORD. Let him get hot! That is up to him.

He sits on the ground.

FRANK. Star?

STARFORD. What you want?

FRANK. What *you* want? You want to sign chiti?

No answer.

You want to drink coffee?

NKWABI. Let him drink coffee. That leave more Pepsi for the rest of us.

STARFORD. I do not want that boss to sign chiti and drink coffee on my behalf.

VIOLET *is lifting a basket of stones to put on her head.*

Not so fast.

VIOLET. What?

She stops, but the basket is heavy.

STARFORD. What have you got in this life?

VIOLET. Not much.

STARFORD. What things?

VIOLET. What I got on.

STARFORD. What else?

VIOLET. A few more things to wear. Why do you ask this?

STARFORD. There's something else you got. You got your work. The shamba grow coffee-beans from your work. But who get those coffee-beans?

VIOLET. Enough! Enough! I am sick of your big talk!

She heaves the basket on to her head and strides off. FRANK and NKWABI go on working with their hoes. STARFORD watches, then joins in as though casually, or trying it out. Gradually he takes up their rhythm so that all three are working as one. VIOLET comes and goes carrying stones.

A bell rings far off. They stop. NKWABI puts his hands to his mouth and makes the sound of a birdcall: a signal to others far off. They collect their things and start to go.

VIOLET. Star?

STARFORD. You walk in front.

They walk on. STARFORD stays.

I will work on it. I will explain it to her better. One fine day.

He walks on, his hoe over his shoulder.

On the road.

STARFORD. See! Kilimanjaro! Something of a landmark. Turisti come from far and wide. Three days to reach the top, it is a simple walk. Last year a team from Italy drive to the top on motorbikes. A ladies choir from Salt Lake City. One time, a Japanese with one leg only, fell in a trance and hopped up all the way.

Across the mountain: Kenya! That sad country. Ten years they fight for freedom. At last they win. Out from his mud hut jail come the king of the freedom-fighters, Jomo Kenyatta, called Mzee in respect for his white hairs. 'Look', say the world, 'you have your country! What will you do with it?' He stand, his red eyes blinking in the sun. 'What would you like?' he ask. 'Capitalism' cry the world. He whispers, 'I agree'. No sooner have the masses won their freedom than they lose it to big business. In the shanty towns they weep with bitter tears. And the old Mzee grow sick and die, sitting on a throne like the Sultan of Zanzibar, watching the dancing-girls.

In our country we are African socialists. We don't meddle in that Kenya business. All we hear is from the men who creep at night time through the border post. They sit here by the road and sell nice things to gangs of mammas walking back from work. Ball point pens. Pond's cream. Imperial Leather soap.

He stops.

What is this? A Rangerover stopped on the track?

By the Rangerover.

STEVE *sits inside examining a road map.*

STARFORD. Jambo!

STEVE. Jambo!

STARFORD. Habari za jioni? (How are you this evening?)

STEVE (*very distinctly*). Do you speak English?

STARFORD. A little. You are looking for the turisti information post?

STEVE. No, the training college.

STARFORD. Very good! I take you there.

STEVE (*who has been warned about giving long and complicated lifts*). Don't let me drag you out of your way.

STARFORD. It is not a problem.

STEVE. Fine. Thanks. Climb in.

He opens the front door. STARFORD *gets in.*

Is it far?

STARFORD. No, no, in this district everywhere is quite near to everywhere else. First, you must turn the car and drive it that way back.

STEVE. Look, I'd be happy to give you a lift. Only I've driven four hundred miles today and I'm looking forward to a rest. I want the Teachers' Training College, is that clear?

STARFORD. Back that way.

STEVE. Not according to the map.

STARFORD. Yes, that is a problem. On that map are many famous mistakes and this is number one.

STEVE. I see.

Pause. Since he can see no alternative:

Anything coming? Silly question.

He turns the car and they drive on, bumping vigorously on the potholes.

The drive to college.

STARFORD. In a few miles we shall drive past a trading store. You will know it by the sign on top say 'Chatterjee'.

STEVE. I don't want to stop.

STARFORD. There is no reason to! It is closed and everything is stolen from the shelf. But when you see it, you must turn to the left.

STEVE. If you say so.

STARFORD. You will see the college at once. It is a building of an English kind. On top is a Christian cross. And at the gate are young people with many guns and pangas.

STEVE. There are?

STARFORD. There must be! In our country we are on a semi-permanent war footing. These young people watch for enemies of many sorts. Bandits. Dissidents. South African spies. But do not worry, all that will be necessary is for you to state your name and business.

STEVE. Right.

STARFORD. To make it more easy, I can explain to them on your behalf.

STEVE. Fine, fine, I'd appreciate that.

STARFORD. Do you mind to tell me your name?

STEVE. Ah, not at all. It's Winter. W. I. N . . .

STARFORD (*who recognises the name*). Winter!

STEVE. Stephen Winter. Steve.

STARFORD. Starford.

STEVE. Glad to meet you. As for my business, I'm a lecturer at the Polytechnic of North London. I've an appointment at the College. Matter of fact, I'll be there a month. I've a letter somewhere from the Ministry of National Education if they'd like to . . .

STARFORD. It is not a problem! And you come to teach?

STEVE. Not quite.

STARFORD. Why not?

STEVE. My job's to find things out. And pass the information on to those who need it. I'm here to learn, if you like.

STARFORD. That is better still. We are comrades together in the same boat! Here we are!

At the gate to the college.

VIOLET, FRANK *and* NKWABI *appear in camouflage jackets, bristling with Kalashnikovs and pangas.*

VIOLET/FRANK/NKWABI. Stop!

STEVE. Jesus Christ!

VIOLET/FRANK/NKWABI. Name and business! Name and business!

STEVE (*to* STARFORD). The name's Winter, got it? I'm here by invitation. I'm English.

He stops the car. VIOLET, FRANK *and* NKWABI *address* STARFORD:

NKWABI. Wind down your window!

VIOLET. Do not get out of the car!

STARFORD. Silence!

NKWABI. No silence! We demand an explanation!

VIOLET. Starford, you must state your name and business!

VIOLET/FRANK/NKWABI. Name and business! Name and business!

STARFORD. *My* name and business?

NKWABI. That is correct.

STARFORD. Bullshit! You see me every day! You know my name and business too much already!

NKWABI. Who are you and what are you doing and why are you sitting in the car with the mzungu?

VIOLET. And why you not walk from shamba like the rest of us?

STARFORD. The mzungu give me a lifti.

NKWABI. He give you a lifti, why he not give everybody else a lifti?

VIOLET/FRANK/NKWABI. Name and business! Name and business!

STARFORD. Madness! Madness! I will put a stop to it!

He leaps from the car, seizes a gun and fires it into the air. VIOLET, NKWABI *and* FRANK *stand dumbstruck.* STEVE *ducks.*

Silence, you foolish children! Our guest is here! Where are your greetings? Where your welcoming gifts? Are these the manners of your villages? I am happy to introduce the distinguished professor from the Polytechnic of North London, Mr. Stiv Winter. He is here to further our education and assist our dynamising role amongst the masses! And all you can do is wave your guns into the air like bandits!

Silence.

That is a lot more like it. Now everybody must shake hands.

They do.

VIOLET. How do you do.

NKWABI. So nice to make your acquaintance.

STARFORD. Welcome to our college.

STEVE. Pleasure.

STARFORD (*to the others*). Good, good, now you have been polite why do you not stand at your guarding post?

They do, annoyed.

Mr. Stiv, we have been expecting you for weeks. Now I will show you to your quarters.

He gets into the Rangerover.

A further short drive.

STARFORD. Take a quiet man or woman. Make him a boss and he becomes an elephant on the rampage. In our country, Mr. Stiv, it is number one problem. We have faith in our leader. And in the masses we have faith as well. But in between, that is another story.

STEVE. So you're a student here?

STARFORD. I train to be a teacher.

STEVE. But you work in the fields?

STARFORD. It is common to all students.

STEVE. Do you do a lot of it?

STARFORD. Each morning. Some afternoons. And now we have a new shamba, it is on the increase.

STEVE. How do you feel about that?

STARFORD. Now you must tell me something, Mr. Stiv. Is it the custom in your country to ask such personal questions?

STEVE. Sorry.

STARFORD. It is not a problem. We have arrived at your apartment. See, the students have formed a welcoming party.

Outside STEVE's *apartment*

VIOLET, NKWABI *and* FRANK *are waiting with their hoes. As the Rangerover approaches, they indicate its movement by travelling smoothly sideways.*

STARFORD *jumps out, unpacks a suitcase and some boxes.* VIOLET, FRANK *and* NKWABI *lift one each.*

STEVE. Leave it please. I'll do it. They're a bit delicate.

They put the boxes down.

STARFORD. Mr. Stiv! You must not carry your bags! We students are here to make you feel at home!

VIOLET. He would not let us!

FRANK. He say to put them down!

STARFORD. Rubbish! Bullshit! You talk like Mr. Stiv was some white boss. No! He come to learn from us. You think Mr. Stiv must come all the way from U.K. to learn from us, and then he must carry his bags on top?

STEVE. If you insist.

He puts his luggage down. The students carry it to the door.

STARFORD (*with charm*). This humble concrete block will be your home.

STEVE *starts to enter.*

One moment please!

STEVE *stops.*

In our country, Mr. Stiv, we do not knock on doors. Most
people do not *have* any doors. How then do we know not to
walk into a room when the people inside are asleep or
making love or saying scandalous things about us which it
would be impolite to hear? We stand at the door and say:
'Hodi!' That is, 'I am here, may I enter without offence?'
And if you are welcome, the people inside will answer:
'Karibu!' That is, 'Please come in.'

STEVE. Fine, fine. 'Hodi!'

From inside the room, MR. KADUMA *replies:*

KADUMA. Karibu!

STARFORD. You see?

STEVE *goes in. The students follow, carrying his luggage.*

End of scene.

Scene Two

STEVE*'s apartment. A table and two chairs.* MR. KADUMA
*stands, his hands lightly pressed together. He is in advanced
middle age, handsome, urbane, perpetually agreeable and
shabbily dressed: his salary is minute.*

KADUMA. Mr. Winter! Welcome to our college! As for you
students, you are not required. I will show Mr. Winter his
bed and thermos flask and then he will recover from his
ordeals.

They put down his luggage. KADUMA *claps his hands.*

Off! Off! Away with all you children to your dormitories!

They leave.

Kaduma.

STEVE, *imagining this to be a form of native greeting, nods politely and places his hands together.*

Matthew Kaduma.

STEVE. I'm sorry. Winter, Steve Winter.

KADUMA. A pleasure.

They shake hands. On the table is a large tin of Africafé instant coffee, a carton of longlife milk, a bowl of sugar, a cup and saucer, a teaspoon and a thermos flask.

Shall I serve coffee?

STEVE. Thank you.

KADUMA. Milk?

STEVE. Please.

KADUMA. And sugar?

STEVE. Just the one.

KADUMA. Heaped up or flat?

STEVE. Like that will do fine.

KADUMA *has put the ingredients together in the cup. Now he adds hot water from the thermos and stirs carefully. He hands STEVE the cup.*

KADUMA. Please make yourself comfortable.

STEVE *sits.* KADUMA *stands erect.*

I am vice-principal of the college. I teach Music, English Lit, and Business Studies and mark all examination papers. Also I must dabble in administration and punish the bad students from time to time.

STEVE. Won't you sit down?

KADUMA *politely notices the chair as though for the first time.*

KADUMA. Thank you.

He sits and flexes his aching shoulder.

Mr.Winter, how old do you suppose me to be?

STEVE. It's hard to tell.

KADUMA. Fifty-nine. And how many hours shamba work do you think I have done today? Six.

STEVE. The staff do shamba work?

KADUMA. One day I will crack in two. One day I think the students will crack as well. But which of us has any choice? The work is voluntary and we are a democratic country.

STEVE. Would you like a drink?

KADUMA. A drink?

STEVE. I've some whisky in my case.

KADUMA. Thank you, it is not my custom.

STEVE. Coffee?

KADUMA. I would like some very much, but sadly no second cup has been provided.

STEVE. Look.

He unscrews the cup-shaped thermos-top. KADUMA *looks at it politely as though it had materialised at that moment.*

KADUMA. How ingenious. I shall follow your advice.

STEVE. I've got a better idea. You drink this. (*The coffee.*) I'll pour myself a Scotch. You don't object?

KADUMA *utters a silent open-palmed gesture of acceptance and self-deprecation, something he will often repeat.* STEVE *gets a bottle of Teachers out of his suitcase and pours some into the thermos-top. Meanwhile:*

KADUMA. Once we have refreshed ourselves, I shall accompany you to the staff room. Mr. Mzoga is there. He is principal of the college. And my senior. And to the students, the boss. You have heard of him?

STEVE. Not yet.

KADUMA. He looks forward to meeting you. At present he is playing darts with the junior members of staff, but he is always happy to receive a distinguished guest.

STEVE. What I had in mind was a drink and a shower, and then bed and maybe meet him for a briefing in the morning.

KADUMA. I understand. You are exhausted.

STEVE. That's all right then?

KADUMA. It may just possibly be all right. But I think that when Mr. Mzoga invites you for a game of darts he expects to see you as arranged. There is no hurry. He will be playing till nine or ten o'clock.

He smiles at STEVE *and sips his coffee.* STEVE *drinks his whisky.*

This is my first cup of coffee today. It has been all go. We started at seven with a staff inner caucus meeting for our principal's benefit. A crisis! Somebody somewhere had forgotten to inform the local chief of security about your visit. Everyone else for ten miles round knows everything there is to know about you, and more, but no, not him, he must discover last night by dint of a chance remark in the bar of the King George Hotel. Who do you suppose had to smooth his ruffled feathers, guide him back to square one, through the proper channels and out the other end, all between morning assembly and midday shamba work? I leave you to answer that question. And if I had failed? You would be driving back to Dar es Salaam, and I would not be sitting here drinking your coffee and welcoming you on behalf of our forgetful principal.

STEVE. I appreciate that.

He has finished his whisky, to his faint surprise, and from now on pours himself more ad lib.

KADUMA. I hope you will say the same when you have seen a little of our college. It was built during the dark days of the imperialist episode by missionaries of the Benedictine order. Their hand may be seen in the mosaic floor of the entrance lobby depicting the Lamb of God, the neon light cross on the roof and the green velvet curtains on the stage of the assembly hall. From which somebody has last week removed a piece of cloth four feet by two, why I don't know but I am told it was to cover his desk. Amongst our modern features is the Party Office conference hall. A visit by you tomorrow would be appreciated.

STEVE. I'll look forward to that.

KADUMA. Furnished two years ago by a construction team from North Korea, it presents an inspiring contrast to the poor conditions prevailing elsewhere in the college grounds. Curtains. A carpet. I do not exaggerate. And, on the walls, portraits in oil of our great President and members of his Cabinet. As seen through North Korean eyes. The paintings arrived from Pyongyang six months after the departure of the construction team. We unpacked them, and were startled. We had not hoped for precise resemblances, but at least we expected pictures of black men. But no such luck, every portrait we unwrapped looked more like a North Korean than the last. Mr. Winter, have you ever seen a North Korean? We hung the portraits. When we look at them, we make the necessary cultural adjustment. And we are instructed. For one people to help another, it's a delicate business. Sensitivities can be hurt. Those Koreans, you don't have to like them as individuals, but as a nation, they are our allies. Oh yes. We stand together in the struggle against oppression. Yet see how close they came to hurting our feelings.

You, Mr. Winter, come from a country which held us like a snake beneath its foot. You must tread with care.

STEVE. I plan to.

KADUMA. When your visit to us was first proposed, the response among our senior staff was negative. In this country, we have a problem of bureaucracy. People don't trust themselves to act with imagination. It is, I am told, a legacy of colonial times.

STEVE. Of course.

KADUMA. I used my best endeavours to point out the benefits you would bring. Your equipment was of course the chief attraction. Your company has promised us television sets, video-recorders, and few people in this district have ever seen such things. Our principal was quick to see the status which these wonders would confer upon the college, and on himself as well.

STEVE. Yes. That's not what I had in mind.

KADUMA. Of course not! Mr. Winter, I have a special interest in the success of your mission. You must forgive the banality of my efforts on your behalf. You have brought your equipment?

STEVE (*indicating his luggage*). There it is.

KADUMA. That's it?

STEVE. Tape-deck, portable TV camera, transformer, cassette-player and twenty-two-inch monitor.

KADUMA. And the quantity?

STEVE. One of each.

KADUMA. For myself I do not care. But Mr. Mzoga expected more.

STEVE. More can be provided. Mr. Kaduma, do you think I should have another drink?

KADUMA. I think you should please yourself.

STEVE (*while doing so*). My visit's an experiment. Will equipment of this kind do any good in a place like this? That's what I'm here to find out. We're not interested in littering the country with electronic hardware that nobody's going to use. That's the beads and bangles syndrome. Handing out goodies, always wanting something in exchange.

KADUMA. I understand, but thank you for pointing it out to me.

STEVE. That kind of thinking should have gone out with Livingstone. Sadly it hasn't. It goes on all the time. Big business. Bigger than ever. We're not like that. We're advanced. Selective. We chose this country, Mr. . . .

KADUMA. Kaduma.

STEVE. We chose it before any other country in Africa. And why? Because we're looking for a progressive country. And in that country, a progressive system of education. Once we've found it, we'll plug in our technology. Any other way, we're simply using electronics to pump the same old ideas into people's minds, only more intensively. And that's wrong, don't you agree?

KADUMA. What is the alternative?

STEVE. We reverse the flow. The electronics help people see themselves. They discover their own culture. A group of women, say, collecting firewood. Students kicking a ball. Record them and then watch the monitor. What does the image tell you? What do you discover from their body-language? What do you learn about the roles of men and women in traditional society?

KADUMA. And this is what you plan to try out here?

STEVE. That's right.

KADUMA. And this is your gift to Mzoga? You have come four thousand miles to show him something he can see from his office window? I think I would try this drink of yours, if there were a glass.

STEVE. Here.

He pours a scotch into the cap of the Teachers bottle, then hands it to KADUMA.

KADUMA. Should I say something? Cheers?

STEVE. I don't myself.

He carries on drinking: he's too tired and hungry to stop.

KADUMA. I told you about our Party Conference Hall. In that Hall, Mr. Mzoga is a simple Party member. We can say whatever we like to him and there is nothing he can do about it. Nothing, that is, till he gets out of that Hall. Then the position is reversed.

In addition to his academic duties, Mr. Mzoga employs all staff and manages all coffee grown on the college shambas and indeed in the district at large. He is principal of the peasants' literacy course and head of the ladies' college. He is chairman of the Party branch and by coincidence Mrs. Mzoga has recently been elected treasurer of the women's section. He runs this district complete.

STEVE. Not me, though.

KADUMA. Of course not. But you want your experiment to work. Why? I don't know, you have given a possible explanation, let us not quibble with it. Mzoga wants the experiment to work. Why? He wants the television sets. There need be no problem as long as you are tactful with him. See him as little as you can. On no account see him tonight, you are too tired. I shall say I found you asleep and no loud noise could wake you.

You talk of the students' culture. Wait till you talk to them. We are a developing country. A young person has no time to think of culture. He has too much work to do! Goats to herd, cattle to feed, little children younger than himself to tend. He must struggle to go to school, trample on others to reach a higher grade. By the time he reaches college he is a battle-scarred veteran. Still he must work. He must spend three-quarters of his time hoeing shamba and study his books by starlight. Some of the students work so hard that they learn nothing at all. You have met Nkwabi. Yesterday I say to him: Nkwabi, why are your marks so bad? He replies, 'A devil sit on my shoulder and whisper the wrong answers in my ear!' In your country you have superstition too. Do you deny it?

STEVE. Not at all.

KADUMA. And you have ignorance on top. But also you have advantages. English people are lazy. They are easily bored. These are great strengths. Boredom is creative. It is the shamba in which your culture is grown. Our students are never bored, I'm sad to say. They feel no hunger for the higher things of life, their lives are too full as it is. I look to you, to show them, with the help of what you have brought . . .

He indicates the boxes on the floor.

. . . a world they do not even know exists. A world where life in all its harshness is enriched by art. A world of culture. They have none of their own, I promise you that.

STEVE. I've met a few.

KADUMA. And you don't agree? Who? Starford?

STEVE. I think that's his name.

KADUMA. He has no culture. But he could pick it up. When he does, I think the sparks will fly.

He stands. The drink has had no effect on him.

I've taken much of your time. Your class tomorrow is in the library. Good luck with it. We have a word in our language: Ndugu. It means a kinsman: nephew, cousin, cousin of a nephew, our grandfathers were easygoing about such distinctions. In modern terms, the word means 'comrade'. We are all socialists here. We use it often. Have I your permission?

STEVE. I'm flattered.

KADUMA. Ndugu Winter, good night.

End of scene.

Scene Three

The Library. If books are to be represented, they comprise several copies of the Reader's Digest and the complete works of Kim Il Sung.

STEVE has almost finished setting up his equipment. NKWABI sits ready for the class.

STEVE. I'd planned to start with a few slides. But Mr. Mzoga was keen for me to show the full range of such equipment as I've brought. The reason's pretty exciting. It seems next week you'll be receiving a delegation from the A.N.C. And I quite understand you'll want to have made a comprehensive start by then. So, I'm sorry you told me your name but I forgot to write it down.

NKWABI. Nkwabi.

STEVE. Well, Nkwabi, when the others are here I reckon we can start.

NKWABI. May I speak?

STEVE. Sure.

NKWABI. This morning was a big speech from an A.N.C. forward coming person. Starford must talk to him.

STEVE. Oh I see.

NKWABI. I go and fetch him.

STEVE. Why don't we wait and see what happens?

NKWABI. Certainly sir!

He goes. STEVE, about to complete his setting-up, finds that something's missing.

STEVE. Shit!

VIOLET comes in.

VIOLET. Mr. Stiv, we have been looking everywhere and everywhere for Nkwabi.

STEVE. He's just gone to look for Starford.

VIOLET. I will get him.

STEVE. Hold it, hold it. Before we start, I'm looking for a
piece of cable about so long, with a plug at each end. It's
the connection between video-player and the monitor.

VIOLET. I have never seen such a thing in this country.

STEVE. Well say if you do. Otherwise we're up er you know
without a paddle.

VIOLET. I will try to find that thing.

She goes. In a flash of inspiration STEVE *realises it might
be in his pocket. He looks. It isn't.* FRANK *comes in.*

FRANK. Good morning Mr. Stiv.

STEVE. Good morning.

FRANK. Mr. Mzoga say this class must finish soon so he can
tell the school what happen when the A.N.C. delegation
come next week.

STEVE. Oh yes, well I appreciate that's very important.

FRANK. No I don't mind to wait. What has happened to the
other students?

STEVE. Just stay where you are. They'll show.

FRANK. It is not a problem.

He goes. STEVE *looks for the connection.* STARFORD
comes in.

STARFORD. Mr. Stiv, I have been looking everywhere for
those people. They are nowhere to be found. It is nothing
personal. Many of the students are keen to see your visual
aids. But there is the A.N.C. delegation next week and they
must first make the garden nice and get ready the liberation
songs.

STEVE. Fine, fine, let's start as we are.

STARFORD. How can we start without the students?

STEVE. Just wait here. I'm sure they'll be along.

> STARFORD *sits.* NKWABI *comes back.*

Come in, come in.

> NKWABI *sits.* VIOLET *comes in.*

VIOLET. I have found Nkwabi.

STEVE. Fine. Let's sit and wait. He'll come in his own good time.

> FRANK *comes in.*

STEVE. Nkwabi, at last. Wouldn't you like to sit down?

> FRANK *sits down.*

STARFORD. Point of order.

STEVE. Certainly, certainly, let's keep it short.

STARFORD. That man is Frank. That is Nkwabi. She is Violet. I am Starford.

STEVE. Starford, Frank, pom pom pom, I've got that. (*To* NKWABI.) Did you find the connection?

VIOLET. Mr. Stiv, it was me who was finding that connection.

STEVE. Let's have it then.

VIOLET. I have never seen such a thing in this country.

STEVE. Great.

What I had planned this morning was a demonstration of audio-visual aids in education. What we have here is a video-player of a light and portable nature, video-camera, basic transformer, a monitor adaptable for tropical conditions and a stock of educational cassettes selected by a team of U.N.E.S.C.O. educational advisers as suitable for application to rural life. What we don't have is a length of cable with a male connection one end and a female at the other. Violet these are technical terms, without which the whole setup is as useful as Pope's nipples.

Pause.

Anyway, we've got to finish in a minute, isn't that right?

NKWABI. Mr. Stiv, is not a problem. Mr. Mzoga have a
change of plan. He have taken the A.N.C. forward coming
person to the King George Hoteli and they will not get back
till after lunch.

STEVE. I see.

NKWABI. We have all morning.

STEVE. Only no equipment. Thrown back on our own
resources. Okay then, who's got an idea?

Pause.

What I sometimes do in these situations is, let's say, a
getting-to-know-each-other game. We might just sit in a
circle and look at the person on our left and say what
animal or plant he or she reminds us of.

Pause.

Another good game is to invent a ritual of some kind.
Anyone here know anything about rituals?

Embarrassed pause.

Fine. I've got it. Story-telling. Violet?

VIOLET. You want me to tell a story?

STEVE. It's up to you but . . . Yes.

Pause.

VIOLET. 'Mastikito'.

STARFORD. Mr. Stiv, this is a little children's story.

STEVE. Give her a chance.

VIOLET. A father and a mother got married. In time their child
was made. Her name was Mastikito. The mother died. The
father marry again and make two daughters, Tatu and Piri.
The second wife is cruel to Mastikito. She make her sweep
the house and cook the food. One day she say, 'Mastikito,
our firewood is empty. Go into the bush and pick up more.'
The young girl, Tatu, sympathise for Mastikito. Quietly and

out of sight she follow Mastikito into the bush. What she see? The second wife has digged a hole and covered it with leaves. Mastikito fall in. The wife fill up the hole and go back home, Tatu see all this. That night she say, 'Mother, where is Mastikito?' Her mother answer, ' She has gone to visit her grandmother.' Tatu say nothing. When all are asleep, she slip out from the house. She find the spot and she dig. And she sing this song:

'Mastikito! Mastikito! My mother has buried you alive! Now I will dig you up!'

And Mastikito sing from under the ground:

'Tatu! Tatu! Dig faster! I will rot and the worms will eat me!'

Two days and two nights she dig. At last she pull out Mastikito. All down her side, down half her body, she has rotted away and the worms are eating her. Tatu take her to the king. The king call the second wife and he say to her, 'You will have two punishments. One I fix myself. All the worms that come from Mastikito, you must eat.' The king's wives collect the worms in a bowl. When she finish to eat, the king say: 'Now come your second punishment. It will be fixed for you by Mastikito.' But Mastikito say: 'There will be no more punishment. What my stepmother have done to me, I forgive.' The king give Mastikito three cows and send her home. He send the stepmother home on top. And this is the story of Mastikito.

Pause.

STEVE. Well. Now. What does this story have to say to us today?

NKWABI. We must respect our elders and forgive them.

STEVE. Exactly, that's the kind of theme which might be buried in it.

NKWABI. It is the moral.

VIOLET. But it is not buried.

NKWABI. It was Mastikito who was buried.

STEVE. Right. I see. Respect our elders. And do we agree with that? Whatever they do?

Pause.

Thank you, Violet. That was very interesting. Actually, when I said a story I meant ideally something true to life. Some real event from our own experience. Not that I want to tell you what to say, that's up to you and the way it takes us. So. What has happened in this district in the last few weeks?

Pause.

Come on, I don't believe that nothing interesting has happened. Starford?

STARFORD. No, nothing interesting has happened.

STEVE. Yesterday I gave you a lift, right? You were coming back from shamba work. Had anything happened that day that hadn't happened before?

VIOLET. Yesterday we start to work on a new shamba.

NKWABI. It is a shamba which the boss have bought.

FRANK. He buy that shamba from Mr. Chatterjee.

STEVE. And why did he do that? Why did Mr. Chatterjee want to sell?

VIOLET. It is because of a strange thing which happen on that shamba.

STARFORD. I don't think Mr. Stiv will want to know this rubbish.

STEVE. No no, if affects your lives, let's hear it.

VIOLET. Mr. Chatterjee hear a voice.

STEVE. What kind of voice?

VIOLET. He hear a voice without anyone at all being there to speak.

STEVE. Who did? This Mr.Chatterjee?

VIOLET. Mr. Chatterjee, Mrs. Chatterjee and their two
daughters Premula and Pearl.

STEVE. Hang on, hang on, I think we're getting a little carried
away here. What *really* happened, right?

STARFORD (*as one exploding a fantasy*). These two Indian
people were running the village shop. And people say they
make big prices up. And nobody want to pay. But there was
no other shop to buy the food in. That was the problem.

STEVE. Good. Now, what we might do in Britain is take a
situation like that and improvise around it. That means,
making up the words ourselves. Do you think we can do
that?

Pause.

No?

STARFORD. Mr. Stiv, in this country we do not do that kind
of thing.

STEVE. Well, how'd you like to give it a try?

NKWABI. It is a problem.

VIOLET. When we are little children we might tell a story and
make up the words, But we don't think you would be
interested.

FRANK. Maybe, as Mr. Stiv is a guest, we should try to
oblige.

NKWABI. I agree.

VIOLET. Me too.

STARFORD. O.K. And I will help.

STEVE. Fine, let's start. Don't worry if you find it tricky at
first.

VIOLET. Who will be story-teller?

STARFORD. I will do that thing.

FRANK (*to* VIOLET). You must be the mamma of the
Chatterjees.

> VIOLET *wraps a sheet round herself Asian style.*
> STARFORD *begins:*

STARFORD. This is the story of the Chatterjee family and
their adventures at the foot of Mount Kilimanjaro. Let it
begin.

VIOLET (*as Mrs. Chatterjee*). Premula! Pearl! You two
daughters are nothing but a trial! Why aren't you like the
black girls in the village? They help their mammas in the
shambas day and night. And what do you do? Nothing. You
sit and read movie magazines and plait your hair. How can
we save enough money to fly first class back to India and
build a temple there?

VIOLET (*as one daughter*). Oh Mamma! We are too proud to
pick up stones and hoe the shamba!

VIOLET (*as the other daughter*). Can you not pay cash to the
mammas of the village to pick up stones and hoe the
shamba on our behalf?

VIOLET (*as Mrs. Chatterjee, sings*).

> Oh to be a mother
> You give birth to your daughters
> That gives you pain
> Then they are lazy and ungrateful
> That is the greatest pain of all!

STEVE. Fine, fine, only Violet seems to be playing all the
parts. Wouldn't somebody else like to . . . ?

> *Without prompting,* FRANK *comes on as Mr. Chatterjee.*

FRANK. Good morning, wife.

STEVE. Frank, well done. Don't be embarrassed, just . . .

ALL. Ssss! (*Meaning 'ssh!'*)

VIOLET. Good morning Mr. Chatterjee. Sit on the sofa set and
tell me how you are happy today.

FRANK. Things are very bad! I work all day selling Pepsi and razorblades to those stupid black monkeys in my shop! I can hardly walk home, so heavy are my pockets from all the money I have taken from them! Now I find none of my women will hoe and tend my shamba! See it is taken care of! I want a big fine coffee-crop next year or I will beat you all till you are flat as poppadoms!

He goes off.

STEVE. This is fascinating. What I'd like to . . .

ALL. Sss!

VIOLET. It is not a problem. I will hire the mammas of the village to hoe and tend my shamba and I will pay them as little as possible to do it. Then my daughters can go on reading Screen Romance and I can sew more bits of glass on to my sari.

STEVE. Hold it a moment. What I'd like to suggest is, let's examine was was actually happening here . . .

He is silenced by hilarious laughter from VIOLET *and* FRANK *as* STARFORD *and* NKWABI *appear dressed as village mammas in kangas, wearing leaves in their hair and with lavishly feminine demeanour. Each carries a hoe. When agreeing about something, or both are amused, one holds his palm out and the other slaps it.*

NKWABI. Good morning Mamma Mpofu! Have you slept well?

STARFORD. I've slept very well, Mamma Mmaka, if you slept well!

NKWABI. Oh I slept wonderfully!

STARFORD. Good, good! And where are you going?

NKWABI. I am going to dig for Mrs. Chatterjee!

STARFORD. Me too! (*Slap hands.*) Is it true she cannot dig her own shamba?

NKWABI. Dig her shamba? She is too lazy to do anything but mark up the prices on the stockings and petticoats she sells.

STARFORD. That woman is one big idle baboon, we must teach her a lesson. What we must do is this. Every time we take out a stone we will carry it across the shamba and bury it in the other end.

NKWABI. Yes! That is the ideal solution! That will do the trick!

VIOLET *meets them.*

VIOLET. You are much too late! To work! I must return to my shop.

She pretends to go, but surreptitiously hides behind a bush and watches.

NKWABI. Quick, let us bury this stone.

STARFORD. And this one!

BOTH. Ha ha ha!

They rush backwards and forwards picking up stones and burying them. VIOLET *sings:*

VIOLET. Oh my shamba!
The mammas pick up the stones
And they bury them back in the ground.
I look at the piles of stones they make,
Too small for me to believe,
Oh to be back in India
Where these devils will not torment me!

She comes out of her hiding-place.

Silence!

The village mammas stop their activities.

Now I have caught you red-handed. Mamma Mpofu, there you are burying a stone. From now on I make a new decision. No more ready cash will be paid to you mammas. The money you have earned, I will knock off from what you buy in my shop and owe on tick. That is how you will get paid.

NKWABI. Jackal!

STARFORD. Hyena!

VIOLET. Say what you like! My profits will rise and rise! Never will you outwit me! I shall own this village complete!

STEVE. Well done. Now what I suggest, is that we look at some of the preconceptions which came up in the course of the impro. Right at the end, we heard that . . .

VIOLET. Mr. Stiv, that was only the beginning.

STEVE. Ah.

STARFORD (*as story-teller*). From that day, Mrs. Chatterjee count the stones with care. But the village mammas had a rude reply.

NKWABI. Now we must punish that wild pig's penis!

STARFORD. Yes! We will bring stones from our own shambas and bury them instead!

NKWABI. Good! Good! Things are getting out of control!

STARFORD (*as story-teller*). Listen now to the story of Mamma Mghamba.

NKWABI *pads himself out to look fat.*

NKWABI. I am Mamma Mghamba, the fattest mamma in the village. I will pack my kanga full of stones so that I can hardly walk. Each stone is there to kill a coffee-bush. Each stone is one more thorn in the foot of Chatterjee.

STARFORD. Mamma Mghamba walk to work. She is so heavy with stones to kill the coffee-bushes that she roll from side to side. When she reach the river-bank, she stagger and fall into the water.

NKWABI. Aaaah!

ALL. Splash! (*Or Swahili equivalent.*)

STARFORD. She shout for help!

NKWABI. Help! Help! Pull me out!

FRANK *and* VIOLET *laugh helplessly at this development.*

STARFORD. Three men with ropes come running to pull Mamma Mghamba from her predicament. But it is a problem.

VIOLET. She is heavier than ever before!

FRANK. She has too many stones in her pocket!

VIOLET. It would be easier to pull out a hippopotamus!

FRANK. We must go and find a tractor!

VIOLET. No, a tractor will cost too much. We must wait three days until she float up to the top.

FRANK/VIOLET. Goodbye, Mamma Mghamba! Good bye!

STARFORD. One week later the funeral of Mamma Mghamba take place.

All four assemble as mourners, drinking, singing, dancing and having a good time.

VIOLET. Friends! Let us honour the memory of Mamma Mghamba!

NKWABI. Yes! Let us eat as much food as we can!

FRANK. Let us drink pombe until we fall on the floor!

NKWABI. Wait! Wait! Who is this I see approaching the hut?

FRANK. It is that yellow witch from the trading store!

STARFORD. How dare she come to us at such a time? If it were not for her, Mamma Mghamba would be getting drunk with us here today!

VIOLET, *back in sari, approaches the hut. The mourners turn their backs on her.*

VIOLET. Hodi! Hodi! Hodi!

STARFORD. Mrs. Chatterjee stand outside the hut and say 'Hodi'. But nobody say 'Karibu' back to her. At last she enter without a welcome.

VIOLET *comes into the hut.*

FRANK. How she cry! How she scratch her face! How she tear her sari!

NKWABI. She has put ashes on her head on top!

STARFORD. She bring with her a box of groceries. What for?

VIOLET. Oh you dear mammas of the village. I come to pay my last respects to Mamma Mghamba. And look, with me I have brought presents for you all. Tins of corned beef. A bunch of bananas. A crate of Pepsi for you ladies and all-day suckers for the little watoto. (*i.e. children, which she indicates by looking affectionately at them and patting them on the head.*)

Please understand I never mean to upset you mammas. From now on I pay you cash once more to hoe my shamba. Yes! Ready cash at last! Just so long as you do not put in too many extra stones.

STARFORD. But Mrs.Chatterjee can do nothing to win approval.

ALL (*sing*).
    You came from over the sea,
    You build a shop in our village
    But your prices are much too high
    And you send our money away.
    Go after it!
    Fly after it!
    Get on an aeroplane and leave us in peace!

    STARFORD, FRANK and NKWABI beat VIOLET and drive her out of the hut.

STEVE. Great! Fantastic! Starford, Violet, you said you couldn't improvise.

STARFORD. All we are doing, Mr. Stiv, is make up what people do when something happen to them.

VIOLET. Anybody can do that.

STEVE. What I'd like now is for us to chat about what we've done. For example, was Mrs. Chatterjee right or wrong or even misunderstood? To what extent was she responsible for the death of Mamma thingummy . . .

STARFORD. Mamma Mghamba fall in the river through her own ignorance.

VIOLET. Rubbish!

FRANK. Mr. Stiv, if you stop a story in the middle, nothing will follow but a fight.

STEVE. You mean there's more?

STARFORD. No! Mr. Stiv does not want to see the next part of the story. It is bullshit.

NKWABI. Let us ask Mr. Stiv.

STEVE. Up to you.

STARFORD. Then somebody else must be the storyteller.

NKWABI. That is not a problem.

He continues the story, changing the mood by his intense seriousness.

See now the strange thing which happen on the tribal shamba.

VIOLET *and* FRANK *present the Chatterjees at home.*

VIOLET. Why, Mr. Chatterjee, do the village mammas curse and beat me? How long must we stay in this village where they hate us so?

FRANK. Silence! We stay here until we have got every shilling we can grasp from them. Where are our two daughters Premula and Pearl?

VIOLET. I have put them to bed.

FRANK. Why do you put them to bed at such a time? Do you not know we have electric light so that we can sit and read magazines long after good people have gone to bed?

VIOLET. I put them to bed because I wish to talk with you. Sit with me on the sofa set and I will tell you something too frightening to hear.

FRANK. Ha ha! Tell me and see how much I get frightened! There is nothing in the world that frighten me!

VIOLET. The village mammas have put a curse on us. They have called on their dead ancestors to chase us out of this house and off the shamba.

FRANK (*to* VIOLET). Why, Mrs. Chatterjee, would the ancestors go to all such trouble to push us off our shamba? To pay us back for that fat mamma who fall in the river? It is rubbish!

VIOLET. This is why. This shamba we have bought is tribal land. We do not belong to that tribe. We do not even have a tribe! The ancestors are angry to see their shamba grow coffee for strangers. That is why they push us off.

FRANK. Rubbish! Mumbo-jumbo! We Indian people have nothing to fear from those black ancestors.

VIOLET. But what is that noise? Listen.

They listen. NKWABI, *sitting at the side, makes a terrifying noise, something like:*

NKWABI. Woooo! Woooo!

FRANK/VIOLET. Aaaah!

FRANK *quakes with comic terror and hides.* VIOLET *looks around in panic.*

VIOLET. Oh Mr. Chatterjee, where have you gone?

FRANK. I am hiding under the table from the ancestors!

NKWABI. Woooo! Woooo!

VIOLET/FRANK. Help! Help! It has happened again! We have heard a voice and there was nobody at all to speak!

VIOLET. Mr. Chatterjee, let us go to bed. We will lock all the doors and put our blankets over our faces, then no ancestor will find us.

FRANK. And our two daughters will sleep with us too.

VIOLET, FRANK *and* NKWABI (*as the daughters*) *get under a blanket and cover their heads.*

FRANK. Now it is night.

NKWABI makes noises of frogs, crickets, etc.

FRANK. The sun is up. Wake up, my wife! See, no ancestor has troubled us!

They throw off the blanket and look around in horror.

VIOLET. Aah!

NKWABI. Ooh!

FRANK. What do I see?

VIOLET. We are not in our house!

FRANK. We have wake up in the middle of the shamba!

NKWABI. Mother, father, how did we get here? Who has carried us out of our house? We are too frightened!

VIOLET. Mr. Chatterjee, see! The village mammas are standing around the shamba pointing and laughing at us!

FRANK. Now they are throwing stones and hitting us!

They react to a shower of imaginary stones.

FRANK/VIOLET/NKWABI. Ah! Ah! Ah!

FRANK. Enough! This village is full of devils! I wash my hands with it! I will sell my house and shamba to Mr. Mzoga at the college. Then I take the money and fly first class to India!

VIOLET, FRANK and NKWABI snap out of character, cheer and dance a conga, African-style, while singing a wordless song of celebration. They do a couple of turns around the room and then sit down abruptly, not with any expectation of applause, so that an odd pause follows.

STEVE. Fine.

They stare at him, non-committal, whether in hope of praise or comment is impossible to say.

Just one thing I'm not quite clear about. That last section, was it made up?

STARFORD. It is true that the boss buy the shamba from Mr. Chatterjee. Yesterday we start to work on it. And that is how I meet you on the road.

STEVE. I understand. But the reason for them to sell up and leave the village, what was that?

They stare at him.

Don't think I'm being personal. I'm interested, that's all.The shamba is tribal land, is that correct? And the ancestors want it back for the tribe?

NKWABI. It is not only the land. On that land are coffee bushes.

STEVE. Yes, I got that.

NKWABI. When the beans are sold, the Chatterjee family get the cash. That is the problem.

STEVE. Problem for who? The ancestors?

STARFORD. Bullshit! This is bullshit like the mammas in the village say to frighten the little children! If that night is like any other night, Mr. Chatterjee is coming back from the King George Hoteli. He is drunk! And he fall to sleep in the wrong place. Or he go to the toilet in the middle of the night and lose the way. Maybe they get a fright from the voice and sleep in the shamba for a safe place.

VIOLET. Then what is that voice?

STEVE. Violet, do you believe this?

She doesn't reply.

Starford, you don't, I can see. Frank?

FRANK *looks at* STARFORD, *then shakes his head.*

Nkwabi, what do you think?

NKWABI. Yes and no.

STARFORD *snorts in contempt.*

STEVE. Fine. I've learned a lot. Let's do one more. How does the story end? What happens next?

STARFORD. We hoe the shamba.

STEVE. Can you show me?

STARFORD. It is a problem. To show how we hoe shamba, we must feel committed to it. And every day we have to hoe shamba in any case, we are fed up with it.

STEVE. Sure, sure, I see.

STARFORD. It is not a good suggestion.

STEVE. No, no, I'm sorry. Well, what happens *then*?

NKWABI. We sell the coffee-beans,

STARFORD. The *boss* sell the coffee-beans.

STEVE. Fine, show me how it's done.

FRANK. You want one of us to act the boss?

STEVE. Yes. Why not you?

FRANK. OK.

FRANK gets up, waddles over to a chair in fat and pompous manner. Lots of laughter. When it's quietened down:

STEVE. Now we need somebody else. Somebody to buy the coffee-beans. Come on, we're being a bit slow suddenly.

VIOLET and NKWABI smile.

NKWABI. Mr. Stiv, we think you should buy the coffee-beans.

STEVE. All right.

He sits opposite FRANK. VIOLET giggles.

What's the joke?

STARFORD. Mr. Stiv, it is nothing to laugh at. What she is too shy to say is, you are the best person to buy the coffee-beans because we are black and you are white.

STEVE. I see. A white man buys the coffee, is that it?

STARFORD. When somebody come in a car to business with the boss for the coffee, yes he will be very likely white.

STEVE. Always the same person?

STARFORD. No, often a different one. You are standing in as it were for all of them. It is a foolish joke. Believe me, it is not the colour of the man that is important.

STEVE. Right, right. But who is this man? Or series of men? What's the name of his company?

STARFORD. We do not know.

STEVE. Violet? Nkwabi? Frank?

STARFORD. Mr. Stiv, we have a problem. It is a problem of commitment, that is, the personal commitment of us, as students, as members of a group. Each morning, many afternoons, we do shamba work. We grow coffee, some vegetables and banana. The vegetable and banana we see for ourselves a day or two later in the market. Mr. Mzoga, he arrange the sale. The price and what he do with the money, he organise that too. We do not know much. As for the coffee, we know nothing. Let me ask you a question. Is that right?

STEVE. I'm sure there's nothing sinister about it.

STARFORD. That is not my point. Why do we work in shamba at all? For a good reason. Out of ten thousand people in this country, how many will go to college? Maybe one. No, less. We are the chosen few. What will we do with our good fortune? Will we share it with our brothers? Or will we come to think that we are better than them? That now we have a schooling, we must have a bigger salary, a suit of clothes, a car? No! We must understand, each and every day, that we are flesh and blood with our brothers in the villages. We work in the shamba same as they do. We must fight for them. We must tell them what we read in our books. We must ask the questions they cannot ask.

VIOLET. Like what?

STARFORD. Like who get the coffee-beans?

STEVE. Right, right.

STARFORD. You agree?

STEVE. Absolutely. Why don't you ask Mr. Mzoga?

NKWABI. That would not be possible.

STEVE. Why not?

NKWABI. On Thursday evening, seven o'clock, Mr. Mzoga hold his open day. At that time, for one hour, students may come to him to ask their problems.

STEVE. It's Thursday today. Why don't you see him tonight?

NKWABI. No-one has ever been known to visit him then. What he would say if we disturbed him in his open day hour, we do not like to think.

STEVE. That's a pity.

STARFORD. I think so too.

STEVE. Violet, do you agree?

VIOLET. I do not mind who get the coffee-beans.

FRANK. Nkwabi? Frank?

VIOLET. May we go now?

STEVE. Sure. I'm sorry about the missing connection. I'll try to cobble something together for tomorrow.

They rise.

STARFORD. Wait! Stop! There is a problem. Chatterjee, he is thrown off his shamba. By who?

VIOLET. The ancestors.

STARFORD. Why?

VIOLET. It is tribal land. They do not like to see the Chatterjees make cash from it.

STARFORD. And now? Who own the shamba?

VIOLET. The college.

STARFORD. And who get the cash? Who get the coffee-beans?

VIOLET. We do not know! We do not need to know!

STARFORD. Do the ancestors know? Do they approve? What if they don't? What will they do to us if they are angry?

Pause.

VIOLET. We must ask.

FRANK. Yes.

VIOLET. We ask the boss tonight.

FRANK. Yes!

STARFORD. And one thing more! Let us not wear our Sunday suits like little children at a confirmation! We will wear our shamba clothes and carry hoes as workers with a strong and fierce demand!

NKWABI. Not me.

STARFORD. Why not?

NKWABI. I do not care to know. I stay away.

VIOLET. Bullshit!

End of Act One.

ACT TWO

Scene One

MR. MZOGA*'s office.* MR. MZOGA *sits at a large desk. He is short, disagreeably fat, carries a stick and wears a smart western-style black suit.*

STARFORD, FRANK *and* VIOLET *approach his office. They wear work clothes and carry their hoes over their shoulders.*

STUDENTS. Hodi!

MR. MZOGA *reacts with astonishment. He looks at his watch, then in surprise at the door. The students repeat:*

Hodi!

MZOGA (*angry and defensive*). Karibu!

The three students enter.

STUDENTS. Shikamoo. (*A deferential greeting.*)

MZOGA. Marahaba. (*Acknowledgement from a superior to an inferior.*) And you better sit down.

They do, in a row, their hoes held upright, blade upward.

Never once in all my years at this college has such a thing befell. See, you wear your working clothes! You wave your dirty hoes above my carpet! Is this some accident? No! It is on purpose to make a fool of me and break the college rules. Do you deny it?

STARFORD. Sir, that is correct.

MZOGA. Now we are talking sense. Point number two: every Thursday I sit in this chair from seven to eight o'clock. I could be mingling with the junior members of staff around the dartboard. I could be sitting with Mrs. Mzoga listening to the political broadcasts. I could be dropping in at the King George Hoteli to read the latest news. But no, I sit and twiddle my toes to wait for a knock at my door in the hope to improve student/staff relations.

And is this all? No! Now I must have my rest disturbed! Of all your workteam, only Nkwabi is a good boy today. You, Starford, are the ringleader of all the troubles in the college. You, Frank, follow him like a jackal. You, Violet, are not too bad, what you are doing with these rascals and their plots I must wait to find out.

One thing I can tell you from the start. Whatever you want from me you will not get it. I don't know why I must be bothered to tell you this. I don't know why you can't work it out for yourselves. I don't know why you disrupt my Thursday open day hour instead. Or why you take up the time I could be devoting to the legitimate demands of students in need of fatherly advice. Students who are anxious to raise their work-targets! To volunteer for consciousness-raising expeditions among the masses! Or give up their spare time on literacy campaigns among the poor mammas of the village! For all I know there are hundreds of such students waiting outside that door this very moment, and I must sit here . . .

His voice rises to a shout.

. . . like an office boy, listening to problems which you are too stupid to solve and too impertinent to keep to yourselves!

He calms down.

Does this answer your question?

STARFORD. No. It does not.

MZOGA. Good. I don't complain. We will continue this meeting before witnesses.

He picks up the intercom on his desk and buzzes the switchboard.

Who's that? Miss Maguluko? Hello hello hello, I can't talk now, I am addressing an ad hoc student delegation and need a couple of staff members to speed the plough. Who is there left in the staff room? Mr. Kaduma, no I don't like him, someone else. Where are the others? I see. In that case, tell them I won't be long and say to that Mr. Kaduma to skip down the corridor as fast as his legs will carry him. Bye-bye for now, be seeing you!

He bangs the intercom down.

This is a pencil. This is a notebook. I will ask Mr. Kaduma to take the minutes. I may want to refresh my memory when I make up the punishment book at the end of the week.

KADUMA *enters via a quick hodi/karibu exchange.*

MZOGA. Sit there. No, there.

KADUMA *sits.*

I want you to tell me, Mr. Kaduma, when was the last time I was approached during my student/staff communications surgery?

KADUMA. Three years ago.

MZOGA. So long? Remind me if you please, what was the point at issue?

KADUMA. As I recall, Principal, some of the students had a query concerning the food in the canteen.

MZOGA. They did? What was wrong with it?

KADUMA. They could not find any meat in the meat stew.

MZOGA. That's right! That's right! (*He laughs.*) That was a good discussion. I let off steam, they let off steam. Who took the minutes on that occasion?

KADUMA. The senior lecturer in contemporary historical studies, Mr. Ng'ong'a.

MZOGA. I remember it well. He let off steam himself. Oh yes. He described the hardships of the students in moving terms. He gave a lengthy lecture on dietary requirements for shamba workers. Can you remind me, Mr. Kaduma, where is Mr. Ng'ong'a now?

KADUMA. He was transferred at your request a fortnight later. He now teaches domestic economics at an infant school in Simbawanga.

MZOGA. There is no school in Simbawanga. Plans to build a school in Simbawange have been unavoidably postponed. Why? Cholera. Tsetse fly. Malaria. To say nothing of the armed hostility of the local tribesmen. The Government has decided to send no bricklayers, plumbers or other socially productive personnel to Simbawanga until these teething troubles have been ironed out. And until that happy day, the wretched Mr. Ng'ong'a will teach piccanins in the bush with one pencil to share round the class and another to scrape the leeches from his legs. What a pity for Mr. Ng'ong'a that he didn't stick to writing the minutes in silence, rather than make speeches about meat stew.

He hands KADUMA the pencil and paper.

Shall we start?

To the students:

Good, what can I do to help?

STARFORD. The Chatterjees sell their shamba. You buy the shamba. We grow coffee in that shamba. Now we ask, who get the coffee-beans?

MZOGA. You want to know who get the coffee-beans?

VIOLET. Yes, we want to know.

MZOGA. Bullshit! No young woman has ever asked such a question. It is much too difficult! That is the kind of question our great leader asked when he led the masses to throw out the colonial oppressor. It is the kind of question those trouble-making monkeys ask at the University when they go on march and take off the day on striki. It is a trick. I see through it at once. Why do you mind so much who get the coffee-beans when you never minded before in your life? I tell you. It is because I buy an extra shamba and you do not like the extra work.

He stands.

Starford. Violet. Frank. You have been chosen as leaders of the masses. You have been given shoes on your feet and a book in front of your nose. There is not a village goatherd boy who would not throw his right hand to the crocodiles for such a chance! A student who is given education and refuse to use it for the benefit of the masses is like a man sent from a village to find water, and when he has found it, drink it himself and leave his fellow-villagers to die of thirst. A student who forget his solidarity with the masses, who think he is too good for manual labour, who threat to stop to work, who forget the tears of his mother, the sufferings of his little brothers and sisters, the commands of his father and village elders, who spit on his grandfather's curse, is lost for ever! He is a traitor! He deserve no mercy! You will go back to work and you will hoe shamba and we will hear no more nonsense about coffee-beans! Does that answer your question?

FRANK. Not exactly.

VIOLET. I don't think so.

STARFORD. No!

MZOGA *glares at them in fury.*

KADUMA. Mr. Principal . . .

MZOGA. Did you say something?

KADUMA. I agreed, as we discussed, to listen in silence, as befits a humble secretary, to this exchange of views. Yet I feel compelled to speak. You are so near to a solution, and yet so far, that a few words on my part might serve to dispel the present misunderstanding.

MZOGA. Keep it short!

KADUMA. It is a well-known fact that you never agree to anything the students ask.

MZOGA. Of course, I don't need you to tell me that.

KADUMA. Why, then, do they ask for less shamba work?

MZOGA. Because they want to *do* less shamba work.

KADUMA. No, Mr. Principal. If they ask you for less shamba work, they know you will give them twice as much.

MZOGA. Your pencil, Kaduma, is lying idle. Come to the point!

KADUMA. School work is hard for them. English is a difficult language. Arithmetic is also a problem, many of them must labour to remember where the numbers go. If they do more shamba work, these irksome studies will be reduced! Mr. Principal, I implore you not to be angry with them for this simple ruse. Young people are lazy. But they are our future. Let us help them to shake off their idle habits. Do not fall for their trick. Reduce their shamba work. Give them more school work. Perhaps a little time off in between so that life is not too hard for them. You will have won the argument and shown that you mean business.

MZOGA. There is a problem.

KADUMA. May I ask what it is?

MZOGA. I never agree with anything you say either.

KADUMA. Perfectly true.

MZOGA. But this time I go along with it. Less shamba work. More school work. I have decided.

KADUMA. Mr. Principal, accept my congratulations.

MZOGA. Violet, you accept your punishment?

VIOLET. (Mumble, mumble.)

MZOGA. Frank?

FRANK. (Mumble mumble.)

MZOGA. Starford?

STARFORD. No! Who get the coffee-beans?

MZOGA *stares at him.*

MZOGA. This boy has gone mad! Always I have hated him worse than death! And since yesterday he is worse than ever!

He picks up the intercom.

Find that Englishman. Tell him to come at once. I want a full account of his activities at the experimental media in education workshop session!

He gets up and paces about in fury waving his stick.
KADUMA *speaks quietly to* STARFORD.

KADUMA. Starford, what are you doing? See how you lead your comrade Frank into danger. And your sister Violet, how near she come to a name in the punishment book. Think of your village! The shame of your mother! The grief of your comrades here!

STEVE enters. MZOGA *greets him jovially at first.*

MZOGA. Karibu, Karibu! Mr. Stiv, you are a busy man. Thank you for gracing me with your time. Please be seated! Put up your feet! Have a glass of water! We have waited for months to welcome you. And to see your media-in-education packages, that is a treat too long in store!

And now I must know: why have the students come running out of your class to gossip and make trouble and bother me with questions about coffee-beans? Can you explain it?

STEVE. Mr. Mzoga, I suggest you ask the students.

MZOGA. Of course, it was the first thing I did,

STEVE. What did they say?

MZOGA. Nothing of interest. The finger point at you.

STEVE. I see. Well, Mr. Mzoga, I know you'll accept what I have to say in a spirit of comradely criticism.

MZOGA. Let us hope so.

STEVE. Here goes then. What's this country about? Self-reliance. People aren't doing things simply because they're told to. They can ask questions. They can ask just why the Party has come to whatever decision it's come to. And maybe they can start to make their own decisions. Insofar as that's practical in a developing country.

I've not discussed this with the students. All that happened
was that this afternoon I set up a couple of improvisations –
that's a well-established educational technique – and
followed it up with a group discussion.

And this problem emerged. They're working nineteen to the
dozen in the shambas. And basically they might as well be
back in the old colonial days. Because they don't know who
they're working for.

You see, Mr. Mzoga, I've got my problems too. I'm here
with a package. A little to start with and lots to follow.
We're happy to give it away, Africa's been ripped for
centuries, it's time it took something back. But I've got to
be able to give the right answers when I get back home. I'll
have to report on the teaching here. Not just the academic
side, you understand. There are other aspects too, the whole
consciousness and participatory side of things.

So you get an idea of the question I'll be faced with. And,
I'm sorry if this sounds crude, the kind of report my team
will want before they formalise your allocation.

And your attitude this evening doesn't help. You've been
asked a question. Have you answered it?

STARFORD. He has not.

STEVE. There you are. I'll do my best. But I know what my
team will say. And they won't be sending television sets.
Blackboards and chalk, more like.

MZOGA *replies with expansive geniality:*

MZOGA. What is all the fuss about? Records for all cashcrop
enterprises, peasant co-operative, state-owned, para-statal
or, as in our own case, ancillary to institutions of Higher
Education, are on display twice yearly at the Ministry of
National Agriculture. I don't know the exact days. You
could ask.

STEVE. Sorry, Mr. Mzoga, but that's five hundred miles away.
Haven't you got the information here?

MZOGA. I was coming to that. We deal direct with the sales team of Kilimanjaro Coffee Ltd.

STARFORD. What is this Kilimanjaro?

MZOGA. It is an agency providing transport services which we cannot afford ourselves.

FRANK. They get the coffee-beans!

STARFORD. Not yet! This Kilimanjaro Coffee, who owns that?

MZOGA. Mr. Stiv, is it kind to confuse these young people with things they cannot understand?

STEVE. They want to know.

MZOGA. It is not a problem. The company is a subsidiary of East African Developments, an autonomous body, chartered by the national government and staffed I may add entirely by national citizens.

FRANK. They get the coffee-beans?

STARFORD. No, no, not yet.This East African Developments, who owns that?

MZOGA. Too complex!

STARFORD. Who?

MZOGA. East African Developments is not owned by anybody. It is a quasi-independent subsidiary . . .

STARFORD (*to* STEVE). What is this?

STEVE. It means it's owned by . . .

MZOGA. . . . . Knightsbridge Investments.

STARFORD. This Knightsbridge, they sell coffee?

MZOGA. No of course they do not sell coffee! They have far too much to do than sell coffee all day!

STARFORD. What then?

MZOGA. This is too much! How do I know? They organise the running of a hotel here and there, they have some interest in the sisal trade, they give advice on contract for cement, you think I can keep track of their comings and goings?

STARFORD. And where do they live?

MZOGA. What difference do it make?

VIOLET. Mr. Mzoga, you get letters from these people?

MZOGA. You think they write me private letters?

FRANK. Any kind of letter. Show us.

VIOLET. Cover the letter part, we do not want to read. Show us the top piece where it say who own the paper it written on. That mean they own the business too.

STARFORD. Show us the names.

MZOGA. No!

STEVE. I'm sorry, Mr. Mzoga. It's difficult to see why not.

MZOGA seethes. Then:

MZOGA. Although I am not privy to their inner councils, once a year, in the course of the festive season, there comes a calendar addressed to me.

He produces it from his desk: it's a month-a-page affair with glossy full-colour photographs. He holds it up and turns the pages, reading the captions:

'February. The soaring skyline of Nigeria's capital city proclaims the Africa of tomorrow.' 'November. Little Jamal laughs to see his father's waterpump.' 'July. Malawian miners in their lunch-break don their colourful regalia.' And here at the back, a personal message from the chairman and his board.

He bangs it down.

See for yourself.

The students cluster round and read:

STARFORD. Who are these people?

FRANK. Let me see!

VIOLET. What kind of names are these?

STARFORD. The duke of what is this place?

VIOLET. Lord who?

FRANK. Wazungu, every one of them!

STARFORD. Is it for them we grow the coffee-beans?

VIOLET. It is worse than Mr. Chatterjee!

STARFORD. It is jackals of big business! Bullshit! We stop to work.

MZOGA. You stop to work?

STARFORD. We stop to work!

FRANK/VIOLET. We stop to work!

FRANK. Let us climb on top of the assembly hall!

VIOLET. Let us sit on the roof and wave our hoes at all the other students!

STARFORD. Let us bang on the roof!

VIOLET. Let us bang ngoma drumming on the roof! Then never will you sleep at all tonight!

STARFORD. We go on striki!

FRANK. Time has come!

VIOLET. Revenge has come from all our ancestors!

End of scene.

Scene Two

Night. Blackness.

Crickets. Frogs. Not a pinch of light.

Out of the blackness and over the sounds of night, the students are heard drumming in rhythm on the tin roof of the assembly hall.

As the drumming grows, the constellation of the Southern Cross is seen, spread wide across the stage.

Scene Three

The following morning. The library. The drumming can still be heard, now more distant.

KADUMA is sitting, a cup of coffee balanced on his knee. He looks cheerful and wears a clean shirt. He is listening to STEVE's tape-recorder with pleasure. From it comes the voice of John Gielgud:

    'What a piece of work is a man! How noble in reason! How infinite in faculty! In form, how moving, how express and admirable! In action how like an angel! In apprehension how like a god! The beauty of the world! The paragon of animals . . . '

    STEVE has come in.

KADUMA. Ndugu Winter, good morning! Forgive my liberties with your equipment. The students returned to me a missing part. I fitted it out of curiosity, and from that moment I was lost.

STEVE. It's only a test-tape. Not much verbal stuff on it really. It's mainly disco.

KADUMA. It will do. You brought some culture after all.

    He sits and smiles at STEVE. Drumming is still heard.

As for the rest, Starford, Frank and Violet are sitting on top of the assembly hall. They are busy drumming on the tin roof. It is a problem.

STEVE. I'm sorry to bother you further. I've bad news. My Rangerover's disappeared.

KADUMA. That is quite true. It has been appropriated by Mr. Mzoga for an urgent official tour to Dar es Salaam for instructions to deal with student revolt. I hasten to add that permission was received by sunrise telephone call to the High Commissioner. Mzoga is distressed. And alarmed. What will the Ministry of National Education say now that he can no longer keep his own students under control? They will get hot with him. Do you know, Ndugu, I taught that man?

STEVE. You'd not told me that.

KADUMA. Oh yes. 'Daffodils' by William Wordsworth. 'What, Mzoga does this poem mean? What is your personal response to its limpid imagery?' 'Oh no Mr. Kaduma, I don't know about such things but I have learned it by heart, will that do?' In a country like this, Ndugu, people like that get on.

I regret I cannot offer you a cup of coffee. Unless you do not mind to share a cup with me.

STEVE. A pleasure.

KADUMA *hands him the cup. They sit drinking by turns.*

KADUMA. Today I can collect my thoughts in peace. Work has stopped. Mzoga has left me in charge. I can't say he did so with a smile. But for me it is a challenge. How am I to get those foolish children off the roof and back to the classrooms where they belong? Have you a suggestion?

STEVE. I'm afraid not.

They sit. The drumming continues.

I heard the drumming all night. I couldn't sleep. So I went for a walk by the waterfall. Looked up at the stars. They're so much brighter here than they are at home. The funny thing was that the only constellation I could recognise was the one I'd never seen before. The Southern Cross. I sat on a rock, and looked, and I thought, yes, this is it. This is Africa. I've finally got here. And I know I've got off to a difficult start. But it's a *start*. I've got the rest of the month. I'm going to enjoy it.

KADUMA. You were out all night? That explains your presence here. You have had no message from Mzoga?

STEVE. No.

KADUMA. Before he vanished, he dictated a detailed memorandum about your visit. Briefly, hospitality has been withdrawn. You must leave this morning. Since your Rangerover is already in use, you will be picked up in an hour by a vegetable lorry bound for Tanga market. With any luck, you will find from there a bus service to Morogoro junction. From there are many tourist cars bound for the capital, if you make yourself conspicuous by the side of the road, you may be offered a lift. Or you may walk, or take another bus, if they are still running. Ndugu, I wish you luck.

It falls to me to thank you for the gift of your equipment. Tell me . . .

NKWABI *outside the room:*

NKWABI. Hodi.

KADUMA. Karibu.

NKWABI *comes in carrying* STEVE's *luggage.*

Your suitcase. How tactless. Nkwabi, I want you to sit down.

NKWABI *finds a seat.*

Did I say anything about a chair?

NKWABI *sits on the floor. To* STEVE:

My duties for the day continue. No, they hot up.

KADUMA *stands. Suddenly a spark of real activity and drive. He looks years younger.*

Listen, Nkwabi. Can you hear anything unusual?

NKWABI. Ngoma.

KADUMA. Drumming, correct. Why?

NKWABI. It is a striki.

KADUMA. A strike, what for?

NKWABI. The new shamba. It grow for who? They say, for jackals of big business.

KADUMA. What is wrong with that?

NKWABI. They do not like it.

KADUMA. Who does not like it? Who?

NKWABI. Mizimu.

KADUMA. English, English!

NKWABI. Ancestors.

KADUMA. Those Chatterjees sleep in their shamba. In the morning the mammas throw stones at them. There is no ancestor required to make them leave the village, you or I would do the same. But why do they sleep in their shamba? Why?

NKWABI. It is for something bad that happen in their house.

KADUMA. What?

NKWABI. They hear a voice and there was nobody at all to speak.

KADUMA. Tell this story to the village mammas! Tell it to the students! Nkwabi, you fool anyone in this college but not me! If Chatterjee hear a voice, then somebody make it. Who?

NKWABI *looks terrified.*

Somebody small. Somebody small enough to hide behind a sofa set. Somebody good at making funny noises!

Mzoga wanted that shamba. For years he try to get it. Already the village mammas hate those Chatterjees. Already

the Chatterjees were in a fright. They needed one little push.
Who give that push?

Nkwabi, little Nkwabi, you were fool enough to help
Mzoga. Do you think he will help you back? Think of your
exam papers. Who mark them?

NKWABI. You, Mzee.

KADUMA. What kind old man forgive you when the devil sit
on your shoulder and whisper wrong answers in your ear?

NKWABI. Is you, Mzee.

KADUMA. What cruel old man can get so angry that he give
you bottom marks of all time? Nought, nought, nought!
Send this boy back to his village! Make him feed goats!
Marry him to the village prostitute!

NKWABI. You, Mzee, you, you, you!

KADUMA. Then tell me: who hide behind the sofa set and go
'Woo woo!' at the Chatterjees?

NKWABI. It was me.

KADUMA. I might forgive you. We shall see. First you must
go up on that roof. You must tell the students this thing you
have done. Tell them that the ancestors were not, this time,
concerned with coffee-beans. Or who they grow for. Or who
hoe their shambas. Out of my sight!

NKWABI *goes as fast as he can.* KADUMA *sits, relaxes,
tired.*

African discipline.

STEVE. Will it work?

KADUMA. They will come down.

STEVE. All of them?

KADUMA. Who can say?

STEVE. Not Starford.

KADUMA. No. He never believed that rubbish in the first
place. He will stay on the roof. Mzoga will get instructions.

And the boy will be expelled. Sent back to his village. He
will become a peasant. With luck, he may find his way to
town and end his days as a low grade garage mechanic. You
care for him? Then why did you not think about his future?
See how he fight to learn. He struggle like an ox in a net.
And all the time, what does he know? His history is old
magazines. His politics is pamphlets scraped together by
failed B.A's. His imagination is like gravel. You could have
taught him. You could have given him culture. And a sense
of beauty. Tell me, Ndugu, in our country, have you seen a
beautiful thing so far?

STEVE. Oh yes.

KADUMA. I forgot. The Southern Cross. You come as a friend
and you congratulate us on our geographical features. Shall
I tell you the most beautiful place in Africa?

The Cape of Good Hope. I travelled there as a student, top
student from Makerere University. Permit for a three-day
course in farm management. A subject which bored me then
as much as it does now. But I wanted to see the world, you
understand. Seven days on the train from Uganda, crammed
among the peasants, labourers wrapped in blankets,
smelling of tobacco and sweat. And at Stellenbosch I got
out. Do you know the place?

STEVE. I've never been to South Africa.

KADUMA. But if you wanted to, you could. Stellenbosch is a
University town. There is a main street lined with trees. On
each side are houses, solid things, built by Dutchmen in the
ancient style. Curved gables, mahogany doors with brass
fittings, whitewashed walls, fruit orchards. History. The sun
shone high but I kept my jacket on. I felt respect. I walked
the streets. I wanted a cup of coffee, and of course nobody
would sell me one. I didn't mind. It was the place of my
dreams. Have I shocked you?

STEVE. Yes.

KADUMA. You may not have noticed this, Ndugu, but Africa
is a land of bullshit. The A.N.C. will visit us in a week. Mr.
Mzoga will make a speech and see the grass is cut. He will

be proud. The students will be proud. Why not? Some of them will join the freedom fighters in the bush. Let them. Let them drill and learn discipline and fire their rifles in the air. Armed struggle! What a sense of purpose it gives! What would we do without it? What would we say to our young men? How could we possibly account for our own mistakes?

STEVE. I'm sorry. I really don't want to hear this.

KADUMA. You do not find it pleasant, once in a while, for two men not to bullshit each other? Tell me, what will you say to your employers? May we look forward to receiving your visual aids? Do you think they will be planted in fertile soil?

STEVE. I'm optimistic. I can see things are wrong here. But you've had your revolution. That's what matters. You've got the right machine. It works. Maybe it could work better, but that's a matter of time. In Britain there's no use fiddling round the edges. It's wrong at heart. There isn't much hope.

KADUMA. And here you believe there is?

STEVE. I think so.

KADUMA (*very pleasant*). Well, it was worth a try. One problem occurs to me. But since you have a conscience, I hesitate to burden it further.

STEVE. What's that?

KADUMA. I have heard of a company like yours, which struggled for years to present the peasants of Thailand with tractors. The poor fellows were using elephants, you see, and from time to time, elephants being what they are, they would refuse to work or sit on people's heads. Why, then, would the peasants not accept the tractors? Finally someone asked them. They explained: if we have a couple of tractors, they are much better than elephants to start with, but after a while, bits fall off them, more and more they collapse, till all we have left is a pile of junk. If we have two elephants, and wait a few years, what have we then? *Three* elephants!

Spare parts, Ndugu. We do not, I believe, have an
electronics factory in Dar es Salaam. Where will we get
replacements?

STEVE. We'll take care of that.

KADUMA. And maintenance? You hope to return, you say.
If not you, then somebody else. One way and another, our
audio-visual aids will keep your company fully occupied.

STEVE. For a year or two, maybe.

KADUMA. For free? Please don't answer that question.
I don't want to learn about nominal service charges and
low profit margins. My curiosity has been exhausted.

'What a piece of work is a man! How noble in reason!
How infinite in faculty!' I agree.

Now we will find the truck. The students have stopped their
drumming. Either they have thrown themselves off the roof,
or they are on their way back to the shamba. We will pause
on our journey to find out. Don't be depressed. You are
young. You will swiftly recover.

STEVE. I still hope we'll meet again.

KADUMA. Not here. You have caused embarrassment. Next
time they will send us a different Ndugu.

STEVE. Then somewhere else.

KADUMA. Where might that be?

STEVE. You won't always be here. You could leave.

KADUMA (*with poise*). And where would I go? What hope is
there for me? No, I must stay in this dreadful place until I
die.

End of scene.

Scene Four

The new shamba. VIOLET, FRANK *and* NKWABI *are hoeing as in the first scene.*

STEVE *comes on and starts to cross the stage carrying his suitcase. He looks downcast and depressed.* VIOLET *sees him and calls out in delight.*

VIOLET. Mr. Stiv!

FRANK. Mr. Stiv!

NKWABI. You go now?

VIOLET. Pole! Pole! (Hard luck!)

FRANK. Pole sana! (Very hard luck!)

ALL. Pole sana! Pole sana!

> STEVE *is now among them. They cluster round him, shake his hand and say affectionate goodbyes.*

STEVE. Where is Starford?

STARFORD. Mr. Stiv!

> *He appears from out of sight carrying a basket of stones.*

STEVE. There you are. I'm on my way. I thought I'd stop and say goodbye.

> *From all, a sigh of condolence.*

STARFORD. Not good-bye. Kwa heri ya kuonana.

> *Applause and agreement from the others.*

STEVE. What's that?

STARFORD. That is: our greetings until we meet again once more.

STEVE. Sorry. I think it's more final than that.

STARFORD. Mr. Stiv, I want your help. There is a piece of shamba too hard for me to hoe. As you are on your way, will you not try it for me?

STEVE. Where?

STARFORD. Just here.

He moves away from the others. They go on with their hoeing and watch. STEVE *joins* STARFORD.

STARFORD. It is nothing. But it is best if you pretend to work.

STEVE *takes the hoe and works the earth with it.*

See, they laugh to see you try. We will not mind, that is their rubbish thinking.

STEVE. Go on.

STARFORD. They say the boss have seen the Ministry. He has had a very bad success.

STEVE. He has?

STARFORD. They make it hot for him.

STEVE. I'm glad to hear it. Star, what about you?

STARFORD. What about me?

STEVE. You're back at work.

STARFORD. That is correct.

STEVE. I understand. But I'm sorry.

STARFORD. Why is that?

STEVE. You went on strike for a principle. You put up a fight. That was good. Now, what? You've jacked it in. Do you think you'll get another chance?

STARFORD. In this country, Mr. Stiv, we think a lot. Also, the way in which we think, it is very complicated. You are good for us. You think in quite a simple way. And you do not know too much. When we meet you, we get a shake-up. But we must not always notice what you tell us! Now I must ask you something.

STEVE. What's that?

STARFORD. If I work here. Then teach a year or two and save up hard. I can in that time put together, let me see. Two hundred pounds English money. With that it may be I can get a flight. And come to your country. Go to a good college. Like you did. And then come home as a better teacher.

But it is a problem. A person in U.K. must write me a letter. That he will sponsor me. And find me a job. And for an address where I can live with him.

STEVE. I see.

STARFORD. You understand what it is I am asking.

STEVE. Sure, sure.

STARFORD. Good. Because I do not like to say it myself.

Pause.

STEVE. Yes, well, I'll do what I can. The main thing, of course, is that you've got it in writing.

STARFORD. That, and the job, and also the place to live.

STEVE. Quite a serious business.

STARFORD. That is why I have entrusted it to you.

STEVE. Fine. Fine. Well, I know where to write to you.

STARFORD. Here.

STEVE. That's right. I'll give it er serious consideration.

STARFORD. You will?

STEVE. Oh yes.

STARFORD *smiles.*

STARFORD. Then I will see you in a year or two.

STEVE. In case there's any problem . . .

STARFORD. No, there will be no problem. Thank you, friend.

He sees the results of STEVE's *hoeing.*

See! Ha ha! You have made it crooked!

He takes the hoe.

I mend it for you.

STEVE. But if there *is* a problem. I'll have done my best. Look, there's the truck. It's been great to meet you, Starford. Good bye.

STARFORD. No, not goodbye. Kwa heri ya kuonana.

Pause.

No, that is too difficult for you. Then you can say it in English. 'Our greetings till we meet again once more.'

He wipes his hand and they shake hands. STEVE *goes.* STARFORD *stands and watches. All wave as the truck drives off. Then* STARFORD *joins the others and they carry on hoeing.*

End of play.

THE CUSTOM OF THE COUNTRY

An earlier version of *The Custom of the Country* was first presented in the Barbican Pit on 12 October 1983. The cast was as follows:

ROGER	John Bowe
PAUL	Christopher Guard
TENDAI	Josette Simon
COUNT ANTONIO DE ROSARIO	Yemi Ajibade
LAZARUS	Bruce Myers
ELIAS	Hepburn Graham
DAISY	Sinead Cusack
WILLEM	Tom Mannion
DR. JAMESON	David Bradley
HENRIETTA	Sara Kestelman
DR. BRINK	Paul Webster
WAITER	Hepburn Graham
JUSTIN	Yemi Ajibade

Director David Jones
Designer Ralph Koltai
Lighting Designer Michael Calf
Music Nigel Hess

Characters
in order of appearance

ROGER DU BOYS, *a gentleman of leisure*
PAUL DU BOYS, *his brother, a missionary*
TENDAI, *Paul's fiancée*
COUNT ANTONIO DE ROSARIO, *a feudal lord*
LAZARUS, *a scholar*
ELIAS, *a butler-boy*
DAISY, *an entrepreneuse*
WILLEM, *a boy of twenty*
DR. JAMESON, *a British agent*
HENRIETTA VAN ES, *Willem's mother, owner of the
    Nooitgedacht Goldmine*
DR. BRINK, *her brother, a lawyer*
A WAITER
JUSTIN, *butler-boy to Mevrouw van Es*

*The play is set in 1890, in the Zambesi Valley and in the town
of Johannesburg in the Transvaal Republic.*

ACT ONE

Scene One

Africa 1890. The Zambesi Valley. Late afternoon.

ROGER *is sitting waiting. He is thirty, handsome, fleshy, sunburnt and at present battered and footsore from travel. He has a small, battered hold-all. It's hot.*

PAUL *calls from out of sight:*

PAUL. Roger!

ROGER. Paul!

> PAUL *comes running on. He's a missionary: twenty-five, lean, fit.*

> My dear fellow! How are you?

> *They embrace, then shake hands.*

> I've been walking bloody weeks. You look well! Fit eh? Surprised to see me? Eh?

PAUL. I'm shattered. Why're you here?

ROGER. Why d'you think?

PAUL. I don't know.

ROGER. We were worried about you!

PAUL. I'm fine!

ROGER. Good, good.

> *Pause.*

> Mother's bearing up.

PAUL. Is there something wrong with her?

ROGER. Well, you know, the leg. I brought any amount of presents from her and letters from various relations but they got lost with the baggage. Well, there's this.

He looks in his hold-all and finds a blue scarf which is wrapped around a whisky bottle.

PAUL. I don't want it.

ROGER. You haven't seen it.

PAUL. I don't want it whatever it is.

ROGER. It's a scarf. Nanny knitted it. I've been using it to guard the breakables. Go on.

PAUL. All right. Thanks.

He takes it, stuffs it in a pocket.

ROGER. Drink?

PAUL *shakes his head.* ROGER *drinks.*

PAUL. They told me another white man had arrived. I was coming to tell him to clear off. I wasn't expecting you. You've put me off my stroke. What happened to your luggage?

ROGER. Porter trouble. Splendid bunch until this morning, then I woke up to find they'd buggered off with everything they could carry.

PAUL. They're frightened of this place. I love it. I've been incredibly lucky. I run my own mission now. I had two hundred converts when I started, but they've drifted off, except for one. There's somebody you must meet. I've fallen in love. Listen.

They do. Drums are beating in the distance.

Drums. Our wedding's tomorrow. The ceremony of course will be an ordinary Congregational one, but the reception's for all the village. There'll be singing. Beer. Dancing-girls.

ROGER. Splendid!

PAUL. No, there's a problem. In this country, when a young woman marries, the chief has the right to sleep with her on the wedding night.

ROGER. Well I'm damned!

PAUL. Sometimes I think I don't mind. It isn't her fault. It isn't mine. Then suddenly my stomach heaves, or I start to cry. What should I do?

ROGER. Easy. Skip the wedding and carry on as was, then you'll still get the fun and it'll be none of his business.

PAUL. There's no 'as was' about it. I love and respect her. If you touch the women round here I'll chuck you out.

ROGER. Don't you trust me?

PAUL. I know you!

He sees someone.

Here she is.

TENDAI *comes on in a white, homemade mission dress. She bobs and claps to* PAUL. *She is eighteen: slight, beautiful, self-possessed, never surprised.*

Tendai, this is my brother Roger. He's come all the way from England.

TENDAI *bobs and claps.*

ROGER. Charming!

TENDAI. Brother, now you are here you must be putting a fire under my husband. Why is he not stopping our custom? Why is he not thinking of a trick? I am rather upset.

ROGER. She's right!

PAUL. What can I do?

ROGER. Run away!

TENDAI. Yes!

PAUL. I can't leave the mission.

TENDAI (*to* ROGER). This is what he is like. Once he is having a thought in his head it become a rock. (*To* PAUL.) No one is liking this place except for you. The wood is too hard to cut, the water is too far to carry. Everybody would be running away this day if they are having a place to run to. We can be running to England, once we are married.

PAUL. That'll be too late.

ROGER. Don't wait till tomorrow, old boy. You're the minister, you can marry yourself any old time you want.

TENDAI. You can marry me now!

ROGER. Exactly! Whyever not? You'll spoil the party, but there's bigger things at stake. A lady's happiness! Honour of the family! Wake up, lad!

PAUL. All right. I'll do it. Under protest.

ROGER. Nonsense, you can't wait.

PAUL. How do you know?

ROGER. I'm your brother.

Pause. Thinks, then lights up.

PAUL. You're right! I want to go back to England! We'll be home by Christmas! Let's get married at once!

ROGER. Look out!

TENDAI. It is he.

ANTONIO *comes on. He is middle-aged, black, dignified, grandly dressed.* TENDAI *and* PAUL *clap to him.*

PAUL. Honoured chief, this is my brother, Roger.

ANTONIO *nods to* ROGER.

ROGER. I like your country. Very good. Your African customs, very nice.

ANTONIO. I am not an African.

ROGER. No?

ANTONIO. No. My ancestor came to this country long ago. It was when my father's father's father was alive . . .

ROGER. That he came?

ANTONIO. No. When they lost the book with the dates in it. Before him was another father, then twins, then a tall man known as the Beheader, and before him, one with three

eyes, two at the front and one at the back, here. This land
belonged to him. He could do whatever he wanted and
nobody could stop him, except his Catholic Majesty, the
King of Portugal. Like him, my name is Count Antonio de
Rosario. Like him, I am a Portuguese, and those customs
done in Portugal in his time, I do today. When my sons are
born, everyone must be happy. When I die, my soldiers will
kill one man in every house in case the people are not sad
enough. As for that king in Portugal, he never interferes,
perhaps he is dead, how do I know? When a young woman
marries, I sleep with her. What is so strange about that, have
you no wedding customs?

PAUL. Nothing like that!

ROGER (*with tact*). Not in the dissenting churches. Show him,
Pauly, how does the service start?

PAUL *catches* ROGER*'s eye.*

PAUL. Oh. Yes. The minister says, 'If any man knows due
cause why these two should not be united in holy wedlock,
let him speak now or forever hold his peace.'

ANTONIO. And what does that person say?

PAUL. Nothing, hopefully, but the marriage isn't legal
otherwise. Gosh. What might happen then . . .

He, TENDAI *and* ROGER *arrange themselves,* ROGER *as
best man.* PAUL *changes places depending on whether he's
being minister or groom .*

. . . is that he says to, say it were me, 'Paul James Jeremy
wilt thou have this woman to thy lawful wedded wife to live
together after God's ordinance in the holy estate of
matrimony, wilt thou love her, comfort her, honour and keep
her in sickness and in health and forsaking all other keep
only unto her so long as you both shall live?' I will.

ANTONIO. The minister will?

PAUL. No, the bridegroom will, that's why I said it.

ANTONIO. What does it mean?

PAUL. Listen again. It goes, 'Tendai', let's say for the sake of
    variety, 'wilt though have this man to thy lawful wedded
    husband, to live together after God's ordinance in the holy
    estate of matrimony, wilt thou love him, comfort him,
    honour and keep him in sickness and in health and
    forsaking all other keep only unto him so long as you both
    shall live?'

TENDAI. I will.

PAUL. Now comes the difficult bit, people often get it wrong,
    but fortunately Tendai has been studying it, let's see if she
    remembers.

PAUL/TENDAI. 'I Tendai/Paul take thee Tendai/Paul to my
    lawful wedded wife/husband to have and to hold from this
    day forward, for better or for worse for richer for poorer, in
    sickness and in health to love, to cherish until death us do
    part according to God's holy law.'

ANTONIO. And then they are married?

ROGER/TENDAI. Yes!

PAUL. No! You need a ring! I've forgotten the ring!

ROGER. Here!

    He gives him his own.

    It's Dad's, last thing he gave me.

PAUL. He takes the ring and says . . .

TENDAI. It is a spell.

PAUL. Not exactly, Tendai, it's a blessing. 'Bless this ring
    O Lord and grant that these thy servants may faithfully
    keep their solemn pledge and abound evermore in love and
    holiness through Jesus Christ our Lord, Amen,' and he gives
    it to the man, who puts it on the woman's hand, fourth
    finger . . .

    He puts the ring on TENDAI's *finger.*

    . . . then we kneel . . .

    They kneel.

. . . and the minister says . . .

He gets up.

. . . you'll have to imagine the man . . . 'Forasmuch as Paul
and Tendai have consorted together in holy wedlock and
have witnessed the same before God and this company and
thereto have given and pledged their troth either to other
and have declared the same by giving and receiving a ring
and by joining of hands I pronounce that they be man and
wife together!'

ANTONIO. That's all?

PAUL. He kisses the bride.

He kisses TENDAI.

So does the minister.

He kisses her again and so does ROGER.

ROGER. And the best man too!

ANTONIO. Now me.

ROGER *steers* TENDAI *away.*

ROGER. I think you'll find, sir, tomorrow's the day.

ANTONIO. True! Ha ha! I am happy to think of this! See, the
women are making beer. We shall be friends tonight!

They all clap to ANTONIO, *as he goes off, then get up
quickly.*

PAUL. Have you travelled without porters?

ROGER. No.

PAUL. Nor me.

TENDAI. I have never travelled, it does not matter, I am
knowing about all these things. North is a wide river, to
East and West are ghosts and witches, we must go South to
the kingdom of Lobengula, that way!

She points.

ROGER. That's not South.

TENDAI. That way!

She points in the other direction.

We shall not be taking food, we will greet people on the path and tell them that we are dying of hunger. Also there will be birds, fruit, berries, mice and caterpillars. We must take two blankets only, a bow and arrows and to make fire we will be finding sticks.

PAUL (*to* ROGER). To rub together.

ROGER. That won't work.

TENDAI. It do not always work but I will not be minding, if I am cold I will hold on to my husband and we will be too happy.

ROGER. Speaking of which: just thought I might examine the dancing-girls, eh Pauly?

PAUL. No time for that! It's getting dark. Let's go!

End of scene.

Scene Two

Johannesburg. Mrs. Bone's new house. An empty room on the first floor. Windows looking down on to the street.

LAZARUS *comes in. He is 28, a Central European Jew, dark, bony and good-looking. He wears a shabby suit and a long black overcoat. He carries his hat in one hand, a bundle of books tied together with string in the other.*

He looks round the room. Another door opens. ELIAS, *the butler-boy, comes in carrying breakfast on a tray and crosses the room towards a bedroom door.*

LAZARUS. Good morning, Elias. The cart's arrived, the driver's ready to unload. These books are mine, they're precious, don't touch them, I'll carry them up myself.

ELIAS. Mrs. Bone say you not to live upstairs.

LAZARUS. What do you mean?

ELIAS. Mrs. Bone say you to live in basement.

LAZARUS. My living quarters have been on the cards for weeks, they are through that door and up a flight of steps, a pleasant former nursery with windows on the park. The basement is a dungeon with green slime running down the walls, it is servants' quarters.

ELIAS. Mrs. Bone say that where you must go.

LAZARUS. I will not! Would you if you didn't have to? When the revolution comes you may quarter me there with pleasure, I shall paint slogans on the walls and use it for peasants' reading classes, but until that happy day, dear friend, don't piss me about. Show me to my room! You won't? Quite right, you're a good fellow, I shall speak to Mrs. Bone myself.

ELIAS stands firmly in front of the bedroom door.

ELIAS. Mrs. Bone up early this morning.

LAZARUS. Unpacking . . . ?

ELIAS. Yes.

LAZARUS. . . . . and measuring up for curtains, that makes sense, what I don't understand is why in that case she is having her breakfast in bed?

ELIAS. Breakfast is not for her.

He goes into the bedroom. LAZARUS looks thoughtfully at the bedroom door. DAISY comes in. She is in her thirties, very pretty, with a small waist. She has the air of being an army widow, which is partly accurate. She carries a handful of letters, etc..

DAISY. I keep finding old trunks the men brought over without asking. Photos of boys at sea and letters from funny old generals. Well I'll stuff them in the grate and up they'll go. From today, everything about my life will be crisp and stylish.

She goes to the window and watches the men unloading below. Meanwhile:

Did you come on the cart?

LAZARUS. I did.

DAISY. Thank God that's done. I'll never move house again.

She shouts out of the window:

Mind that sofa!

To ELIAS, *who has come out of the bedroom.*

Go and take charge. And hurry!

ELIAS *goes.* DAISY *puts the letters and photos in the grate. To* LAZARUS:

You're looking very blue.

LAZARUS. Where am I sleeping?

DAISY. Why?

LAZARUS. I'm a latent consumptive.

DAISY. You're going in the basement.

LAZARUS. Are you trying to kill me?

DAISY. You can come up here to report on business but you can't sit about and read. There isn't room.

LAZARUS. The house is enormous!

DAISY. You won't like it. It'll be frightfully grand.

LAZARUS. Why should I mind if it's . . . ?

DAISY. Dammit you're my secretary!

LAZARUS. You don't treat me like a secretary.

DAISY. I do and I will.

LAZARUS. What are my duties? You never say, you throw me bits and pieces of work and then you snatch them away while I'm still thinking about them. Where's my salary?

DAISY. I give you money!

LAZARUS. I don't want money, I want the same amount of money every week. In an envelope. I want . . .

DAISY. You're not good enough! For half the bother I could have a *proper* secretary, *and* he'd have a home to go to.

LAZARUS. Good, fine, do that!

DAISY. Don't think I won't! I'm thinking about it! I think about it all the time. I'm sick of seeing a light under your door and knowing you're working late. I don't want to know about you. I don't want to know about the business. You can look after the firm and our relations will be strictly at arms' length.

LAZARUS. You're treating me like a rejected lover.

DAISY. You are a rejected lover.

LAZARUS. I resent that! How long since we slept together? A year?

DAISY. Ten months. There's a man in my bedroom. If you can't be nice to him, stay out of his way.

LAZARUS. Why should I not be nice to him?

DAISY. Because you're a shit. He's a big, blond farm-boy and he's so stupid it's like heavenly innocence. I woke at four this morning and I looked at the window and thought, what's that? Then I remembered: my window, my walls, my dressing-gown on an unfamiliar hook. The light hit his face at an odd angle. It flattened it out like paper, with holes punched in for eyes. Then it got brighter and the bones stood out. Broad nose, hard bristles, jawbones thick as elbows.

The bedroom door opens and WILLEM *comes in, still buttoning up his shirt and stuffing the tails into his trousers. He's aged about twenty, heavily built, with a black eye.*

WILLEM (*of* LAZARUS). Who's this?

DAISY. A friend. Don't you want a bath?

WILLEM. Hell no. Will you be at that place tonight?

DAISY. I don't know.

WILLEM. Can I come here?

DAISY. Let's meet as fate decides. Or not. Will you find the door?

WILLEM. Bitch.

He goes out. Silence for a moment. The doorbell rings.

DAISY. I didn't say he was nice.

LAZARUS (*with infinite compassion*). Oh Daisy!

DAISY. Everything drags me back.

She stands, moves to the bedroom door. ELIAS shows in Dr. JAMESON and leaves. JAMESON is thirty-five, balding, Scots. Clubroom manner.

JAMESON. Mrs. Bone?

DAISY. Yes?

JAMESON. Remember an old pal? Leander Jameson.

DAISY. Dr. Jim! It's a rotten time to call. Where've you been?

JAMESON. Matabele . . . (land).

DAISY has vanished into the bedroom and closed the door. To LAZARUS:

She seems disturbed.

LAZARUS. She's busy. She's burning letters from her old lovers. I should come back next week.

JAMESON. Who are you?

LAZARUS. By vocation I am a scholar. But Mrs. Bone is kind enough to provide my lodgings. In return I check her accounts and offer advice. Were it not for me, she'd be in debtors' prison and her business would be bankrupt.

JAMESON. I find that hard to believe.

LAZARUS. Two years ago, she had one house, three girls and a nasty overdraft. Then she met me. I'm her genius. I push her on. In times like these, you must expand, expand, expand. I understand the world, you see, thanks to a lifetime of study and analysis. Now she owns a string of brothels and I still haven't finished my book.

DAISY *comes in with a bottle of champagne.*

DAISY. I haven't settled in enough for tea, but look what I found in a trunk. *Un souvenir des années oubliées.*

She gives LAZARUS *the bottle.*

Open it!

JAMESON. May we speak freely?

DAISY. My secretary and I work hand in glove.

JAMESON *goes to the door he came in by and opens it.*

JAMESON. Come in.

TENDAI *comes in, still in her mission dress, now ragged and torn.*

DAISY. She's lovely. I'll take her on like a shot.

JAMESON. That's not the plan. This young woman is a potential source of vital intelligence. She needs a refuge for a week or two. Your name caught my attention as I was running my eye down the list of applicants to the Polo Club. It struck me at once that the presence in one of your houses of a strange young woman would pass unnoticed.

LAZARUS. How many brothel-keepers do you have in the Polo Club? A full team?

JAMESON. None, strictly speaking. But exceptions can be made for public service. I'm the Chairman, Mrs. Bone. Do as I say, and I'll sail you in like a frigate. Shall I go on?

DAISY. Please do.

JAMESON. For the last three months of my travels among the Matabele, Tendai – her name – has been my prisoner. My pioneer column discovered her in the course of a raid on rebel tribesmen and rescued her from a burning village.

LAZARUS. Who set fire to it?

DAISY. Shut up or get out.

JAMESON. The village was not her home. She had arrived there in the company of a white man, an English missionary. It seems he'd taken a fancy to her, married her and eloped, travelling some few hundreds of miles from her homeland in the North. Now we come to the point. Her home is Monomatapa.

LAZARUS. Indeed?

DAISY. Don't say you've heard of it.

LAZARUS. The city-state of Monomatapa was founded by sixteenth-century Portuguese explorers somewhere in the valley of the Zambesi. Over the centuries, it lost contact with the modern world . . .

JAMESON. . . . though Dr. Livingstone wrote in his journal of a mysterious lost kingdom, a place of feudal lords and gold mines.

DAISY. I see!

JAMESON. I need hardly add what a prize this territory would be for the British Empire. But before I can bargain with the fellow in charge, I need a go-between, a man he trusts, in short, the missionary. Fortunately we have him over a barrel.

DAISY. How?

JAMESON. He's married a darkie. I'll have him sent down for two years if he doesn't oblige. First we must find him. She is the bait. Bath her, dress her, show her round town and I guarantee he'll come knocking at our doors within the week.

DAISY (to TENDAI). Where is he now?

TENDAI. I am not knowing. When there are coming white men with guns and hunters, everyone run away. I look for my husband, there is nothing but fire, the village is burning. The soldiers bring me to this doctor, he is saying nicely he will bring me to my husband, it is a trick, he travel me for three months, then bring me to this large village, then this house.

LAZARUS (*to* JAMESON). You're a brute.

DAISY. Get out.

LAZARUS *chooses a book from one of his bundles and goes. Meanwhile:*

(*To* TENDAI.) What's his name?

TENDAI. Paul.

DAISY. Paul what?

JAMESON. She doesn't know. Either she's forgotten or the chap went native. I've prepared a list of unconnected words which I'd like you to fire at her unexpectedly from time to time. It may be that the darker regions of her mind will disgorge the missing syllables when properly stimulated. But I run before my horse to market. Will you look after her?

DAISY. Absolutely.

JAMESON. Watch her. Guard her. We struggle against a bitter irony of history: that nine-tenths of Africa's gold has been discovered beneath the feet of stubborn Boers. "Like some brave Crusoe on an isle marooned, The Empire bleeds; but gold will stop the wound!" Don't worry about the Polo Club. Good day.

He goes.

DAISY. What an awful man. (*To* TENDAI.) Sit here.

TENDAI *does.*

Are you thinking about Paul?

TENDAI *nods.*

Tell me: when you sleep with him, does it make you happy?

TENDAI. We have never sleep together. We have had no chance.

DAISY. Darling, you must find him!

TENDAI. Even if I am never finding him, I will be loving him always.

DAISY takes out her handkerchief, blows her nose. LAZARUS comes in.

LAZARUS. What is it?

DAISY. Nothing to do with you.

He waits.

I'd so looked forward to today. When I first came to Jo'burg I had nothing. Now look. Five houses, clothes from Paris, not blinking bad. And I feel dreadful. It's her. She's got everything I haven't.

LAZARUS. Perfect love?

DAISY. We believe in it, do we?

LAZARUS. I'm persuaded it exists.

DAISY. Come away with me. We could go to Greece. Or take a steamer up the Nile to see the Pyramids. I won't molest you. I'll sit on the deck in an old sun hat and read the Baedeker. We'll do whatever makes us happy together.

LAZARUS. Daisy, you and I will be happy together when we're dead.

DAISY. Then there's no hope for me.

LAZARUS (*as one explaining to a child*). You'll find somebody. Someone handsome. Simple enough not to notice when you hurt him. Too honest to suspect your love affairs. A little lacking in feeling generally would be a help and not too clever. I hope you find him.

DAISY. You liar, you'd be jealous and upset.

LAZARUS. If I can get on with my work, if it makes you less horrible to me, then the sooner you start looking the better.

DAISY. I will.

LAZARUS. Good.

DAISY. I'll start on Monday.

LAZARUS. Monday, what's the matter with you, start now. Go to the window and look.

DAISY goes to the window. LAZARUS opens a book.

(*To* TENDAI.) You're really going to like it here.

DAISY. You could leave.

LAZARUS. You're meant to be looking.

DAISY. You don't like me.

LAZARUS. I do, but I disapprove.

DAISY. You insult my friends.

LAZARUS. They're dreadful people.

DAISY. Why stay?

LAZARUS. I live my life for very little reason except to see the wicked on this earth destroyed. *I* can't destroy them, who am I against such legions? They must destroy themselves. There, I can help. Help them guzzle, screw, grow rich. Help them ravage us till our lives are too cruel to bear. The world will become a slaughterhouse. The lame and the halt will be pursued by sprinting Alsatians. The blind will be crushed under carriage-wheels. Then the trumpet will sound. We will rise.

DAISY. Ssh! I think I've seen him. He's just come out of the barber's and he's looking in a window.

LAZARUS goes to the window, looks.

LAZARUS. Him?

DAISY. Why not?

LAZARUS. In the blue scarf?

DAISY. That's the one.

LAZARUS. Your perfect love!

He laughs.

How odd!

DAISY. You're jealous!

LAZARUS. Not in the slightest. It's remarkable.

She takes his hand.

DAISY. Stay for lunch.

LAZARUS. I live in the basement.

DAISY. Don't sulk. You can eat up here. We'll finish this.

She picks up the champagne bottle. To TENDAI:

Are you thirsty?

LAZARUS. She won't like it.

DAISY. Give her a chance.

She pours TENDAI *some champagne, which* TENDAI *likes.*

She'll live with me. She'll be my lady's maid. (*To* TENDAI.)
What's his name? Paul. I'm calling my fellow Paul as well.
Cheers.

They drink.

End of scene.

Scene Three

HENRIETTA*'s goldfields. An open space. The surface
buildings of a goldmine can be seen in the distance.*

HENRIETTA *van Es is talking with her brother,* DR. BRINK.
*She is a handsome, broad-shouldered woman in her forties,
plainly but expensively dressed. He's a stout man with a spade
beard, in frock coat and hat.*

HENRIETTA. They wrote to me last week. I said no. They
came to call. I said, speak to my lawyer. Now here you are,
and I discover you're on their side.

BRINK. If you're trying to raise the price, you're a fool. These are your own people, Hennie. Boers to a man. We can't pay more.

HENRIETTA. I don't want to sell.

BRINK. Half a million pounds! At least let's walk back to the house and discuss it.

HENRIETTA. Let's stay where we can see what we're talking about.

She looks out.

When my husband first brought me here to Nooitgedacht, all this was God's veldt. Long grass, native tracks, far as the eye could see. Virgin land. That was a good year. We built the house, we filled the dam. We'd fall on our pillows half-dead at midnight, get up again at four. We were young, we were in love. Twelve months later he was dead, and that summer I struck gold. I love this farm. I love the goldmine even more. You could double the price and I'd still say no.

BRINK. Hennie, listen. From the day that gold was found in our republic, we have been under siege. Foreigners take our land. Week by week, more is sold, less belongs to the people. As long as a woman owns this farm, it is in danger. Those English are scoundrels. They'll take every low advantage of your tender feelings and you'll be too weak to resist them.

HENRIETTA. What nonsense you talk! When we were children, who could fight, who broke in the horses, who cut a bullet from her own arm?

BRINK. You're still a woman.

HENRIETTA. True. My husband left me eighty-seven pounds, three shillings and sixpence. And the farm, and some advice. He said, 'Don't sell the land, Hennie.' He said, 'Bring the bible, put it on the bed.' He was very thin by then. He said, 'Everyone's talking gold. Everyone's selling up. Believe me, my girl, they'll be the losers. I want to know before I die that there's one sane person left in the Transvaal even if it has to be my wife. Now swear.' I said 'I'll swear to nothing.' I kept the land because it suited me, and now I'm rich. I run the mine like my kitchen. Nothing's wasted, everything comes back as something else. At night I light a lamp and sit up adding figures till my spectacles pinch my nose too much to continue. I'm clever. That's what I like the most, finding how clever I am. And it's hard. I miss Hendrik. I miss the company. I wake up at night and tiptoe down the stairs and cook big dinners. When they're too old to eat I throw them away or give them to the natives.

WILLEM *calls from out of sight.*

WILLEM. Ma!

HENRIETTA. There's my son. He's my worry. He's my cross. I've seen him in town. Drunk, loud, fists in all directions.

WILLEM *comes on.*

Where have you been? Say hello to your uncle Frans. He's a big man now, he's in the Senate.

WILLEM. Afternoon uncle.

HENRIETTA. I waited up for you. I fell asleep over my book. I've a headache from the lamp. Where did you stay?

WILLEM. With a friend.

HENRIETTA. Have you been drinking?

She grabs him.

WILLEM. Ma!

She sniffs.

Don't wriggle! I can smell it. And there's something else.

She sniffs again.

HENRIETTA. Perfume. Where did you sleep? Don't lie.

WILLEM. I've met a woman.

HENRIETTA. What's her name?

WILLEM. Daisy.

BRINK. Mrs. Bone?

HENRIETTA. The woman is married?

BRINK. Divorced, I believe, or some such. People like her don't trouble with such distinctions.

HENRIETTA (*to* WILLEM). Where will you be tonight? I'll tell you. Here. I'm going with your uncle to the President's banquet. I shall sleep at the house in town. This is a family business, one of us must stay.

WILLEM. That's not fair.

HENRIETTA. Talk to him, Frans.

BRINK. Look here, young Willem. Don't you add to your mother's troubles. You drink, you fight. Now you consort with a notorious woman. My godfathers, boy, is there no one your own age? Leave her alone, you understand me?

WILLEM. Yes, uncle.

BRINK. That's better. (*Confidentially.*) I'll talk to you later about this. As for tonight . . .

To HENRIETTA:

. . . let him go out if he wants. A couple of beers, a headache in the morning, it's to be expected.

HENRIETTA (*to* WILLEM). Do what you like.

WILLEM. I needs some money.

HENRIETTA. Then you must wait. My purse is in the house.

WILLEM. Where?

HENRIETTA. Where you can't find it!

WILLEM. Let's go.

He pulls her by the hand. She pulls away and hits him hard over the face, then turns away in silence.

BRINK. Your mother's upset. Here's a guinea.

WILLEM. You's a friend, Uncle Frans.

BRINK. Be off.

　WILLEM *goes off.*

HENRIETTA. I've lost him. How? Have I done wrong? Am I being punished?

BRINK. You wanted power, and you destroyed your womanhood to get it.

HENRIETTA. It's not too late. She's older than him, you say? Then it won't last. He'll come home. There'll be his dinner laid and a mother waiting.

BRINK. And the mine?

HENRIETTA. I'll sell. I shall come to your office at three o'clock on Thursday. Whatever you've drawn up for me, I'll sign. Good, that's done. Shall we return to the house?

BRINK. With pleasure.

HENRIETTA. There's a melktert waiting for your tea. It was baked by the maid, but I taught her myself and she's nearly got it right. Come.

　End of scene.

Scene Four

The Criterion Hotel. Upstairs room. At the back are big, shuttered windows leading to a long balcony. A door at each side. There's a small bar. A waiter is up a ladder, hanging up bunting in the orange, white and green of the Transvaal Republic.

Dr. JAMESON is smoking a cigar and reading the Johannesburg Star. After a moment:

JAMESON. Waiter! A brandy and soda.

WAITER. Yes baas.

He climbs down the ladder and goes to the door. It opens and WILLEM *comes in.*

Ah, no!

WILLEM. Quiet, you!

He pushes his way in.

JAMESON. What's the difficulty?

WAITER. The manager say, sir, this young baas very bad. He not allowed to drink in this hotel.

WILLEM. You're all mixed up! There's a gentleman's agreement between me and Mr. Baas Manager. I don't drink in the bar downstairs, and he don't serve me.

WAITER. Please, my baas . . . !

WILLEM *gives the waiter a push, then several more.*

WILLEM. Hasn't you got no sense, you bloody monkey? I'm not in the bar, I'm here!

The waiter, infuriated, pushes WILLEM *back. More would follow but:*

JAMESON. Young man! If I may vouch for your behaviour, I'll be honoured.

To the waiter:

My card. If in doubt, present it to the manager. Now get me a brandy. (*To* WILLEM.) Won't you join me? (*To the* WAITER.) Two.

The waiter pours two brandies, which he will deliver before going back up the ladder.

Leander Jameson. Call me Dr. Jim.

WILLEM. Willem van Es.

JAMESON. Van Es? The heir perhaps to the Nooitgedacht goldmine?

WILLEM. Not any more. My ma's selling up.

JAMESON. To whom? I ask for interest merely.

WILLEM. To Boers. She'd never sell out to English. Sorry!

JAMESON. I'm not offended. Narrow nationalism is not my creed. I believe in brotherhood, the nations united under the banner of progress. Besides, I am a Scot. *Why* is she selling?

WILLEM. Because of me. I drinks, I fights, I likes old woman. She says she wants to take me off to Europe and renovate my mind.

JAMESON. Someone's coming. Not a word of our conversation.

BRINK comes in. He is dressed for the banquet in a frock coat and top hat, with all his medals and a sash in the colours of the Republic. JAMESON walks quickly up to the balcony, saying loudly:

Thank you for the light!

BRINK. Willem!

WILLEM. Uncle Frans!

BRINK. Your mother suspected you might be here. We're on our way to the banquet, and she asks me to say that if you're sober you may come in the carriage and watch the parade from the Town Hall windows.

WILLEM. Uncle . . . !

BRINK. That's an order. (*To the* WAITER.) Boy, get those flags up straight. (*To* WILLEM.) It's a scandal. An English hotel with an English manager. He drags his feet and hopes his insolence will go unnoticed. Now I want a brandy.

WILLEM (*calls*). Waiter!

The waiter comes down and serves BRINK a brandy. Meanwhile:

BRINK. Your ma has spotted Mevrouw van Roodeport and I can't stand that woman's cackle. Tell me, my boy, if I was to say the words "an attractive woman", what would you think of?

WILLEM. I likes them mature, uncle.

BRINK. I'm old-fashioned. In my young days, the saying was 'Black for pleasure, white for repentance'. There's a place for both in a man's life, did the minister never tell you?

WILLEM. Yes, uncle.

BRINK. So what do you young fellows think of black girls these days?

WILLEM. I likes them but they gives me a conscience.

BRINK. That's what they're there for! Why else did the Lord provide them?

TENDAI *comes in left, bathed, dressed and spruced up.*
JAMESON *comes down to meet her.*

Just look at this!

JAMESON *is there.*

JAMESON. Gentlemen, this African is in my care. Dr. Brink, I'm surprised at you. Tendai, what are you doing?

TENDAI. I am being sent by Mrs. Bone to arrange her table.

WILLEM (*aside*). She's coming here!

BRINK. The impudence to show her face in public! Willem, come.

WILLEM. I wants to stay.

BRINK. Then I shall tell your mother I could not find you. The truth would break her heart.

DAISY *comes in with* LAZARUS. *She sees* BRINK.

DAISY. Frans, what a great surprise. I can't talk now.

BRINK. Good evening.

He tips his hat and goes. DAISY *sees Dr.* JAMESON.

DAISY. And Dr. Jim! This table will be fine. Tendai, it wouldn't do for you to sit, but you may stand behind my table like a proper butler, won't that be fun.

She and LAZARUS *have taken their seats. To* LAZARUS:

What are you staring at?

LAZARUS *has spotted* WILLEM.

LAZARUS. That boy.

DAISY. I've seen him.

LAZARUS. What's his name?

DAISY. You met him this morning.

LAZARUS. You slept with him last night.

DAISY. Willem. I'm cutting him dead. Hold my hand, I'm feeling awful. Everything's catching up.

JAMESON *has taken a seat at their table.*

JAMESON. Are you well?

DAISY. Yes, terribly happy. It's foul downstairs, like a horrid English pub. The streets are packed, is something on?

JAMESON. The Battle of Blood River.

DAISY. Jesus, where?

JAMESON. It's the anniversary celebrations. President Kruger will lead a torchlight procession past these very windows, accompanied by leaders of the church, widows in weeds and young men in allegorical loincloths.

DAISY (*calls to the* WAITER). Hurry up, we're thirsty!

JAMESON *indicates* WILLEM, *who is skulking.*

JAMESON. There's your young friend. What price he joins us?

LAZARUS. Why not?

JAMESON (*calls over to* WILLEM). Bring a chair!

DAISY (*to* LAZARUS). Traitor.

LAZARUS. Be nice to him.

DAISY (*to* JAMESON). I'm under strain. (*Of* LAZARUS.) He's no help. I've put him in charge of an empire worth thousands of pounds and all he can do is sit and read the wine list.

LAZARUS. I'll go out shortly.

DAISY. So you say.

LAZARUS. I'll visit the houses, check the receipts, what do you think I've been doing every Saturday night for the last year and a half?

DAISY (*repentant*). I know, I know.

LAZARUS. Can't you subside a little?

JAMESON (*to the* WAITER). The '73.

WAITER. Sure, baas.

DAISY (*to* WILLEM, *who has joined them*). Goodness, it's you! The light was in my eyes.

JAMESON. And how's our dusky princess?

LAZARUS. She wants her husband.

JAMESON (*winks*). So do we!

LAZARUS. She's most unhappy.

DAISY. She is *not!*

LAZARUS. She wants to observe the crowd and find her husband.

DAISY. That's all she thinks of.

WILLEM (*to* LAZARUS, *of* JAMESON). Is *he* with *her?*

LAZARUS. Certainly not.

DAISY (*to* WILLEM). Move your knee.

JAMESON. And how's her memory?

DAISY. Not a flicker.

WILLEM (*to* LAZARUS). Not a boyfriend?

LAZARUS. No.

JAMESON. Are the words not helping?

DAISY. Words what words?

WILLEM (*to* LAZARUS). Who are you?

JAMESON. I left a list of words to jog her memory.

WILLEM. Are *you* her boyfriend?

DAISY. I've been too busy.

   LAZARUS *rises.*

LAZARUS. Daisy, I'm off.

DAISY. For God's sake stay.

WILLEM. He wants to go.

   The waiter is pouring wine all round.

DAISY. The '73, that's perfect.

LAZARUS. It's Saturday night! The houses will be packed, beds will collapse, glass will shatter, squaddies will break down the doors and nobody will pay.

DAISY. Wait till ten.

JAMESON. Quiet please!

WILLEM (*to* WAITER). Another bottle!

LAZARUS. Ssh!

JAMESON. Words!

DAISY. He's starting.

   Pause.

JAMESON (*to* TENDAI). Empty your mind of all thought.

WILLEM. That won't be hard.

DAISY. Shut up.

JAMESON. Now girl, you must do as I say.

DAISY. She has.

WILLEM. Has what?

LAZARUS. Emptied her mind of all thought.

JAMESON. It's not like turning down the gas, you know. The process requires intense mental effort.

DAISY. Look at her if you don't believe me!

They look at TENDAI.

Tell me, Tendai, are you thinking of anything?

TENDAI. What?

DAISY. You see?

JAMESON. I'm not convinced. She looks like this all the time.

DAISY. Exactly!

JAMESON. She can't be thinking of nothing all day.

WILLEM. Why not?

JAMESON. She'd forget her name and bang into closed doors.

LAZARUS. It is a complex process. The object of love has been absorbed into the deepest layer of the mind, while day-to-day thoughts have risen to a superficial level.

DAISY. She can remember or forget them as she pleases. (*To* TENDAI.) Isn't that so?

TENDAI. What?

JAMESON. Hem hem.

LAZARUS. He's starting up.

Pause.

JAMESON. Man!

TENDAI. Paul.

JAMESON. Moustache.

DAISY (*to* WILLEM). And keep your hands to yourself!

LAZARUS. What was the word?

TENDAI. Moustache.

JAMESON. And what's the answer?

TENDAI. Paul.

JAMESON. Ah ha!

DAISY. Has Paul a moustache?

TENDAI. I am not knowing.

JAMESON. She *must* be knowing!

DAISY. Not at all! If you're really, really in love, you don't waste time wondering if people have moustaches or not, you have a spiritual bond. I always knew love was like this. Tendai, where do you want to be?

TENDAI. Outside.

DAISY. To wander the muddy streets, to peer at the face of each young stranger. To cry 'Paul, Paul, Paul', till some kind soul takes pity. Go!

TENDAI *bobs and claps and goes. Meanwhile:*

JAMESON. Most frustrating.

LAZARUS. And cruel of you, Daisy, to raise her hopes.

DAISY. They're better that way. We're the lucky ones, she and I: to love and never to meet the bastard. Willem, I'm not sleeping with you tonight.

WILLEM. Oh shit.

He cries.

DAISY. *My* Paul is standing looking in a window. This is what he generally does, in fact I've never seen him any other way. He's just had his hair cut, and the man's made a good job of it, which is lucky because as long as I live it will stay precisely at that length. What he's doing, what in fact he *does*, is slide his finger down the inside of his collar where the cuttings scratch. Then he huffs up his coat and walks away. He's a perfect lover and I'm perfectly content.

ROGER *comes in.*

Oh rats.

JAMESON. Ah, Roger, there you are. (*To the others.*) Allow me to introduce a new acquaintance. Mrs. Bone, Lazarus something, Willem van Es. (*To* DAISY.) Or have you met?

DAISY. I don't believe we've had the pleasure.

ROGER. I'll say we have.

DAISY (*to* LAZARUS). Get rid of him.

ROGER. We met at Sophie's.

DAISY. I've never heard of her.

WILLEM. Sophie's is a bar.

LAZARUS (*to* WILLEM). Daisy owns it.

ROGER. You played the piano.

DAISY. *What?*

ROGER. You bought champagne.

DAISY. I did not!

LAZARUS. Nor did she play the piano. Nor does Sophie's exist. Nor do pianos exist. You, they, and everything else that doesn't suit her are hereby abolished. Nor did you sleep together.

ROGER. I seem to remember we were most compatible.

LAZARUS. You would be.

DAISY. Bastard!

LAZARUS. Don't lie!

DAISY. All right then! He said would I. I said yes but he'd have to wait till closing time. He said when's that. I said four. He said what did I do till then, so I took him into my office and sucked him off while I was cashing up. I took him home . . .

ROGER. I think we might draw a veil . . .

DAISY. He fucked me twice, I fell asleep, he woke me up for another fuck, then he fucked me over breakfast and he fucked me again in the hall on his way out. There's something peculiar about him.

JAMESON. He certainly fucks a lot.

DAISY. No, what it was, was that each fuck was really several rolled into one, because when he comes, he stays in and then starts fucking all over again as though he hadn't. You're all being very quiet! I'm going outside.

She goes out towards the balcony.

LAZARUS. I'll come with you.

DAISY. Do what you like!

LAZARUS (*to* ROGER). Don't be discouraged. She likes you really.

WILLEM. Shit I'll murder you!

He dives ROGER, *who defends himself ably. A fight would follow but:* HENRIETTA *comes in, simply but grandly dressed for the banquet and wearing her real diamonds.*

HENRIETTA. Willem!

WILLEM. Ma!

JAMESON (*aside*). Mevrouw van Es!

HENRIETTA. Fighting!

WILLEM. I'm sorry ma. I lost my rag.

JAMESON (*to* ROGER). Fancy a drink?

He ushers ROGER *out.* LAZARUS *goes out and joins* DAISY.

HENRIETTA. Your uncle came down to the carriage wearing his liar's face. I knew you were here . . .

TENDAI *comes in, opposite door to* ROGER, *sad and disappointed.*

. . . and this girl confirmed it.

She indicates DAISY.

Is that her?

WILLEM. Yes.

HENRIETTA. Dry your eyes.

She wipes his face.

Go downstairs. Wait with your uncle.

He goes. To TENDAI:

Ask your madam if she can spare a moment.

TENDAI *approaches* DAISY, *bobs and claps and gives her the message. After a moment,* DAISY *comes into the room. She's nervous.* TENDAI *follows, but keeps her distance.*

HENRIETTA. I saw you arriving. I thought you very pretty. You know my son?

DAISY. Not really.

HENRIETTA. Then I don't understand.

DAISY. I slept with him last night, but it didn't mean much. I've slept with all the men you've seen tonight, and only one meant anything to speak of. Do you mind, I think I need this.

She pours herself some wine, the glass clattering as her hand shakes.

Dr. Jameson says you're a tycoon, if that's the word.

HENRIETTA. Not any more. On Thursday I shall visit my attorney, and by the evening I shall have sold nearly all I own. I shall be nothing but myself. Myself as mother, which was my reason for selling. And myself as whatever else a woman can be in a town like this. I have slept with only one man. I did so for the last time on the sixteenth of October nineteen years ago. Till then, every night for three years, and we had made love, though not slept, twice in the open air before our marriage. Once, after a family party, I experienced great pleasure as he penetrated me. At other times, through no fault of his, my mind would drift. That one time I thought for many years to have been an accident. God had made me rich, I got my pleasure from business. Pleasure with men was in my thoughts, but I never considered it practically until tonight. When I do.

DAISY. You mustn't!

HENRIETTA. I expected different advice.

DAISY. Oh, you don't know. Were you pretty when you were her age?

She indicates TENDAI.

Looking at you, I'd guess you're more attractive now. I was a great beauty. If a man saw me, he wanted me, simple as that. He'd smile, or brush my elbow in a friendly fashion. What the nuns at school called 'little attentions', 'course they didn't stay little very long. I thought everybody in the world was being asked to go to bed, how would I know, I'd only myself to go by. I thought it was something you said 'Yes' to so's they wouldn't go on about it, like eating the fat off the plate. What bothered me was why was I getting upset? Was I doing it wrong? Why was I always crying afterwards while they were whistling merry tunes and so forth? The answer, as I soon found out, was that they didn't think much of me.

She sees LAZARUS, *who has detached himself from the balcony.*

Lazarus, come here.

He does. She goes on.

They were treating me like shit. So I treated them like shit straight back and I still do. I'm not sleeping with any more men, it makes me too horrible.

LAZARUS. You are horrible, that's why you do it.

DAISY. You hate me!

LAZARUS. Not at all, it's what you're like, just do me a favour and don't pretend otherwise.

DAISY (*of* HENRIETTA). She's otherwise! Nineteen years without a man.

LAZARUS. Daisy, you are the slave of your desires, and your term of servitude will end, in my opinion, when you have burned them out, and not before.

HENRIETTA. I understand that.

DAISY. Well, as we used to say: swap.

She kisses HENRIETTA *lightly, to both their surprise.*
DAISY *gets her handkerchief out and blows her nose. To*
LAZARUS:

Silly sod, look what you made me do.

The festivities outside grow louder.

Listen, there's the band! The parade's going past! Tendai,
go and look.

TENDAI *goes out on to the balcony.* BRINK *and* WILLEM
come up from downstairs.

BRINK (*to* HENRIETTA). The crowd's too thick, we'll have
to watch from here. It's not the company I would have
chosen, but there's . . .

HENRIETTA *cuts him off:*

HENRIETTA. I'm enjoying myself!

They go on to the balcony.

DAISY (*to* LAZARUS). That man. That Englishman. He's one
in a million. Sign him up.

LAZARUS *slaps his forehead in wildly regretted
forgetfulness.*

I pay you money to think of things like that!

She goes to the balcony. Calls to the others:

What's happening? Are the boys in loincloths here?

The procession is now going by: music, cheering, chanting.
DAISY, HENRIETTA, WILLEM *and* BRINK *go out on to
the balcony and look out into the street. The English party
is separate from the Afrikaans one, which cheers much more
enthusiastically.*

ROGER *and* JAMESON *enter, both drinking.* LAZARUS
sees them, edges down towards them and eavesdrops.

JAMESON. So you're a patriot?

ROGER. I should say so.

JAMESON. Have you private means?

ROGER. I play cards for a living.

JAMESON. That's the sort of thing I'd rather not know. Do
you shoot?

ROGER. I can't afford to these days.

JAMESON. The experience is what counts. Do you carry a
gun?

ROGER *pats his jacket.*

ROGER. Want to see it?

JAMESON. I'll take your word for it. Have you any idea of the
wealth of this republic? Any notion of the use it could be
put to in enlightened hands?

ROGER. Can't say I'd thought about it.

JAMESON. You'd class yourself as a man of action rather than
one of nature's Hamlets? Excellent. This town could be
captured by a handful of trained men. I am raising a small
subversive army under the guise of the Sons of Albion
Sports and Rifles Club.

ROGER. Not illegal is it?

JAMESON (*with bottle*). Have another.

ROGER. Any chance of a uniform?

JAMESON. That might follow. What do you say?

ROGER. Well I'll see how I go, but I generally say yes to things.
I like it here. Charming young ladies, splendid people.

DAISY *calls from the balcony:*

DAISY. Dr. Jim! Come quickly!

JAMESON *goes up to the balcony, annoyed. Music and
cheering are heard.*

WILLEM. There he is!

BRINK. The President!

ALL. Hooray! Hooray! Hooray!

LAZARUS buttonholes ROGER.

LAZARUS. Ignore that man. Notorious crackpot. I have a post to offer which is far better suited to your talents.

From the balcony:

JAMESON. That's it.

DAISY. We've seen enough.

LAZARUS (*to* ROGER). We can't talk here. Come down to the bar. I'll buy you a drink.

He stands back, shows ROGER out. DAISY calls to him:

DAISY. Where are you going? (*To* TENDAI.) Order the carriage.

She moves quickly to LAZARUS. TENDAI goes out quickly, opposite door to ROGER. The others drift back into the room.

JAMESON. Most intriguing.

BRINK. An inspiration!

JAMESON. Though the crowd was smaller than I had expected.

DAISY (*to* LAZARUS). I've seen him again. Paul. My Paul. He's down in the street.

LAZARUS. Shall I collect him for you?

DAISY. Don't you dare.

HENRIETTA (*to* BRINK). I'm too tired for the banquet. Take Willem. Sit him beside you and make him behave. I'll sleep in the house in town.

BRINK (*to* HENRIETTA). Who'll drive you home?

DAISY. I will. Don't be embarrassed. We can draw the blinds.

HENRIETTA (*to* DAISY). I'll be happy to be seen with you, Mrs. Bone. I'll meet you on the steps in just a moment. I must gather my thoughts.

She moves up to the balcony. BRINK *and* WILLEM *have gone.* JAMESON *goes out after them.*

LAZARUS. Daisy, one moment.

On her way out, she stops.

Why don't you want to meet him?

DAISY. Because if I do, he won't be perfect.

She goes. LAZARUS *stands alone.*

LAZARUS. True.

He goes out quickly after her. The opposite door opens and ROGER *looks in.*

ROGER. Hello?

HENRIETTA *comes down from the balcony. She looks at him steadily, approaches him. Lays a finger on his lips.*

ROGER. Who are you?

WILLEM *comes in. He sees them.*

WILLEM. Ma?

HENRIETTA *leaves, perfectly composed.* WILLEM *leaves after her. The opposite door opens and* PAUL *comes in. He looks dishevelled and pale and is wearing his blue scarf.*

PAUL. Roger?

ROGER. Paul!

They embrace.

What are doing here?

PAUL. I don't know. I was told to come up and wait. Where is she?

ROGER. Who?

PAUL. Where's Tendai?

ROGER. Don't you know?

PAUL. They said in the village that you'd rescued her. I've been searching for months. What happened?

ROGER. The soldiers took her away. I followed them. Then one of the prisoners got away. He said she'd been shouting at them. She'd been screaming. She wanted them to take her back to you. They took her out of sight. Then he heard a shot.

PAUL. It could have been someone else.

ROGER. I found this.

He takes off his ring. Gives it to PAUL.

Pauly, she's dead.

PAUL *sits, turning the ring over in his hands.*

Go on. Be angry. Cry.

PAUL. I can't. That's what you always told me. That I didn't have any feelings. Well I don't.

The door opens. It's LAZARUS. *To* PAUL:

LAZARUS. Thank you for waiting.

PAUL. What do you want? Why have you brought me here?

LAZARUS. There is a woman who admires you.

PAUL. What?

LAZARUS. Her character is flawless, her beauty untouched by the passage of years, her body a palace of pleasures to which you alone in the wide world have the key.

PAUL. Could you say that again more simply?

ROGER. For God's sake, there's a beautiful woman who wants you to go to bed with her.

Pause.

PAUL. Where does she live?

LAZARUS. I'll take you.

ROGER. Where's he going?

PAUL. Where will I be?

LAZARUS (*to* ROGER). I'll tell you later. Call on me in two hours' time at this address.

He's scribbling it on a piece of paper.

Basement window, the light will be on, I shall be writing, tap on the glass. Now say good-bye.

ROGER *and* PAUL *shake hands.*

ROGER. It's been remarkably brief, old chap.

PAUL. We'll meet in the morning.

LAZARUS *ushers* PAUL *out.* ROGER *is left alone: he feels it. He picks up a half-finished glass and drains it. Goes to one of the doors, opens it, calls down the stairs:*

ROGER. Waiter!

At once the WAITER *rushes into the room from the opposite door. He stands panting, as one about to announce high drama.*

That was quick. I'll have a . . .

WAITER. Run!

ROGER. What?

WAITER. He's coming!

ROGER. Who? Where?

WAITER. Run! Run!

The door behind ROGER *opens quietly.* WILLEM *is there with a rifle. He aims it at* ROGER. *The waiter ducks and hides.* ROGER *spins round, draws his revolver and fires. Loud explosion.* WILLEM *is knocked across the room, his rifle firing into the air. He lies groaning.* ROGER *stares at him.*

ROGER. He's dead.

WAITER. Not quite yet. Will take a minute.

He goes quickly to both doors and bolts them. Points to the window.

Out that window, climb down railing, then a small jump. Quick!

Knocking is heard on the door. Voice call in alarm. 'Hello?' 'What's happened?' etc.

ROGER. Thanks for the help. I'll . . .

WAITER. Go!

ROGER runs to the balcony and disappears over the railing. WILLEM is still groaning. The waiter picks up a chair and breaks it over his head. WILLEM falls silent. When the waiter is satisfied that he's dead, and the banging and shouting from behind the door are louder than ever:

WAITER. I'm comin'. I'm comin'. The door it stick bad, my baas. I'm a-comin'!

He goes in no hurry to open the door.

End of scene.

Scene Five

HENRIETTA*'s bedroom. Later that night. A large bed. HENRIETTA, in her nightdress, is sitting on the bed reading her family bible. Candles burning. There is a knock on the door.*

HENRIETTA. Come in.

JUSTIN, the family butler-boy, comes in.

Is Master Willem not back yet?

JUSTIN. Not yet, madam.

HENRIETTA. I gave him my place at the President's banquet. I wanted to come home and think about my life.

JUSTIN. Is that all, madam?

HENRIETTA. Justin, how long have you worked for me?

JUSTIN. Have I done a mistake?

HENRIETTA. You're a good and faithful servant. When I die you will inherit fifteen shillings.

JUSTIN (*tries not to sound patronising*). It's too much, madam. Shall I put out the candles?

HENRIETTA. I'll do them myself. When Master Willem returns, tell him to come up and say good night.

JUSTIN goes. HENRIETTA reads from her bible:

'And Jesus said: let he who is without sin cast the first stone.'

She puts the bible away, gets up, blows out the candles and gets into bed.

Darkness. A dog barks in the street below. Then:

A creak from the shutters. They open slowly and a figure creeps in. It's ROGER. He moves quietly across the room.

HENRIETTA. Don't move.

ROGER stops.

I mean it.

She comes out from the bed carrying a large antique shotgun.

It's my father's shotgun. I'm a frontier woman, I don't play about. Drop your gun on the bed. Slowly.

He does.

Don't move. All right, I've found it.

She does.

Who are you?

ROGER. An Englishman.

Pause.

I said . . .

HENRIETTA. I heard you. Where were you tonight?

ROGER. Does it matter?

HENRIETTA. It matters to me.

ROGER. At a hotel.

HENRIETTA. Light a match and hold it close to your face. I want to see the kind of man I'm dealing with.

He lights a match, holds it near his face. She recognises him, but he doesn't recognise her.

Can you see me?

ROGER. No.

HENRIETTA. Good. Why did you come here?

ROGER. I needed a place to hide. They're after me.

HENRIETTA. Why?

ROGER. I've shot a man.

HENRIETTA. Did you kill him?

ROGER. I think so.

HENRIETTA. I should call the police.

ROGER. They'll hang me.

HENRIETTA. Very likely. Was it over a woman?

ROGER. Yes.

HENRIETTA. Another man touched her and you lost your rag. My God, you men are fools. Were you seen breaking in?

ROGER. I don't know.

HENRIETTA. You'd better hide in here.

ROGER. Is there a cupboard?

HENRIETTA. Too small.

ROGER. A closet?

HENRIETTA. There is. But unfortunately the key has been mislaid. You can hide in the bed.

ROGER. Where will you sleep?

HENRIETTA. With you.

ROGER. I . . .

HENRIETTA. Would you rather I called the police?

ROGER. I'll take my boots off.

HENRIETTA. Please.

Pause in the dark. Then a loud clunk.

Ssh! Put the second one down quietly.

He does.

All right, that's enough. Get in. Which side do you like?

ROGER. I'm easy.

HENRIETTA. Move across then.

ROGER. Two pillows or one?

HENRIETTA. There is only one.

ROGER. I'm sorry.

HENRIETTA. You get used to it.

She gets into the bed. Pause.

I wonder how often you've done this before? Shared a bed with a woman you've just met?

ROGER. What makes you think I've done it even once?

HENRIETTA. Something about you. Something I'm not used to. In your face, in your voice.

ROGER. To be honest, which is what I feel I should be, death being round the corner for example: there've been many. Not just beds. Carpets, tabletops, little rooms round the back. I'd say, since you ask: a thousand? God I'll roast. But I've never been so frightened.

HENRIETTA. There'd be another difference if it wasn't dark.

ROGER. Would there?

HENRIETTA. Since we're being honest, yes. I've a big plain face. Hands like a labourer.

ROGER. I've been to bed with a labourer. Does that upset you?

HENRIETTA. No. Would you be upset to know how old I am?

ROGER. Forty?

HENRIETTA. Not a bad guess.

ROGER. What's the answer?

HENRIETTA. I told you, it's not a bad guess.

ROGER. I saw a woman today who was older than that.

Pause.

Are you still there?

HENRIETTA. What was she like?

ROGER. Quiet. Dressed up, but nicely so. Poor skin, with beautiful deep eyes. Rather animal.

HENRIETTA. Did she attract you?

ROGER. Yes.

HENRIETTA. Let me touch you. There.

Knocking is heard on the door downstairs.

ROGER. They're here.

HENRIETTA. It doesn't matter.

Muffled voices downstairs. Footsteps up the stairs and along the corridor. Light under the door. A knock.

HENRIETTA (*as one half-asleep*). Who is it?

BRINK. Hennie, it's me.

HENRIETTA. It's too late to call, Frans, go away.

BRINK. Can I come in, please?

HENRIETTA. Wait.

She hides ROGER *under the sheets and blankets, then opens the door and goes back quickly to the bed.* BRINK *comes in with a brace of candles.*

HENRIETTA. I'm sleepy now. Did you want to tell me about the banquet?

BRINK. Hennie, something very bad has happened.

JAMESON *and* JUSTIN *come in carrying* WILLEM.

HENRIETTA (*to* WILLEM). It's you! What are you playing at?

She looks more closely.

Oh my God!

BRINK. He's been shot. The doctor was there. He tried to revive him, but it was too late.

JAMESON. Death was instantaneous. The bullet perforated the left lung, causing massive haemorrhage. There's some bruising on the head. He'd been fighting, it seems.

HENRIETTA. Fighting who?

BRINK. That Englishman. It's the wages of sin, Hennie. They were both connected with Mrs. Bone.

HENRIETTA. Why blame her? It could be any woman's fault. It could be mine.

BRINK. Hennie, the police want to speak to you.

HENRIETTA. I've nothing to tell them.

BRINK. The murderer was seen running this way. They want to know, have you heard footsteps, seen a stranger?

HENRIETTA. No. No, nothing worth bothering with. We'll bury my son tomorrow. No feast, no mourners, it will be as though he'd never lived. I shall return to Nooitgedacht and stay there.

BRINK. We've a meeting on Thursday, Hennie. Do you want it postponed?

HENRIETTA. Cancel it! I won't sell the mine. Why should I? Take him downstairs. I'll follow shortly.

They go, leaving the candles. She waits till they have closed the door.

You can come out now. No, wait.

She turns away from the bed.

Turn your face away from me. Keep it like that.

ROGER *comes out of the bed. He doesn't look at her.*

Get dressed. You'll find some money under the pillow. You must leave the country. Take what you need.

Knocking on the front door below.

That's the police. Wait till they're inside, then go out the way you came.

Pause. She listens.

Now.

ROGER *has put his boots on. He takes money from under the pillow and goes to the window. Stops.*

ROGER. Look at me.

She turns to face him.

I'd like to see you again.

She turns away. Stands still, doesn't move. He leaves by the window.

End of scene.

Scene Six

DAISY*'s new house. Same night. Same room as before, now looking warmer and more comfortable.* DAISY *is sitting reading a novel. A knock at the door.*

DAISY. Come in.

> TENDAI *comes in with* DAISY*'s supper, which includes a bottle of champagne, on a tray. She kneels and starts travelling towards* DAISY *on her knees.*

Oh do get up, you make me feel like Uncle Tom's Cabin.

> TENDAI *stands:*

TENDAI. I am sorry, honoured grandmother.

DAISY. Call me 'Mrs. Bone'. We're friends, remember?

> TENDAI *puts down the tray.* DAISY *looks at her thoughtfully.*

I lost a husband once. Well, twice, but it was the first that mattered. He was a subaltern in the Essex Regiment. Lieutenant Pollock. He was posted to Cyprus to protect the Suez Canal, and that's where he got his ticket. Mr. Bone was a confidence man. He looked like a hired bouncer and he had an office in Kimberley where he dealt in I.D.B. That's 'illicit diamond buying', it means making your wife go on long train journeys with uncut gems stuck up unmentionable places.

> *She turns down the lamp and picks up a big bunch of keys.*

I'm locking up. Come and watch. You can do it yourself tomorrow.

> *She goes out.* TENDAI *follows. Another door opens:* LAZARUS *shows in* PAUL.

LAZARUS. This is the room. Supper! Champagne!

PAUL. Is it for me?

LAZARUS. Who else?

> *He opens the champagne, pours a glass.*

PAUL. What if she comes in?

LAZARUS. She *will* come in!

PAUL. What do I do?

LAZARUS. Whatever you want! She won't resist!

He shakes PAUL's *hand with emotion.*

Dear friend, I tremble for you. No I don't, you're in luck.

He goes. PAUL *drinks.*

PAUL. Why do people do this?

DAISY *comes in, locks the door, turns and sees* PAUL.

DAISY. Help!

PAUL. Don't scream!

DAISY. What do you want? Jewels? Money? I've nothing, I'm a poor widow.

PAUL. It's me.

DAISY. Who? Turn up the lamp.

He does. She recognises him.

Oh God.

PAUL. Are you ill?

DAISY. A little faint. Don't touch me!

PAUL. Don't you want to know why I'm here?

DAISY. I don't want to know anything.

Pause.

Who brought you here? Don't tell me. Twenty-eight, shabbily dressed, strikingly repulsive? That's my ex-secretary. He was disappointed in love and his emotions were unhinged. *Why* did he bring you?

PAUL. To sleep with you.

DAISY. Get out. I mean it. I'm sorry you've been inconvenienced.

PAUL goes to the door and tries to open it.

PAUL. It's stuck.

DAISY. Push!

PAUL. It's locked.

She realises she is carrying the keys.

DAISY. Stay where you are.

She searches among the keys.

Have you far to go? Where's your hotel?

PAUL. I don't have one.

DAISY. Are you staying with friends?

PAUL. I haven't got any.

DAISY. Try this.

She gives him the bunch, a large key prominent on it. He unlocks the door.

Your jacket's wet.

PAUL. It's raining. Goodnight.

He goes. She recovers, then sits and picks up her book. Can't concentrate. Goes to the window, looks out, can't see him.

DAISY. He's gone.

The door opens and PAUL comes in, embarrassed to the point of fury.

PAUL. The *front* door's locked.

DAISY. Don't shout!

PAUL. Do you think I want to be here?

DAISY. Quiet!

Pause.

You've been dreadfully stupid.

PAUL. I know!

DAISY. I lead a secluded life. I don't like surprises.

PAUL. Would you let me out please?

DAISY. All I was going to say was, since it's raining, you could sleep in the attic. I can make you up a bed in no time.

PAUL. I wouldn't dream of it.

DAISY. As long as you don't . . . dismiss the thought entirely. Are you hungry? You must be famished, and I stopped you eating. Finish your supper. I might sit up, I have a book to finish.

PAUL sits.

PAUL. I can't.

DAISY. Are you ill?

PAUL. I think I've drunk too much,

DAISY. Nonsense. You're under strain. Let me feel your forehead. Hot, I thought so.

PAUL. Do you think I could have a cup of tea?

She puts her hands on his shoulders.

DAISY. Relax your shoulders. They're the seat of the nervous system.

She massages his shoulders.

There. It's an Eastern technique. A famous explorer learned it high in the mountains of Tibet. Take your jacket off.

PAUL. I hate to be such a nuisance.

She gets his jacket off and starts to massage his shoulders again.

DAISY. Close your eyes and imagine your muscles stretching and coming apart like the strings of an old tennis racquet. I won't talk. I won't ask questions. Who you are. What your name is. Tell me nothing. You won't need that tie.

She takes off his tie.

Bother, the stud's gone. Do you wear old shirts because you like them?

Undoing his shirt.

They had some in Green and Musgrove's window this morning. Creamy silk with the finest stitching down the front. Shall I order you one'?

PAUL. I couldn't accept it.

DAISY. You'd be doing me a favour.

She has got his shirt off.

There, that's better. More champagne!

PAUL. I'm really not used to it.

DAISY. You're meant to finish it once you've opened the bottle. I might have a glass myself, I'll ring for another, no I'll share yours.

She drinks. Aside:

God, this is exciting.

She starts massaging him again, removing his undershirt in the process.

My husband was in the diplomatic corps. We entertained superbly. The windows blazed all night. Breakfast would be served to a small circle of favoured friends. Scientists, novelists, young poets, while he played Chopin studies on the piano. He left me well provided for, I'm happy to say. How are you off for money?

PAUL. I haven't got any.

DAISY. You must have some.

PAUL. About five shillings.

DAISY. You'd be humouring me splendidly if you'd let me help you. What would you say to two hundred pounds?

PAUL. Two hundred pounds!

DAISY. All right, two-fifty.

PAUL. How can I thank you?

DAISY. You're thanking me now. Just being yourself. Being here. I saw you this afternoon, did my secretary tell you? You were checking your parting in a window. Not just the parting, your face, your whole expression as though you hadn't seen a mirror in ages. I wondered if you'd been in prison? Not for anything wrong. Standing in for a friend perhaps, or bombing a building.

She looks at a spot on his back.

What's this? It looks like a pineapple.

PAUL. It's a birthmark.

DAISY. How strange. Everything else about you is perfectly blank. Like new white china.

She runs her hands over his body. PAUL is now greatly aroused.

PAUL. I'd better go!

DAISY. No, no!

PAUL. You should have chucked me out when I first arrived.

DAISY. I did.

PAUL. I was in love with someone. And I lost her. So I'd nothing left. There was a boy at school who stuck a knife through his hand when his mother died. That's how I felt tonight. I wanted to go to bed with you because it was nothing to do with love. It would be cruel and ugly, but at least I'd feel it. I'm so ashamed.

DAISY. No, no.

PAUL. A woman of your background . . .

DAISY. I shouldn't worry about that . . .

PAUL. Goodnight.

DAISY. I'm not what you think. Why do you suppose I've been topping up your glass? Lying like a cheap watch? I want you.

Pause.

That was all rubbish about my husband. What I was in those days was on the game.

PAUL. And now?

DAISY. It's not that different. I'm nothing. So there's nothing to be afraid of. There really is an attic by the way. I'll ring for the girl, if that's what you want.

She goes to the bell-sash, touches it hesitantly.

Do you think you could make your mind up?

They move together. He moves her down to the sofa, roughly and awkwardly. She cries out quietly in distress.

Oh don't, oh don't.

End of Act One.

ACT TWO

Scene One

LAZARUS's *basement. Two doors. Books, maps, both modern and antique, travel photographs, diagrams of the human body, a globe, a big monochrome reproduction of Botticelli's Primavera. A small bed somewhere. Air of a Renaissance magus's study.*

LAZARUS *is working at his writing-table, his reference-books ranged round him. It's morning but the shutters are closed and a lamp is burning. From outside, the sound of church bells.*

DAISY *comes in. She is about to go out and is dressed in black.*

DAISY. Open the shutters, you'll strain your eyes. It's a gorgeous day.

LAZARUS. I've been working all night.

She opens the shutters. Church bells louder.

In Russia, when the Christians rang their Sunday bells, we locked our shutters locked, rather than spur them on to any additional acts of piety. Bricks through the window, shit on the doorstep. And at Easter we sat three days in the dark, knowing the Good Friday sermon by repute. The subject: Christ's pain. The thorns, the nails, the mother's tears. At the climax of his speech, the priest would cry, 'Kill the Jews! They murdered Christ!' The people would cheer and jump to their feet: this was the bit they liked. As they reached the door of the church, the priest would shout . . . this was the bit they didn't like . . . 'Stop! Not *this* year.' They shuffled back to their places. Too bad! Better luck next Easter! They waited. We waited.

DAISY. Is that what you're writing about?

LAZARUS. I am writing a history of human folly, naturally
my own experiences are included. Is that why you have
descended to my cave of the Nibelung this morning, to
inquire about my masterpiece? No, I don't think so. How
was your lover or have I got the sack?

DAISY. You're getting a regular, regular salary.

LAZARUS (*surprised*). I am?

DAISY. He's terribly nice. Amazingly beautiful with his
clothes off. He'd never had a woman before and he was
awkward for a bit, but very open and unembarrassed once
he got going. He says he loves me. I said I wouldn't hold
him to it, but I think I might have to. He's just how I
imagined. Cheer up.

LAZARUS. I'm working.

He is indeed studying a book.

DAISY. Aren't you pleased?

LAZARUS. Why are you dressed in black?

DAISY. Dr. Jim has sent an urgent message. Willem has been
shot dead. He's lying in his coffin at his mother's house and
the hell of it is, that Dr. Jim wants you and me to meet him
there immediately. And *you've* got to bring some books.

LAZARUS. What kind of books?

DAISY. He doesn't mind about the subject-matter as long as
their combined weight is a hundred and seventy-three
pounds.

LAZARUS. What for?

DAISY. *I* don't know.

LAZARUS. Do I get them back?

DAISY. Presumably. Take the carriage. I shall drag my battered
limbs across the park and meet you there. Am I looking
respectable? I don't feel it.

She goes. LAZARUS *weighs a book in his hands. Stops.*

LAZARUS. She'll get bored. She'll throw him out like all the others. Why do I even mind? But I do, I do.

A knock on the door to the street. ROGER *looks in.*

What happened to you last night? I said come in two hours, now I'm in a hurry, be quick.

ROGER. Where's my brother?

LAZARUS. Nobody told *me* he was your brother.

ROGER. Can I see him?

LAZARUS. Not today. He's resting. He's thrilled with his present arrangements and asks not to be disturbed. And you, was your evening pleasant, how did you spend it?

ROGER. I'm in a hole, old boy.

He has got out a half-bottle of brandy. Drinks.

I slept in a bush. Got up, came here, round the backs of houses. You said you had a proposition.

LAZARUS. I do.

ROGER. Fire away.

LAZARUS. Put down your bottle and I'll tell you. I hear you like women?

ROGER. To sleep with.

LAZARUS. That's all that's needed. Under my guidance, Mrs. Bone has built up a corner in houses of entertainment. Her women are voluptuous and much desired, not by the riff-raff, but by doctors, senators, the pillars of our community. And in classic fashion, her success has opened up a second market. For once the brothels are full of husbands, who is to satisfy the wives? The next and logical step was to open a house where women can pay for men, and this she has done, situated not three blocks away, discreetly fronted by a retailer in durable kitchenware. The women flock to it, which leads by a pleasantly neat contradiction to its only weakness, the difficulty of keeping staff. Men have signed up for six-month contracts and been carried out on stretchers in a week. All posts are vacant. Are you interested?

ROGER (*secretly thrilled*). What's the salary?

LAZARUS. Pound a week.

ROGER. That doesn't sound very much. What about meals?

LAZARUS. Fix your own, what's the matter with you, I thought you couldn't get enough of it?

ROGER. I can't. I can't. I just don't like being taken for granted. When do I start?

LAZARUS. Today.

ROGER. Today's Sunday.

LAZARUS. I know today's Sunday, what are you, some kind of a work-to-rule? Get out of here, I'm fed up with you, you're wasting my time.

ROGER. Stop! You've convinced me.

LAZARUS. Shake!

ROGER. You're a sport.

LAZARUS. No, I'm a puritan. Does that surprise you? I study, I write history, this doesn't interest you, why should it ...?

He pauses.

I've done terrible things. I see it in literal fashion as pushing everything I most detest up an enormous wheel. One with a distinct high point beyond which it falls. Into the flames. And in that apocalyptic turning, the poor and humble will be raised. There will be paradise on earth. Meanwhile: shall we go?

ROGER. You'd better tell Paul I'm on safari.

LAZARUS. Paul?

ROGER. My brother.

LAZARUS. Your brother's name is Paul? Tell me, for interest, is he an adventurous fellow, has he travelled up North?

ROGER. Two years in the Zambesi Valley for the L.M.S.

LAZARUS. The London Missionary Society? Is that a celibate order? Or might he, in the course of his duties, marry a local girl?

ROGER. Exactly what he did, old boy. First-class recipe for disaster and a speedy escape was called for.

LAZARUS (*to himself*). I see!

He goes to the door and calls:

Elias!

To ROGER:

To work! I can't come too, you must accompany yourself.

He writes out the address and gives it to ROGER:

Left out the door, past the excavations you will see a row of shops, a dilapidated crone will let you in, name of Mrs. Blaney. Explain your purpose and wait.

ELIAS *opens the door without knocking.*

ELIAS. What is it now?

LAZARUS. Tell Mrs. Bone's new maid to come down here, and say to the driver I shall want some help with books.

ELIAS *goes.* LAZARUS *addresses* ROGER:

Still here? Be off! I shall be there by one. Good day.

He shows ROGER *out and starts selecting a few books.*

Tendai and Paul! Poor Daisy.

He laughs.

No, it's not funny. She'll go mad.

He laughs again. TENDAI *comes in.*

Come in, come in, have you tidied Mrs. Bone's bedroom yet this morning?

TENDAI. No, big brother.

LAZARUS. Or seen anything unexpected? No? An uneventful
day like any other? I believe you, good, you will spend the
morning out. I have an errand for you. Visit each one of
these addresses.

He gets a bunch of cards out of a cardboard box-file.

Knock on the back door, and ask whichever servant should
attend, to tell their madam we have squeezed her in this
afternoon at the usual place.

He deals out cards.

Mrs. van Rensburg at two, Mrs. van Heerden at two-thirty,
Mrs. van Jaarsveld at three o'clock and Mrs. van Niekerk
thirty minutes later.

He gives her a big stack of cards.

You do the rest, it's half-hour intervals except for Mrs.
Brink, says it's an emergency, give her an hour. Go at once.
When you return, I want you to come directly to this room.
I shall meet you here at noon.

TENDAI *claps, bobs and goes out with the cards.*

We're getting on. Disaster looms! But I won't have it hurt
the girl.

End of scene.

Scene Two

HENRIETTA*'s parlour.* WILLEM *is lying on a table. An
empty coffin. Dr.* JAMESON *is in attendance with his black
bag.* HENRIETTA *is addressing* DAISY, *who has just arrived.
The shutters are closed and the room is dark.*

HENRIETTA. I planned to give up everything for this boy.
Now I know what I am: a simple farmer's widow with a
head for business. I'm not to trouble myself with more than
that. It is impossible for you and I to be friends, but thank
you for calling.

DAISY. I'm sorry.

She embraces HENRIETTA.

HENRIETTA. I must leave now. I'm on my way to my brother's house, and from there to the funeral.

JAMESON. If Mrs. Bone would care to stay for a moment's quiet reflection, I would appreciate the support.

HENRIETTA. As you wish. My butler-boy Justin is stationed in the hall to receive late callers. Tell him if there's anything you need.

JAMESON. I thought you said the house would be empty?

HENRIETTA. Apart from him, it will be.

She goes.

JAMESON. Well, no rush. The undertaker's men aren't due till one.

DAISY. That's not for hours! I don't want to stay and look at this!

She looks at the body.

What happened?

JAMESON. He was shot a moment or two after you left the Criterion Hotel, the attacker being that upper-class dolt for whom you made such claims. I patched up the wound, sent an S.O.S. to his uncle at the President's banquet, and when the boy fell silent, brought him here to his mother and signed the death certificate.

DAISY. Most appropriate by the look of him.

JAMESON. He's alive.

DAISY. Alive?

She looks more closely at WILLEM.

Are you sure?

JAMESON. Oh yes. Body temperature is low and the pulse is imperceptible, but there's no rigor mortis and his pupils respond to light. He's in shock.

DAISY. Tell his mother!

JAMESON. In good time. I sat up half the night. Alone, with him. I peered into the blackness. I saw Africa. I saw the ruined city of Prester John. I saw the palace of the Queen of Sheba, the tower on its side, baboons playing leapfrog in the courtyard. I saw the hidden cave beneath a waterfall where thirteen Portuguese conquistadors sit as they did in life, around a table in their golden armour. I saw savagery, darkness, ghosts. I saw the beast approaching the dying fire. I saw the magical dawn. This young man has been given to us by destiny. His mother owns a goldfield. Not one-tenth of it has been prospected and already she is a millionaire. A company which owned it could build a railway from the Cape to Cairo on the profits. She will not sell.

DAISY. She's selling on Thursday.

JAMESON. So she promised, to a consortium of local burghers. Her reasons were personal: she wished to devote her life to her only son. When the boy was killed, she cancelled the sale. She is a dual personality. The plan is this. The funeral will take place, Thursday will come and go, and she will keep the mine. Shortly afterwards, we will produce the boy alive and kicking. Blissful reunion, an orgy of maternal sentiment, and *at that moment* an offer will be made to buy the goldfield by a company of international repute. I'm a trained psychologist. I can tell you now, we'll get it.

LAZARUS *comes in.*

Where are the books?

LAZARUS. They're in the cart.

JAMESON. Is the servant in the hallway?

LAZARUS. He's polishing the floor.

JAMESON. Damn!

DAISY. Why?

JAMESON. The plan is for the body to be discreetly removed, and the coffin filled up with books to an equivalent weight.

LAZARUS. With books!

JAMESON. We shall remove the so-called victim and revive him in a secluded part of town. Daisy, your house will fit the bill to a T. A foolproof scheme, with but one flaw: with the servant in the hall, we can neither get the books into the house nor the body out.

LAZARUS. My books are my life.

DAISY. Don't whine.

LAZARUS. I have rescued books from libraries burned down by lynch mobs. I have stolen them from shops no Jew could enter. Giordano Bruno, *Italian Dialogues*, three volumes found separately in Vilna, Soho and New York.

JAMESON. Have we a problem?

LAZARUS. No! I've no objection! Bury my books! Bury me if you want! Daisy, you will remember this day.

He walks away from them to a far part of the room.
JAMESON looks out through the doorway. DAISY looks at the body.

JAMESON. Still polishing. If he's anything like my wallah he'll be a good half-hour.

DAISY *files her nails.*

Which reminds me: when I got home last night, I found a letter from the Cape Town office of the London Missionary Society.

DAISY. He's trying to find our famous Paul.

LAZARUS. Ah hah.

JAMESON. Tendai's husband was one Paul du Boys.

DAISY. Peculiar name.

LAZARUS. Is there a photo?

JAMESON. Sadly not. But they've provided a description.

He consults his notebook.

Age twenty-five, hair brown, height five eleven inches. inches.

DAISY. Hardly narrows the field.

JAMESON. And there's an entry, under distinguishing features.

DAISY (*idly*) 'Wooden leg'.

LAZARUS. 'Finger missing'.

DAISY. 'Birthmark shaped like a pineapple'.

JAMESON. Exactly.

DAISY (*shocked*) What?

JAMESON. How did you know about the pineapple?

DAISY. I didn't. It's what sprung into my head.

JAMESON. A remarkable bullseye.

DAISY. Wasn't it just, I'll try again. Where is it on his body? I would say it's on his *left leg*.

JAMESON. It's on his shoulder.

DAISY. Is it really, age twenty-five, five foot eleven, well we'll keep a lookout. Lazarus, where was Tendai when you left the house?

LAZARUS. She's out on an errand.

DAISY. When is she back?

LAZARUS. At noon.

DAISY. Jesus it's twenty-to!

To JAMESON.

You must excuse me. I have to get home at once.

JAMESON. You'll stay till the job's complete.

DAISY. I'm ill. It's the dark. I can't see.

She falls to the ground and screams:

Oh God!

LAZARUS. Give her a sedative.

JAMESON. With pleasure.

He slaps DAISY *hard across the face. She calms down at once. The door opens and* JUSTIN *looks in carrying his polishing-rag.*

JUSTIN. Is the madam sick?

JAMESON. A glass of water.

JUSTIN *goes.*

There's another solution, if we're pressed for time.

DAISY. We are.

JAMESON. There's a body too few in the coffin and one too many in the hall. Ergo:

DAISY. Kill the butler-boy? I can't stand mess.

JAMESON. I've brought my bag. It will be clean as a whistle. (*Of* LAZARUS.) Is he all right?

DAISY. He'll do as I say. I'm game.

JUSTIN *knocks at the door and comes in with a tray and a glass of water, which he gives to* DAISY.

DAISY. Thank you.

JAMESON. Are you well, old fellow? I'm a doctor, you know, if there's anything not shipshape I could set it right.

JUSTIN. No.

JAMESON. No what?

JUSTIN. I am not sick, baas, but my wife is.

JAMESON. Oh I'm sorry to hear that, I must make a point of visiting her on my rounds tomorrow.

He winks at the others.

One more question and then I won't detain you. Have you had an injection?

JUSTIN. No baas.

JAMESON. Why, that will never do! Everyone should have an injection every three years, it makes you simba simba, very strong. Would you like one now?

JUSTIN. Ah no baas.

JAMESON. Not scared of a little needle are you?

JUSTIN. No baas. No money baas.

JAMESON. Don't worry about that, this is bakshee, bonsella, cheapo cheapo, just roll your sleeve up, ladies needn't watch, and I'll prepare the medicine.

LAZARUS (*hesitant*). Stop.

JAMESON. Lazarus, I think you should stand by the door. There!

He has the needle ready.

Isn't that splendid? One day everyone in Africa will have a needle and then no-one will ever get sick. Daisy dear, you won't like this.

DAISY. You're wasting time.

JUSTIN. Will it hurt, baas?

JAMESON. Light pricking sensation possibly, if it's worse than that, you'll know it's doing you good.

LAZARUS *is shaking with horror. He speaks quietly.*

LAZARUS. Bury my books. Please, bury my books.

JAMESON *puts in the needle.* JUSTIN *winces at the prick and smiles at the others in embarrassment. He gets up, rubbing his arm, smiles, takes the glass from* DAISY *and walks to the door. The pain becomes worse and he stops. As it becomes agonising, he falls to the floor.*

LAZARUS. Daisy, help him.

DAISY. Watch the door.

LAZARUS *checks the door.* JUSTIN *dies.* JAMESON *examines the coffin.*

JAMESON. Somewhere there should be a dozen screws. What's this?

He counts them.

DAISY (*quietly to* LAZARUS). You knew about Paul already.

LAZARUS. Yes.

DAISY. Whose side are you on? I'll sort out Tendai the minute we're back. She's a toffee-nosed little miss, I'm sick of her. I'll pack her off to one of the houses with strict instructions for her to be fucked to pulp.

LAZARUS. You frighten me.

DAISY. I'm in love.

JAMESON. . . . . eleven, twelve, all present and correct, but no screwdriver.

Pause.

Just have to bugger up a new scalpel then.

End of scene.

Scene Three

LAZARUS'*s basement. Later that week. It's day outside, but the shutters are closed.*

LAZARUS *is working at his table, looking unaccustomedly sunny.* WILLEM *is propped up in a chair, still unconscious.* TENDAI *is completing the process of bandaging him from toe to top in strips of torn sheeting, and sticking twigs and leaves into the folds of the material. Before the scene is far advanced, she will have swathed his head, so that he's completely mummified but able to move.*

LAZARUS *stops writing, then closes his reference books one by one.*

LAZARUS. I've finished my book. What time is it?

TENDAI. The sun is there . . .

She indicates.

. . . it is half-way through the morning.

LAZARUS. What day of the week?

TENDAI. Friday.

LAZARUS (*of his book*). I've surprised myself. I thought the wicked got punished like apples fall off trees. But they don't. They're inventive, they think ahead. We are forced to intervene, mm? I've found your husband.

TENDAI *stares at him.*

I've found Paul. He's alive and well. I know where he is.

TENDAI. I will be seeing him when?

LAZARUS. Quite soon. No-one must know, especially not Mrs. Bone or the doctor. I've seen them kill a man. How is your patient, is he still sick?

TENDAI. He is not sick, he is being away from his body for a while. Many people in my village are doing this thing.

LAZARUS. Lucky for you the doctor gave up. Keep trying. Play for time.

A knock at the door and ROGER *looks in. He's unrecognisably muffled up in a coat and scarf and has a hat pulled over his face.*

ROGER. Let me in!

LAZARUS. Who's this?

ROGER. It's me.

He unwraps himself. He looks very ill.

LAZARUS. You look dreadful!

ROGER *sees* TENDAI.

ROGER. My God!

TENDAI. Brother!

They embrace.

ROGER. Oh child, don't cry.

LAZARUS. Of course she must cry, what do you think she is, a machine?

TENDAI (*to* ROGER). My brother Lazarus has found my husband. Have you seen him?

ROGER (*to* LAZARUS, *cautious*). Have I seen him?

LAZARUS. Yes but you don't know where he went on Saturday night.

ROGER (*taps his nose*). Say no more!

LAZARUS (*to* TENDAI). You said you were running short of leaves.

TENDAI. Leaves, roots and also bark from a special tree that grow only in my country.

LAZARUS. Half way through the morning, eh? Good, fine, you can go and look for them. Say goodbye to your brother-in-law, he'll still be here when you return.

TENDAI *claps and bobs, collects a spade and goes.*

Your brother is here. Every night and every afternoon, Daisy and he are cavorting like bunny rabbits. Tendai doesn't know. He doesn't know about her. Half my time is spent with Daisy comparing timetables. This morning Daisy and he have gone shopping, so the girl's allowed into the park to dig up roots. Mostly she's locked up here like Mrs. Rochester. Daisy's trying to put her in a brothel. Luckily the girl has found a new vocation, she can revive this zombie, so she claims. Personally I doubt it but I've made a resolution, it is to protect the innocent and punish the guilty. Who do I think I am? I'm under strain. I want your brother out, I want shot of the lot of you. What can I tell the girl, his wife, will she take him back? What's her personality, has she got one? Are you listening?

ROGER (*sleepy voice*). Next please.

LAZARUS. What?

ROGER *wakes and points to an empty spot on the table-top.*

ROGER. There's a mouse on the table!

LAZARUS. You're delirious!

He shakes ROGER and slaps him.

Wake up!

ROGER *does.*

ROGER. And another thing, I find it helps, is sorting out those little details that distinguish them. Mrs. van Wyk has a wart on her chin, Mrs. van Alphen a squint . . .

LAZARUS. Lie down!

ROGER. It's my morning off!

LAZARUS. Just for a moment. Gently, gently.

LAZARUS *helps him on to the bed. Meanwhile:*

If the work is making you ill, you'd better stop. It could be dangerous.

ROGER. I'm not a quitter.

LAZARUS. There is a theory, offered first by Galen, that at the climax of physical union, the male partner dies.

ROGER. That's bees.

LAZARUS. Just for an instant! But too many instants in too short a time might, as it were, mount up with permanently fatal results.

ROGER. We thought that at school, only it was sneezing in those days.

LAZARUS. Nobody sneezes twice an hour, eight hours a day, four days on the trot, I see the returns don't forget. The theory was revived by St. Augustine, who said not only that death took place but that it was the chief attraction. 'The pearl in the oyster' was the phrase he coined. Are you listening?

ROGER *is asleep.*

Asleep. He won't give up. 'Once more unto the breach, dear friends . . . !'

The door opens and DAISY *comes in, dressed for town.*

DAISY. Blimey, those shutters.

She sees ROGER.

Jesus! Get him out!

LAZARUS. He works for you.

DAISY. I know that. Cover him up. Dr. Jim's on his way down. If he sees him, he'll have an apoplectic fit, the man's wanted for murder.

LAZARUS. He's sick. He's dying. He's been abominably exploited.

He covers ROGER *with a sheet.*

'Terminal venery' was the mediaeval phrase. As for the zombie, no change. Tendai has gone to find a special bark, she says it can't fail.

DAISY. Bollocks. I don't know what the doctor's thinking of. She's taking advantage, she's trying to avoid the knocking-shop. Paul and I are meeting at Quinn's Tearooms. Then we're seeing a Mr. Tennyson at Cook's. We're planning a lengthy cruise to start next week, either the West Indies or the Med, I'll let you know. It was a struggle getting him out of the house this morning, but Dr. Jim was late by a stroke of luck so they missed by inches. Look out!

Dr. JAMESON *comes in.*

JAMESON. How's the patient?

DAISY (*pointedly*). No change.

JAMESON. Let me see.

He examines WILLEM, *taps him a bit, lifts one of his hands and lets it drop. He's disappointed by the lack of progress.*

Tch tch tch and I was counting on a full recovery by this evening. I'm holding a reception at the Grand Hotel. His mother will be there and the plan would be to produce the boy in front of witnesses. But would he create the right impression in his present state? A ticklish problem. Daisy, will you attend?

DAISY. Of course.

LAZARUS. Am I invited?

JAMESON. Daisy may bring whoever she's a mind to.

TENDAI *comes in with leaves, twigs and bark. The spade is thick with newly-dug-up earth.*

TENDAI. I have found the medicine!

DAISY. Oh for God's sake!

JAMESON. May I examine it?

TENDAI *gives him a piece, then goes to* WILLEM *and starts chewing bits of the bark and sticking it into his bandages.*

Gotu Kola bark. A natural stimulant for subjects in trance. Quite fascinating. Where did you find it?

TENDAI. I am looking in a very big field quite near.

LAZARUS. She means the park.

DAISY. She's been *digging up the park*.

TENDAI. In that field there is a house, and there I find this tree that grow only in my country.

JAMESON. What kind of house?

TENDAI. It is big and made all of window and it is being hot inside.

DAISY. Oh my God, it's the tropical plants house.

JAMESON. Most resourceful.

DAISY. She'll get us all arrested.

JAMESON. To business please? Tonight, my dear, I'm relying on you to lay on the charm like butter. I have a guest of honour.

DAISY. Who?

JAMESON. Count Antonio de Rosario. Tendai, you'll know the name.

TENDAI. I am listening.

JAMESON. A Portuguese landowner, the last in line of those who overran the Monomatapa Kingdom in the days of Elizabeth. I received a note from him last night, the very penstrokes quaking with fear. Progress is advancing upon his feudal domain, his natives are snapping at the bait, he's after a deal. He gets a Pioneer Column to protect him from his loyal subjects and we get the digging rights, it's all quite neat.

TENDAI *falls to the ground.*

LAZARUS. She's fainted.

DAISY. She'd been munching that bark, it's obviously a dud.

JAMESON *looks at* TENDAI *and* WILLEM:

JAMESON. At times like these I do miss my practice. Daisy, you look delightful.

DAISY. I have an appointment.

DAISY *and* JAMESON *go.* LAZARUS *bends over* TENDAI.

LAZARUS. Wake up.

TENDAI. Are they gone?

LAZARUS. Yes.

TENDAI. This man Antonio, it is he who is wanting his custom.

LAZARUS. What kind of custom?

TENDAI. A woman who marry, first she must play a game with him. You must bring my husband. I must leave this man with the special bark, we must, 'pfft, go.

LAZARUS. It won't be easy. Mrs. Bone's a determined woman. Can you walk?

TENDAI (*tries it*). Yes.

LAZARUS. Thank God for that! There's a job to do and I can't postpone it any longer. Go to the chemist on the corner of Rissik St. Ask to see the assistant manager, a Mr. Potash. Give him this money.

He gives her a big bundle of notes.

He will hand you a parcel. Bring it to me. On no account eat the contents, they contain a rare South American poison. I meanwhile must find Quinn's tearoom. Paul is waiting for a friend. I shall find him and bring him back before she gets there.

TENDAI. She?

LAZARUS. I'm thinking aloud. Pay no attention. Go!

They leave together quickly. LAZARUS *turns the lamp down before going. The room grows darker. A dog howls in the distance.*

ROGER *tosses and turns in his sleep. Pulls the sheet off his face and sits up. He lights a match. Looks round. The match burns his fingers and he drops it.*

ROGER. Where am I?

WILLEM *sits up in his bandages and sees him.*

WILLEM. Who's that?

ROGER. Who's that?

WILLEM. Light the lamp!

ROGER. I'm trying, dammit!

He scrambles to light the lamp. He and WILLEM *stare at each other.*

Are you dead too?

WILLEM. I was.

ROGER. I've had the smell of it. I've been at the door of hell.

WILLEM. I've been through and back.

ROGER. What was your impression?

WILLEM. Worse than here.

ROGER. Don't move.

He touches WILLEM.

You're real.

WILLEM. Oh yes.

ROGER. Do you know me?

WILLEM *nods.*

ROGER. Then I need your help. I'm nine-tenths damned and there's a woman who can save me.

WILLEM. A woman?

ROGER. She had a son. A worthless oaf but she loved him.

WILLEM *contorts in misery,*

Don't turn away. Will you help me find her?

WILLEM. Does she like you?

ROGER. I slept with her once. And then, not slept, I held her in my arms. She's heavy, large-breasted . . .

WILLEM (*a cry of despair*). Ah!

ROGER. Have I put my foot in it?

WILLEM. I know where she works. I'll take you there.

ROGER. Good fellow. But you can't go out looking like that. Put on this coat. And this.

He gives him LAZARUS*'s black overcoat and floppy black hat: they make him look like an anarchist of the period.* ROGER *muffles himself up.*

Help me up, I'm still quite shaky. Ha! You're not that steady either! Easy does it. Careful. That's my boy.

They leave by the street door. LAZARUS brings in PAUL by the other door.

LAZARUS. Come in and wait.

PAUL. Where's Daisy?

LAZARUS (*looks around*). Where's your brother?

PAUL. Is my brother here?

LAZARUS. Where's the zombie?

PAUL. Is my brother a zombie?

LAZARUS. Your brother is fine. Sit down. Or stand. Don't go!

He leaves by the door into the rest of the house. After a moment, TENDAI comes in from the street, breathless, carrying a parcel wrapped in brown paper. They see each other.

PAUL. Is it you? Are you really alive?

She kneels and claps to him. He embraces her.

Oh Tendai.

TENDAI. I knew you would come.

PAUL. I've missed you.

TENDAI. Antonio is in this town, the Doctor Jim is making me to see him this night, we must quickly run, 'pff'.

PAUL. There's someone listening.

LAZARUS opens the door and pops his head in.

LAZARUS. It's only me.

He disappears back.

TENDAI. That man is helping us. The woman of this house is jealous of me, she is hating me.

PAUL. Daisy?

TENDAI. Do you know her?

PAUL. Well, I . . .

TENDAI. She is loving somebody. Is it you?

PAUL. She's just a friend. She's taught me a lot. She's had a fascinating life. She's lonely now and a little bit sad. She hates getting old. Don't let's talk about her.

TENDAI looks closely at him.

TENDAI. You must write a letter now to say good-bye.

PAUL. Oh yes.

TENDAI. But not so she is thinking you are loving her back.

PAUL. I'll keep it simple. I'll say we had to leave in a hurry.

He takes a pen and paper and writes a few words. TENDAI looks over his shoulder.

TENDAI. Yes that is good.

LAZARUS comes in.

PAUL. Did you know she was here?

LAZARUS. Yes.

PAUL. Bastard.

LAZARUS. I accept that. You must leave by the midnight train. I can let you have one hundred pounds, here, take the lot.

PAUL takes the money and starts to count it.

Tendai, where's my parcel?

She gives it to him.

Good girl. (*To* PAUL.) Why are you counting it?

PAUL. I'll pay you back from England.

LAZARUS. You don't have to.

PAUL. I'd rather, frankly.

TENDAI. You must give this letter to Mrs. Bone.

She hands LAZARUS the letter.

LAZARUS. All right.

TENDAI. We are going, big brother. Stay in happiness.

LAZARUS. Goodbye, my dear. (*To* PAUL). Good day.

They go. LAZARUS *reads the note.*

Oh poor, poor Daisy.

He unwraps the parcel. Inside is a big presentation chocolate box with ribbons and artificial flowers. He places it carefully in a prominent place. DAISY *comes in, agitated. She's been running.*

DAISY. You're here!

She looks round.

Christ, where's the zombie?

LAZARUS. I don't know.

DAISY. Paul wasn't at the tearoom. He'd been and gone, they said, a man arrived and headed him off. Was that you? Is there something happening that everybody knows about and I don't?

LAZARUS. You always say that.

DAISY. I swear to God, if you've been acting out of order you'll die screaming. I've got friends you don't know about.

LAZARUS. Read this.

He gives her PAUL's *note.* DAISY *holds it in her hand but doesn't look at it.*

DAISY. Oh Christ, let it be all right. What does it say, is it terrible?

LAZARUS. Read it.

DAISY. I can't wait to see him again.

LAZARUS (*of the letter*). Go on!

DAISY. All right.

She reads the letter. Smiles with relief.

It's fine. It's utterly fine. He says that he can't wait to see me either. Suspicious old cow that I am.

She moves to the door, then stops, suspicious.

I *think* that's what it says.

LAZARUS. It says 'I can't wait to see you'. And he didn't, he went. His wife went too, they're not coming back. I think this is something you must face.

Pause.

DAISY. Still, it comes as no surprise.

LAZARUS. Who are these friends of yours I don't know about?

DAISY. Oh, they exist. Mind if I sit down?

LAZARUS. Why should I mind if you ...?

DAISY. I mean, it's your room, I'm not going to be careering in and out, you do what you like. Nothing to drink is there?

LAZARUS. I'm sorry.

DAISY. Do you know: he was forever leaving notes. Stuck to the looking-glass, under the breakfast tray. Things like, 'I wrote this at four in the morning after I'd been looking at you for half an hour.' Or, 'I really do love you.' 'Cause he had a ready wit.

She stops, crumples a bit.

Oh I can't bear it.

LAZARUS. Daisy, as there is nothing to drink, can I offer you a chocolate.

DAISY. What blinking chocolate?

LAZARUS. They're in here. It's a special box.

DAISY *stares at the elaborate wrappings.*

DAISY. Who's it for?

LAZARUS. You. It's a token of my appreciation. I don't know why they dress it up like this.

DAISY. It's weird.

LAZARUS. Well, never mind that.

He has opened the box. He looks at the chocolates.

LAZARUS. Ah, delicious! Have one.

DAISY. Mm?

LAZARUS. Eat.

DAISY (*calm*). What's in them?

LAZARUS. Praline, caramel, nougat . . .

DAISY. Don't patronise me.

LAZARUS. I don't know what you're talking about,

DAISY. Look at me.

He does.

You've always wanted to kill me, haven't you? It's the only thing you could never hide.

LAZARUS. If you don't trust me, I'll eat one myself.

DAISY. I know you will.

LAZARUS. It doesn't mean much. Still:

He picks a chocolate and eats it.

Now you.

DAISY. Don't rush me.

LAZARUS. Those have got nuts in them.

DAISY. This one.

She eats it.

LAZARUS. Have you thought about the butler-boy?

DAISY. What you say that for?

LAZARUS. That was my plan, you'd eat one, then I'd say, 'Have you thought about . . .'

DAISY. I see. No. Is yours a bit funny?

LAZARUS. Unfamiliar.

DAISY. So's mine. Hold my hand. Reckon they'll get far, those two?

LAZARUS. I don't see why not.

DAISY. If they try to catch a train, they'll be arrested.

LAZARUS. Why?

DAISY. Mixed marriage.

LAZARUS. What makes you think that they'd be spotted?

DAISY. There's only one train a day. I suggested to the Chief of Police that he keep an eye on it.

LAZARUS. You never told me.

DAISY. I should think not.

LAZARUS. I'd run after them but I can't move my feet. Why didn't you say, earlier?

DAISY. I wish I had. Also l think, sod them. I do love you, you know. I was only playing silly buggers.

LAZARUS. Ssh.

DAISY. How many of these are you supposed to have?

LAZARUS. He didn't specify.

DAISY. Go on, then.

They each take one. She fumbles with her chocolate.

I'm not cheating, the wrapper's stuck. You're meant to say something.

LAZARUS. You always knew.

DAISY. You never bloody said it though.

LAZARUS. Yes, I love you. I can't describe how much. My mind, my whole body.

DAISY. I know. Something's happening. Hold tighter.

LAZARUS. I can't.

End of scene.

Scene Four

HENRIETTA's *office. A small space isolated in darkness.*
ROGER, *enveloped in hat and coat, and* WILLEM, *covered in*
LAZARUS's *hat and coat, are waiting.* HENRIETTA *comes in*
and sits behind the desk.

HENRIETTA. Gentlemen, I've kept you waiting. If you won't
make appointments, that's what you must expect. You may
sit. You may even remove your hats.

They both do. ROGER *is revealed and she recognises him.*
WILLEM *can't be recognised, being still wrapped in*
bandages, twigs and leaves.

(*To* ROGER.) You'll need more than a hat if you want to
avoid the police. I thought you were leaving the country.

She buries her head in her hands, then composes herself.

What do you want, more money?

ROGER. Let me speak to you alone. Not in an office.

HENRIETTA. I'm busy. And I've nothing to say that can't be
said in public.

ROGER. I wanted to say I was sorry.

HENRIETTA. I loved my son. Let me tell you something,
mister, you could get down on your knees on that carpet and
beg forgiveness and it still wouldn't help.

WILLEM *applauds, his padded hands making little sound.*

What's wrong with your friend?

ROGER (*as one making allowances*). He's receiving medical
treatment.

HENRIETTA. I'm glad to hear it.

ROGER. When I saw you first, you were simply a woman
who'd walked into a room. I didn't think, yes, I want her, or
I do but she doesn't, or who's that with her . . .

HENRIETTA (*soft*). Do you think I want to listen to this?

ROGER. It's hard on me too. You looked at me strangely. You put your hand up against my face. I can feel it now. I looked at your eyes, your shoulders. I wondered who you were. I wanted to see you again.

HENRIETTA. You did.

ROGER. You saved my life. If I could pay you back, I would. But all I can offer you is worry and regret. All I can say is, here's one more catastrophe for you to cope with. I want to marry you. Various warnings are in order. I've no money. My family was for several centuries very rich, then came my father and his discovery of the Stock Exchange. Where we'd live I can't imagine. I can't stay here for reasons you know. Women you know about as well. I'm not very bright. At school I was a decent half-back, at Oxford I was a drunk. On the positive side . . . I'm single. I'm er . . .

Thinks.

. . . I'm a good shot.

HENRIETTA *stares at him.*

Sorry. I'm decent company in a bar or at a racetrack and I'm sometimes quite persuasive. I don't know about now.

HENRIETTA. It must be hard, being poor at your time of life. I'm rich. Does that surprise you?

ROGER. I didn't know.

HENRIETTA. Perhaps you don't read the newspapers. I own a goldfield and associated industries. If we married, they will belong to you, such is our law. In return, I want no back-answers, and a good impression on my business colleagues. The police are no worry, I can pull strings. Oh, I accept. Is that quite clear? This evening I am attending a reception for a visiting Portuguese at the Grand Hotel. Meet me in the private room at eight precisely. I shall make an announcement in the course of the dinner.

WILLEM *is banging his head on the desk in despair.*

Your friend appears to be distressed. Get him to a doctor.
Good afternoon.

ROGER *intercepts her on her way to the door. He puts his
arms round her and kisses her. After a moment:*

No, I'm upset. Tonight.

She goes.

ROGER. The Grand Hotel eh? Things are looking up.

WILLEM *is staring at him.*

Pity you can't join us.

WILLEM. Don't worry. I'm coming with. I want to see the
fun.

End of scene.

Scene Five

*The private room of the Grand Hotel. A blaze of artificial light.
A large pair of double doors leads to the ballroom, from where
we hear the sound of a small band playing a polka, laughter
and conversation. There's another smaller door at the side.*

*In the room is a long table with a banquet laid out on it.
DAISY and LAZARUS are at opposite ends, drinking
champagne. DAISY is dressed in white and is stretched out
languorously. LAZARUS wears a beautifully-tailored pale suit.*

JAMESON *shows in BRINK. He looks around the room.*

JAMESON. There's no-one in here. We can talk without being
disturbed.

He sees DAISY's champagne-bottle.

Champagne?

BRINK. No thank you.

JAMESON *pours himself a drink.*

JAMESON. Acting on an anonymous tip, the police have arrested the missionary du Boys, along with his native wife, attempting to catch the midnight train to Cape Town.

BRINK. I can't help them.

JAMESON. Why should you? Nevertheless. In a few moments' time we shall receive our guest, the overlord of the ancient kingdom of Monomatapa. I wish to acquire his territory for the Crown and I have this problem, that the fellow's a blue-blooded Portugee. Du Boys ran a mission there for twelve months. I need his help for the duration of the evening.

BRINK. Take him.

JAMESON. May I?

BRINK. We are not bigots! We only object when you meddle in our affairs. The Zambesi Valley is a thousand miles away. You may swallow it tomorrow for all I care, and the more it occupies your time, the happier we shall be. No-one will touch those two, till you give the word.

JAMESON goes to the small door at the side. Meanwhile:

DAISY. If I opened another bottle, do you think they'd see it flying up and popping its own cork?

LAZARUS. What about your glass?

DAISY, who is holding her glass raised, glances at BRINK.

DAISY. It doesn't seem to bother them.

LAZARUS. We don't bother them at all.

JAMESON shows in TENDAI and PAUL, who are in leg-irons.

JAMESON. I can offer you two a pardon for your marriage. All you must do, du Boys, is persuade our guest of the benefits of a British presence. Is that quite clear?

The side door flies open and ROGER bursts in, muffled-up and unrecognisable. WILLEM follows him in, still in his bandages and in hat and coat. ROGER *sees* PAUL *and* TENDAI.

ROGER. Oh Crikey!

LAZARUS. There's the zombie!

JAMESON (*to* ROGER *and* WILLEM). Gentlemen, this is a private function.

ROGER. I've a meeting here at eight.

JAMESON. At eight? It's eight already. Where is our guest?

HENRIETTA *comes in from the ballroom, dressed splendidly and heavily bejewelled.*

HENRIETTA (*to* ROGER). Excellent, you've arrived.

WILLEM *starts trying to yank* ROGER *away into the ballroom.*

JAMESON. Mevrouw, excuse me for one moment.

He goes out into the ballroom.

HENRIETTA. Frans, I have something to tell you.

Loud boos are heard from the ballroom. WILLEM *goes on trying to pull* ROGER *away.*

BRINK. What's that noise?

HENRIETTA. Dr. Jameson has been in this town too long. There'll be a riot before the night is out. (*To* ROGER.) Don't go!

BRINK. What do you wish to say to me?

HENRIETTA. Tonight I shall announce my second marriage. I wish to introduce you to the groom.

BRINK. Hennie!

ROGER. Delighted to make your acquaintance.

BRINK *stares startled at the entirely muffled-up* ROGER.

HENRIETTA. At present he is observing the normal security precautions. Take that look off your face, I've been looking at it forty-four years, I've had enough!

WILLEM, *distressed, takes off his hat and coat, revealing his bandaged face and body.*

WILLEM. Where's the drinks?

HENRIETTA. Through there. Think twice before you ask a girl to dance. There's an ugly mood about.

JAMESON *comes back in. To* WILLEM:

JAMESON. There you are! I'd been wondering where you'd got to. Stay for the dinner. I'll explain.

WILLEM *has opened the big doors and started going out. His bizarre appearance is greeted with loud cheers and hoots, from which he shrinks like Boris Karloff in Frankenstein when the house is on fire.*

HENRIETTA. What does that fellow expect in such a get-up. (*To* WILLEM.) Go!

WILLEM *goes out.*

JAMESON (*to all*). Count Antonio has arrived.

BRINK. At last!

A general move to the door. But:

JAMESON. Wait! There is an unforeseen development. The commissionaire didn't want to let him in, I was forced to pull rank.

HENRIETTA. Why?

JAMESON (*darkly*). Follow me.

HENRIETTA, BRINK *and* JAMESON *go out.* ROGER *takes off his disguise.*

PAUL. Roger!

TENDAI. Brother!

They embrace in silence.

DAISY. Should we really be watching?

LAZARUS. Does it upset you?

DAISY. Not a scrap, it's wonderful.

TENDAI. We are being arrested.

PAUL. But they'll let us off if I do what the doctor says.

TENDAI. Whatever that man is saying, it must be something wicked. If you are helping him I will be leaving you for always, 'pfoo!'

PAUL. Then we'll go to prison!

TENDAI. I am not minding. After prison I will be loving you even more.

ROGER. Listen! It's all gone quiet!

Quiet from the ballroom. ROGER muffles himself up again. WILLEM comes in:

WILLEM. The Count is black!

BRINK, JAMESON and HENRIETTA come in flanking ANTONIO, in his best regalia. As JAMESON passes PAUL:

PAUL. The answer's no.

JAMESON. Then I can't help you.

To all:

Pray be seated.

They sit round the table. DAISY and LAZARUS have to give up their seats. Everyone checks sideways at ANTONIO, not used to sitting at a table with a black man. JAMESON rises:

It falls to me, your highness . . .

He looks in annoyance at the card on which he's made his notes, realising that he'll have to change his speech as he goes along.

. . . to welcome you to this gathering of our most prominent citizens. I must offer you an apology, since two of our intended guests . . .

DAISY (*to* LAZARUS). This is us!

JAMESON. Mrs. Dorothea Bone . . .

LAZARUS. Dorothea!

JAMESON. . . . and the historian Mr. Lazarus Bryze . . .
Brikzy . . . Brikotizwy? passed away unexpectedly this
afternoon following a food poisoning incident.

DAISY. I think that was very nicely put.

JAMESON. To happier subjects! (*To* ANTONIO.) Do you
drink, sir?

ANTONIO (*pointing to the champagne*). Beer.

JAMESON. Ah . . .

BRINK (*who is much better at all this*). Yes it's beer, give him
some beer.

JAMESON *pours* ANTONIO *some champagne.* ANTONIO
*is intrigued by the smallness of the measure, but drinks it
and smiles. Everyone applauds, except for* TENDAI *and*
PAUL. ANTONIO *points to a vase of flowers.*

ANTONIO. Water.

JAMESON. Certainly.

He passes ANTONIO *the vase.* ANTONIO *removes the
flowers, throws them away and washes his hands in the
vase. He passes on to the person on his left, who does the
same. The vase continues to circulate, with people washing
their hands in with varying degrees of aplomb or
embarrassment.* JAMESON *continues:*

To business! I have here a document. All that is required is
for you to sign it . . . or place some other mark of identity . .
. and we shall have concluded a treaty between two great
nations, Victoria's Britain and the Kingdom of Monomatapa.

ANTONIO *gives* JAMESON *a bit of food with his fingers.*
JAMESON *eats it.*

Most kind. Our military exchange will for the time being
consist of a British Pioneer Column posted around your er
villa . . .

He winks at the others.

. . . and our community of wealth will be symbolised by the granting to the British South Africa Company of what are loosely called mineral rights, this is all quite standard. In addition: it is my privilege to offer you . . .

He reaches under the table.

. . . a presentation set of that masterpiece by England's greatest poet, Elizabeth Barrett Browning, *Sonnets from the Portuguese* . . .

Applause, ooh's and aah's around the table, like a TV game show.

. . . a pension of . . .

He consults his notes.

LAZARUS. He's knocking it down!

DAISY. Isn't he just!

JAMESON. . . . four . . . (*Thinks.*) pounds . . . (*Thinks.*) a month.

Applause and cheers.

(*Making this bit up.*) And in addition, the exclusive use of her Majesty's Royal Yacht. When available.

Applause and cheers, but:

ANTONIO. One more thing and I sign.

JAMESON. What might that be?

ANTONIO *points at* PAUL *and* TENDAI.

ANTONIO. That husband and that wife, have they yet sleep together?

JAMESON. One assumes so.

BRINK. Ask them!

PAUL. No!

ALL. Ah!

ANTONIO. Then I must have my custom. The woman marry, first I take her.

JAMESON. I'm certain that that could be arranged. Will you place your mark?

He offers ANTONIO *a fountain pen.* ANTONIO *examines it. Meanwhile:*

DAISY. Paul?

LAZARUS. Try again.

DAISY (*soft, intimate voice*). Paul?

PAUL *looks at her in surprise.*

PAUL. Where are you?

DAISY. I'm dead. I'm in hell.

PAUL (*who has always wanted to know*). What's it like?

DAISY. Just like the nuns at school described it. Howling, burning alive.

LAZARUS. If you've ever seen a book thrown on a fire, and the leaves turn up and blacken. Imagine your skin like that.

DAISY. Only growing from underneath.

PAUL. Why aren't you crying?

DAISY. Darling, we're screaming our heads off this very minute, only they fix it so's you can't see. Pauly, don't let her go. Remember you and me. It's the most terrible thing, my darling, to be in love with somebody and lose them even for a moment. Can't you feel it? Can't you feel the pain? Pauly, it hurts, it hurts!

PAUL *stands and addresses everyone.*

PAUL. I have something to say. This woman is mine. If that man touches her, I'll kill him. She's my wife!

A storm of appreciative applause from everyone except ANTONIO.

JAMESON (*to* ANTONIO). The feeling's unanimous, sir. Here at least this lad has shown a decent instinct. Your custom has no place in the civilised world. Abandon it!

ANTONIO (*with resignation*). I have wives at home.

He places his cross on the treaty. More applause.
HENRIETTA *rises.*

HENRIETTA. I have an announcement to make.

All listen.

For eighteen years I have run a goldmine. Men have been
hired and dismissed, by me. I have done all this, not as a
woman, but as a creature disguising her womanhood to fit
men's ideas of power. Tonight I refuse all this. I will be
strong and rich and I will love. I have promised an English
gentleman my hand. Here he is.

ROGER *unmuffles himself and acknowledges everyone's
attention.*

Let me tell you what he has done to deserve this. This
afternoon he burst into my office and made certain
suggestions. He broke into my bedroom at night. He
murdered my son.

Shocked pause.

ROGER. It is, nonetheless, with the greatest pleasure that I . . .

HENRIETTA. Silence!

ROGER. Oh.

HENRIETTA. I loved my son. And I swear on my husband's
grave to give this gentleman what my son received from
him . . .

She produces, from her reticule, ROGER's *revolver, and
aims it at his head.*

. . . and with the same weapon! No one move! I've been
called weak like a woman! Let anyone who doubts my
strength, my love, my duty, cover your eyes with your
napkins as I blow his brains out!

WILLEM. Mother!

HENRIETTA *looks around wildly.*

HENRIETTA. Willem! Where are you?

WILLEM. Here ma!

He unwraps his bandages and reveals his face.

ALL. Ah!

WILLEM. I doubted you! Forgive me!

HENRIETTA. Son!

They embrace. Applause from everybody. HENRIETTA *detaches herself.*

And yes! I shall marry this man tomorrow!

ROGER (*at once*). I accept!

Applause and cheers. ANTONIO *rises.*

ANTONIO. Now that so many have found what they wanted, why are these two so sad?

He indicates TENDAI *and* PAUL.

JAMESON. The details are embarrassing.

ANTONIO. She is my subject! I demand to know!

BRINK *rises.*

BRINK. On behalf of our President, our nation and our heritage, these two young people have committed no unusual crime, and none we care to punish, provided always that they leave our Republic on the midnight train, and that you, Dr. Jameson, and your soldiers, embark without delay for Monomata-whatever-the hell-it's-called.

ALL. Monomatapa! Hooray!

Everyone cheers, except for TENDAI *and* PAUL, *who embrace.*

DAISY (*to* PAUL). The train will be waiting. I should bunker off before they change their minds. And get a sleeper!

TENDAI *rises.*

TENDAI. Good people, one moment.

They fill their glasses and listen.

To ANTONIO:

Honoured Chief, you are a black man possessed by the spirit of a white. Cast it out, and you can mend the damage you have done.

To HENRIETTA:

Honoured mother, your husband is good for one thing only. If he does not do it enough, you must throw him out and keep your bride-price.

To WILLEM:

Little brother . . .

To ROGER:

. . . big brother . . .

To JAMESON:

. . . honoured healer . . .

To BRINK:

. . . bearded father . . .

To PAUL:

. . . husband of my heart, and all you white people. Now I am married into your family you must respect me. Honour my father, my brothers, their wives, their children, their most far relatives. But treat us like dogs, and we will rise. My bones will rise from the earth and drive you into the sea.

To DAISY *and* LAZARUS:

Those who are dead, I can be fixing you easy. One year from today, I will send people to dance round your grave and beat drums, and you will rest with your ancestors in peace.

She claps her hands. All clap in response.

End of play.

THE DESERT AIR

The characters in the play are fictional. Their story was suggested by true events described by Basil Davidson in Special Operations Europe (*Victor Gollancz, 1980*).

An earlier version of *The Desert Air* was first presented by the
Royal Shakespeare Company at The Other Place, Stratford-
upon-Avon, on 5 December 1984, with the following cast:

THE HIPPO	Geoffrey Hutchings
MAJOR CARP	Andy Readman
THE COMMANDER-IN-CHIEF, MIDDLE EAST	Godfrey Kenton
GENERAL MONTGOMERY	David Whitaker
COLONEL JENIFER	Myles Hoyle
TIM PAGAN	Peter Eyre
MISS FIGGIS	Polly James
ADRIAN WOOLF	Nicholas Woodeson
PETER CRAGO	Nicholas Farrell
CAPTAIN EDDIE FERGUSON	Martin Jacobs
DR. BABIC	John Burgess
MR. DJORDEJEVIC	Peter Theedom
TWO MEN IN BOWLER HATS	Jonathan Scott-Taylor, Andy Readman
A TAXI-DRIVER	Charles Milham
LUKA	Stephen Simms
BOGDAN	Jonathan Scott-Taylor
PETKO	Andy Readman
JOSIP	Myles Hoyle
MILA	Cecile Paoli
JELKO	David Whitaker
MR. LLOYD-LEIGHTON	John Burgess
COLONEL VEATER	Myles Hoyle
FRANCIS BOTHWELL	Martin Jacobs.

Other parts were played by members of the company.

Director   Adrian Noble
Designer   Chris Dyer
Lighting Designer   Wayne Dowdeswell
Music   Colin Sell

Characters
in order of appearance

GENERAL BERNARD MONTGOMERY
THE COMMANDER-IN-CHIEF, MIDDLE EAST
AIDE
COLONEL JENIFER, *O/C Whiteworks*
TIM PAGAN, *an officer in Dangerous Operations*
    Groundforce
MISS FIGGIS, *a senior secretary*
COLONEL GORE, *later Brigadier Gore, known as the Hippo*
CAPTAIN ADRIAN WOOLF, *O/C Jugoslav/Canadian*
    volunteers
CAPTAIN EDDIE FERGUSON, *Australian, a liaison officer*
    to Jugoslavia
MAJOR PETER CRAGO, *an officer in the Jugoslav section of*
    DOG
DR. BABIC, *envoy in Cairo of the official Jugoslav resistance*
LUKA,
BOGDAN,
PETKO,
JOSIP, *Jugoslav Canadian Volunteers*
MILA, *a Polish refugee*
COLONEL PARROTT, *of SIS.*
MR. LLOYD-LEIGHTON, *of the Foreign Office*
COLONEL VEATER, *of an unknown outfit*
BRIGADIER FRANCIS BOTHWELL, *liaison officer to the*
    Jugoslav Partisans
LT. COLONEL CARP, *previously assistant to the Hippo*

Staff-officers, taxi-drivers, waiters, restaurant customers,
Intelligence officers, Jugoslav/Canadian volunteers, etc.

The play is set in Cairo in 1942/43.

ACT ONE

Scene One

Cairo, 1942. A parade ground. Officers enter and assemble in informal deferential order. The COMMANDER-IN-CHIEF *enters with his* AIDE *and takes the next most senior position.* GENERAL MONTGOMERY *enters, followed by aides.*

MONTY. Good morning, gentlemen.

Greetings follow according to rank. A map is set up on an easel, showing the intended battle area. MONTGOMERY *demonstrates his tactics on it with his baton.*

We shall launch our assault on Rommel's forces from the North. Rommel must suppose that we shall launch it from the South. The element of surprise is crucial. Our forces, poised for the Northern thrust, must be invisible to the enemy. (*To the* COMMANDER-IN-CHIEF.) Eh?

COMMANDER-IN-CHIEF. Quite so.

MONTY. And what have your chaps come up with?

COMMANDER-IN-CHIEF (*to his* AIDE). Captain.

AIDE. The celebrated illusionist, Mr. Jasper Maskelyne, has been working on the problem of the tank. We consider the tank, of all our armoured vehicles, the hardest to render invisible. Have you a moment now, sir, to inspect the prototype?

MONTY. Absolutely.

Soldiers with white tapes cordon off MONTY *and the other officers. Meanwhile:*

AIDE. Will you stand back please? (*To* MONTY.) If you wouldn't mind, sir. (*Calls to others.*) Very well back.

Everyone stands back. To another officer:

Ready?

OFFICER (*calls*). Tank, please.

Pause. Flies buzz. It's hot.

MONTY. Tch tch tch.

Two huge doors open and with an immense din and clanking a tank rolls in, completely invisible, as described. Clouds of dust which make everyone cough. MONTY *taps the tank with his baton, making a solid clang. All applaud, amazed, except for* MONTY.

MONTY. Very adequate. I must congratulate Mr. Maskelyne. Where is he?

AIDE. Inside the tank, sir.

MONTY (*loudly*) Very well done, Mr. Maskelyne.

MASKELYNE (*faintly from inside the tank*). Thank you very much, sir.

Officers applaud in delight. MONTY *addresses all present:*

MONTY. The battle of El Alamein will be a roughhouse. The German soldier is a bonny fighter and the only way to beat him is to kill him in battle. The secret is morale. We shall raise the character of our soldiery to the highest pitch. They look to us for strong and determined leadership and by Jiminy they shall get it.

ALL. Most refreshing/Bags of binge/Just what-the-doctor ordered/Mighty shakeup/keen as mustard/Greyhounds in the slips/ etc.

MONTY. Get rid of this.

The tank drives off, making clouds of dust and a tremendous noise, as before. MONTY *and the other officers leave. The scene dissolves.*

Scene Two

Darkness and a hurricane bombardment. Flames, explosions, whizzing shells. A BBC radio announcement is heard:

'It has been announced that at 21.40 hours last night, the Allied Forces in North Africa launched a major attack on the German lines. Fighting is furious . . . '

A tranquil scene appears:

Lieutenant Colonel PAGAN*'s office at Dangerous Operations Groundforce.* PAGAN *and Colonel* TOBY JENIFER *are drinking cups of tea. Both were merchant bankers in peacetime. Tim* PAGAN *is 43, cool, ascetic, subtly nervous. He is at this stage of his life neat and meticulous in his dress and manner.* JENIFER, *a year or two older, is a portly, worldly figure. He is in mid-flow:*

JENIFER. . . . so we put out a story that the English Channel had been covered in some kind of oil-slick and that it would burst into flames upon command to repel the enemy forces.

PAGAN. Did the Germans believe it?

JENIFER. Who can say, Tim, but the British public did. And the following week I got a telegram. Duty called, and could I fly out to Cairo to provide some equally cheerful scenarios about the new offensive?

MISS FIGGIS *comes in, Early forties, wispy. She carries an armful of files.*

FIGGIS. May I disturb you? These are the briefing folders. Will you sign, please?

PAGAN *signs in her little book of who's got what. She opens the shutters to admit more light. Meanwhile:*

PAGAN (*to* JENIFER). Tell me Toby, are you free for lunch?

JENIFER. Oh, not today. I'm meeting a colleague of ours from peace time. Reggie Matheson. And then tonight I'm dining at Government House.

PAGAN. What I'd like to chat about won't take long.

He gives MISS FIGGIS *her book back.*

That will be all.

He waits till she's gone.

We have a new director here at D.O.G. A regular officer from the General Staff. One Colonel Gore. Known as the Hippo, not just aptly, really quite profoundly on some atavistic level. Hell-bent on running the show himself and he hasn't the touch for it and I honestly think he needs to be contained in some way. Kept very busy perhaps or given nothing to do. I wondered, since you happen to be in Cairo, if I might pick your brains?

MISS FIGGIS *comes back in.*

FIGGIS. It's me again. You asked me to say when Dr. Babic had arrived. I'll take your cups.

She comes into the room and starts to clear up. Meanwhile:

JENIFER. Shepheards, Long Bar, half past twelve.

PAGAN. I'll see you there.

There's a knock at the door.

Come in.

Captain ADRIAN WOOLF *comes in with a file. He's 30 or so, wears spectacles, looks incongruous in uniform.*

PAGAN. Woolf, the very fellow. Show Colonel Jenifer downstairs and sign him out.

ADRIAN. This way, sir.

WOOLF *and* JENIFER *go.*

PAGAN (*to* MISS FIGGIS). One moment, please.

The others have gone.

Does the Hippo plan to join us?

FIGGIS. It's hard to say. He's frisky this morning. He burst in on the cipherines and made some unsuitable jokes. And then he kept the package.

PAGAN. Package?

FIGGIS. Didn't you hear? A rather common young Major arrived on a motorbike. A Major Carp. He brought some papers, and the Hippo wouldn't let me enter them in the daybook.

PAGAN. No no no, we can't have secret info floating about unfiled. Please talk to him.

THE HIPPO comes in. He's a short, stubby, resentful, regular soldier. PAGAN *rises.*

HIPPO. Who's that old fart in the corridor?

PAGAN. Colonel Jenifer. He and I were fellow bankers. And the best of friends. Do stay if you wish, but . . .

HIPPO. Thank you.

He sits in PAGAN*'s chair.*

PAGAN. Excellent, excellent. You'll be meeting Captain Ferguson, who's to be parachuted into Jugoslavia tonight. And Dr. Babic, who is the Jugoslavs' official rep in Cairo.

FIGGIS. Your briefing folder.

She offers THE HIPPO *a file of papers.*

HIPPO. What are these?

FIGGIS. Documents on the current state of play in Jugoslavia.

HIPPO (*to* PAGAN). Do you think I'm stupid?

PAGAN. Certainly not. I find them useful.

HIPPO. Thank you. I have my own.

He puts the folder aside, and takes from his briefcase a sheaf of blue papers. Examines them. PAGAN *looks meaningfully at* MISS FIGGIS. *She peers over* THE HIPPO*'s shoulder at the papers.*

What are you gawping at?

FIGGIS. Should I not put those papers through the system?

HIPPO. They're secret.

FIGGIS. We are a secret unit.

HIPPO. Out!

She goes.

Nosey old cow.

ADRIAN *comes back in, with his file.*

What d'you want?.

ADRIAN. I'm sorry, sir. (*To* PAGAN.) You asked for a memo, sir, on discontent amongst our Volunteers. It's here. Collected fruits of an open discussion . . .

HIPPO. Damn you, hoppit!

ADRIAN *goes quickly.*

Bolshevik. Hebrew Bolshevik. Spot him a mile off. Get rid of him.

PAGAN. Captain Woolf can't help his appearance. I happen to know his father and he's highly capable.

ADRIAN *opens the door and shows in Captain FERGUSON: Australian, young, self-reliant. He's in full battledress. With him is Major PETER CRAGO, late twenties.*

PAGAN. Come in, come in. (*To* THE HIPPO.) Colonel, you've not met Captain Ferguson. Colonel Gore.

FERGUSON (*to* THE HIPPO). Nice to meet you at last, sir.

PAGAN *speaks into his desk telephone:*

PAGAN. Will you send in Dr. Babic, please? (*To* CRAGO.) Is everything in order, Major Crago?

PETER. We're driving Eddie to the airfield in time for a drink in the Wing-Commander's office. Take-off's at eight. He'll be dropped at approximately three a.m., as long as the weather holds and the pilot can see the signal fires.

PAGAN. Anything else?

. PETER. I only wish I was going.

PAGAN. Certainly not. This is a serious mission. Proper
soldiers are required, not over-excited academics. Eddie, sit
down. You're kitted up, I see?

He gets out a bottle of scotch and pours FERGUSON *a
glass.*

FERGUSON. I've been packed for days, sir.

PAGAN. Splendid.

FERGUSON *drinks. Nobody else gets one.*

FERGUSON. I've been writing letters all morning. Bit of a
dodge, to stop my dear old mum from wondering where
I've got to.

Appreciative laugh all round.

Every month, Peter's gonna post one back to Melbourne, so
she gets a colourful account of what a fine old time I'm
having in Cairo.

PAGAN. Quite a feat of the imagination.

Another appreciative general laugh.

HIPPO. Yes, there's a limit to what one can say about food and
fucking. Where's that Jug?

*MISS FIGGIS shows DR. BABIC in and leaves. He's
middle-aged, well-groomed but shabby, a Belgrade
University lecturer perhaps.*

PAGAN. Dr. Babic, thousand welcomes. May I present our
new Military Director, Colonel Gore. Captain Ferguson.
Major Crago, GSO 2 Jugoslavian desk. I've been meaning
to say, Dr. Babic . . .

DR. BABIC *is found a seat.*

. . . that in real life, I frequently corresponded with a Mr.
Tomas Babic of the Imperial Bank, Belgrade. Are you
related?

BABIC. My brother.

PAGAN. Is he well?

BABIC. He was killed in the bombing.

HIPPO. Can we get on, please?

PAGAN. You have a statement, Doctor?

BABIC. Thank you.

He takes out his notes:

In April 1941, when Jugoslavia was invaded by the
Germans, a resistance army was formed under the
leadership of a mighty patriot, General Draza Mihailovic.
He and his gallant Chetniks have waged a bitter struggle
from their stronghold on Mount Durmitor. I speak on his
behalf, to thank you, Captain Ferguson, for joining him in
arms.

PAGAN. I am honoured to affirm his Majesty's Government's
support for the Chetnik army in its gallant struggle.

He looks at his watch. THE HIPPO *sings under his breath
in pantomimed long-suffering:*

HIPPO. Oh God our help in ages past . . .

PAGAN. Do you wish to add anything, Colonel?

HIPPO. No.

PAGAN. Then, Dr. Babic, it remains for me to thank you for
attending and for . . .

HIPPO. You're pulling our legs, of course, about the gallant
struggle? Because the word at GHQ is that the Chetnik
army hasn't fired a shot.

FERGUSON. Isn't this what I'm meant to be finding out?

HIPPO. Shut up!

FERGUSON. I thought that . . .

HIPPO. Nothing to do with you.

BABIC. Excuse me. This young man, he must find out what?

An awkward pause. PAGAN *addresses* DR. BABIC *as one
reasonable man to another.*

PAGAN. I cannot deceive you, Dr. Babic. Captain Ferguson's primary purpose is to find out whether the arms, explosives, heaven knows what else, which we've been sending the Chetniks for the last twelve months have been put to use.

BABIC. Is there some doubt about this?

PAGAN. Confirmation is required. The machine of war is a creaky engine. One moves through a Sargasso Sea of checks and balances. If, or when, Captain Ferguson reports that the resistance is in fact resisting, we shall, as promised, send a full-scale military mission in support.

BABIC. And if he does not?

PAGAN. Then not. Till the picture changes.

Pause.

BABIC. This is embarrassing. Draza Mihailovic is not a Balkan warrior from the comic books. He is an officer of the Royal Serbian army. He takes no pleasure in the spilling of blood. I speak of the blood of peasants. Already the Germans have slaughtered half a million. Women, children. These are killings in reprisal. What is the use of reckless attacks on enemy targets, when the results have not been calculated?

HIPPO. What's the use? *What's the use?* What the fuck do you think we're here for?

BABIC (*with spirit*). It seems to me, you're here to prompt my countrymen into premature engagements which you don't want to risk yourselves.

HIPPO. Exactly. 'Cause it's not our fucking country. Bollocks to this. If you aren't up for reckless attacks on enemy targets, who is? Somebody tell me. Or I'll send this wombat (*Ferguson*) to some sensible bloody country. What about Greece?

FERGUSON. I don't speak Greek.

HIPPO. Be quiet.

FERGUSON. I only speak Australian and Serbo-Croat.

HIPPO. *Shut your cakehole!* Crago! You're the expert. Speak!

PETER. We don't exactly know what's happening there, sir.

FERGUSON. Not *yet*.

HIPPO. I'll kill you.

PETER. There's a radio station, which the Nazis jam. It seems to report a separate force, quite different from the Chetniks. But we don't know much about them.

HIPPO (*grotesque pantomime*). Good Jugs, bad Jugs, which is which?

PAGAN. Might I suggest, this very complex picture can't be approached as though it were a game of cowboys and Indians. Colonel Gore, you have a briefing folder, given you by the excellent Miss Figgis. Please consult it.

THE HIPPO *pushes his folder aside.*

As for you, Major Crago. Radio Free Jugoslavia is a Soviet propaganda stunt. According to them, the heroic masses have risen by the thousand, Hitler trembles, ammo-dumps are rocketing into the sky like bonfire night. We don't believe it. There may be scattered groupings here and there. If they exist, they will be drawn into the major effort under Chetnik leadership.

BABIC. Impossible. Those men are bandits from the mountains. Never will there be peace till they are destroyed.

PAGAN. Bandits or no, General Mihailovic will invite them to regroup beneath the Chetnik banner. Captain Ferguson will so instruct him.

FERGUSON. Thanks a bunch.

BABIC. Enough! I radio tonight. My people will light no signal fires, he cannot land. Who do you think we are to order us so? Are we your allies? Or are we merely foreigners?

HIPPO. You are foreigners. *You* are a very funny foreigner. Who pays your salary? The British Government. If you don't like us you can fuck yourself.

*He reaches into his pocket, produces a pillbox, takes a pill.
To everyone:*

I have familiarised myself with the Jugland picture. Captain
Ferguson will join the Chetniks. He will report his findings.

He turns to DR. BABIC:

A military mission of gigantic strength will follow. Men,
supplies and cash.

BABIC. Is this a promise?

HIPPO. Gentleman's honour.

BABIC *is about to embrace him in thanks but:*

Hands off! Ferguson, bugger off fast. Crago, your shirt's
hanging out.

PAGAN (*to* FERGUSON). Eddie, good luck. (*To* BABIC.)
Doctor we shall . . .

HIPPO. Yes, yes, yes.

FERGUSON, CRAGO *and* DR. BABIC *leave.* PAGAN
stays. THE HIPPO *takes another pill. Clasps his swollen
stomach in pain.*

HIPPO. Look at that gut.

He pats it.

Blown up like a fucking football. Know how big it is? A
bile-duct? Size of a thumb. Gawd only knows what this
one's up to.

PAGAN *looks at his watch.*

That woman.

PAGAN. Do you mean Miss Figgis?

HIPPO. Whatever her name is. Give her the chop.

PAGAN. Miss Figgis is our resident filing wizard. She has a
private system all her own. It's really very effective.

HIPPO. DOG is not a village library. It's a machine of war.
It will be honed and tuned and shook into shape in the

Monty fashion. And keep that greasy Jugoslav out of my sight in future.

PAGAN. I certainly shall. He isn't used to being spoken to in that fashion.

HIPPO. Carrot and stick.

PAGAN. When does he get the carrot? The military mission you announced? I hardly think you'll send it, if it can't be justified.

HIPPO. It will be justified! By me! To the CiC if necessary.

PAGAN. How? How? I challenge you to find a smither of proof of action. How I do wish you'd read your briefing folder. Jugoslavia isn't a country. It's a sort of horrible salad made of incompatible ingredients. Dr. Babic is a Serb, and rather a nice one. Most of the Serbian Jugs are totally mad. They have beards down to their waists and bore you to death about a battle which they actually lost in 1389. The Bosnian Moslems go round sucking up to the Germans, the Croatian Catholics practically are Germans. The Montenegrins are stone age lunatics with swivelling eyes, the Albanians make Al Capone look like a pillar of public probity and the only people all these so-called Jugs have any desire to kill are other Jugs.

HIPPO. Stick to essentials, will you? Look at Ferguson. Eh? What's his rank? Miserable bloody Captain. What does that add to the greater glory of DOG? Sweet Fanny Adams.

PAGAN. You're hardly suggesting that we build up the mission merely in order for the officer in command to be promoted?

HIPPO. Jumping Jiminy Crickets, that's the point! Each of our missions to each of our Balkan clients must be commanded by an officer of senior rank. Now listen to this. Before I change my mind.

PAGAN *falls silent.*

I bring you tidings of an elevatory nature.

PAGAN. What?

HIPPO. You have been promoted to the rank of colonel.

PAGAN. Have my duties altered?

HIPPO. No.

PAGAN. Have I done the state some service which I'm
unaware of?

HIPPO. I doubt it.

PAGAN. Then why the change?

HIPPO. Part of the broader picture, Colonel. I've been
mugging up on Europe. Major Dummett heads our mission
behind the enemy lines in Greece, Major Pincher heads our
mission in Albania. It is essential for their standing among
the locals that they rise to colonel. You're their senior
officer and must rise accordingly.

PAGAN. Merely technical? Then I shan't object.

HIPPO. Object? Object? Is that my thanks?

PAGAN. I didn't sign up in order to be promoted.

HIPPO. So you despise me as a wangler.

PAGAN. The rank is irrelevant to me. As for the wangling,
it's a side of Army life I'm unfamiliar with.

HIPPO. Don't tell me you never bloody wangled. You're a
banker.

PAGAN *smiles at the naiveté of this remark.*

PAGAN. Oh no. It isn't like that at all. There's a lot of nonsense
talked about merchant banking. One's dealing all the time
with friends. With men of one's social circle. So one acts
on trust. If you can't trust friends, you might as well shoot
yourself. If they can't trust you, you do shoot yourself.
It's different I know for the professional soldier.

He looks at his watch. Takes out a bunch of keys.

Twelve fifteen. I must lock the office. About Miss Figgis.
Can I not let her stay pro tem? I'm sure you'll find her less
annoying if she's kept on a shorter rein.

HIPPO. Do what you like.

PAGAN. I will.

He's pleased.

Thank you.

HIPPO. Care for lunch?

PAGAN. I'm meeting a friend at Shepheards, I'm afraid. I'm sorry.

HIPPO. You'll have a snort, though?

He opens the whisky.

PAGAN. Just a small one.

HIPPO. Where's your crockery?

PAGAN *takes a couple of glasses out of a drawer, then produces two silver hairbrushes from the usual place and starts brushing his hair.* THE HIPPO *pours drinks.*

Where to eat? Perennial problem. The Anglo-Egyptian club is full of brainy buggers. Groppi's is full of queers and Jewboys. I hate them. I hate lots of people. Women who deny their femininity. Wogs who deny their wogness. People who get their pictures in the papers. Tall men.

He closes the shutters. Meanwhile:

Has it occurred to you, that most great men are short and stumpy? Napoleon. Churchill. Stalin, Hitler. Monty is a stumpy. He is five foot four of concentrated zip and vigour. And I've always thought of Jesus as a stumpy. I couldn't enter a church if I thought he was one of those long, tall, pointy bastards. Drink.

PAGAN. Oh, thank you.

They drink.

HIPPO. Tell you what. Why don't I toddle along to Shepheards with you? Meet your chum and treat you all to a bite?

PAGAN, *appalled at the thought of introducing* THE HIPPO *to Toby* JENIFER, *replies with tact:*

PAGAN. He's rather a bore. We could eat elsewhere, you and I.

HIPPO. I'm comfy here. And you?

PAGAN. Oh yes.

He sits, disconsolate. THE HIPPO *spreads himself, begins a fantastically involved and boring story:*

HIPPO. I remember when I was in Addis Ababa . . .

He holds out the bottle. With resignation, PAGAN *holds out his glass.*

End of scene.

Scene Three

Cairo. Out of doors. The usual racket: traffic, donkeys. street-vendors, the lot. PETER CRAGO *meets* ADRIAN WOOLF.

ADRIAN. Major Crago?

PETER. Captain Woolf.

ADRIAN. Our taxi, sir.

There is a taxi waiting. They climb in.

Ready, driver?

TAXI-DRIVER. Yes, please.

ADRIAN. Straight down the Giza Road as far as the Pyramids.

TAXI-DRIVER. Five piastres.

ADRIAN. Right you are, let's go.

The taxi sets off and on they drive with much bouncing on potholes and avoiding deadly traffic.

TAXI-DRIVER. I show you Pyramids ten piastres.

PETER. Do explain.

ADRIAN. We do not wish to see the Pyramids. Lovely though they are. Our destination is a stucco-fronted house quite near called Sunrise Villas.

TAXI-DRIVER. Sunrise Villas is no longer girlie house.

ADRIAN. We know that, thank you.

TAXI-DRIVER. Sunrise Villas is now top secret house for men who train to fight the Germans in Jugoslavia.

ADRIAN. Well take us there all the same, would you be so kind?

They settle down as the taxi drives on, swerving and bumping.

PETER. You can drop the sir.

ADRIAN. Oh good.

PETER. You can call me Crago.

ADRIAN. Can I indeed, well let me tell you, Crago, that I thought your conduct was appalling.

PETER. When?

ADRIAN. Oh don't pretend. Remember the day you started at DOG?

PETER. Of course.

ADRIAN. I was in the map room reading the *New Statesman*. And you took one look and leapt into Pagan's office and said, 'I ought to warn you, sir, that I have just observed a well-known Communist on the premises, Adrian Woolf.'

PETER. That's exactly what you were at Trinity.

ADRIAN. That's what I told him. And he said, he knew there was lots of that about at Cambridge and it wouldn't be fair if my career was blighted by an adolescent phase. I mean, how insulting! I could have lost my job.

PETER. I was doing my duty.

ADRIAN. Rot.

A blare of horns as an approaching car nearly crashes into them. They duck, then continue:

I can't help wondering what your interest is in me. Or Sunrise Villas.

PETER. Last resort. I'm trying to swing a place on a mission to Jugoslavia.

ADRIAN. Will there be a mission to Jugoslavia?

PETER. Not on present form.

ADRIAN. Why, what does Ferguson say?

PETER. He found the Chetniks. And they won't let him off Mount Durmitor. He's seen no evidence of fighting and it's all a washout.

ADRIAN. How can I help?

PETER. I thought there was a just a chance that some of your chaps might have some inside info on the situation.

ADRIAN. What's the point? You'll only bin it.

PETER. No I won't. I'll tell old Pagan. And if that doesn't wake him up, I'll pass it on to the Brigadier.

ADRIAN. What Brigadier?

PETER. Didn't you know? The Hippo's been promoted.

ADRIAN. Goodness me. And when was his aggrandisement exactly?

PETER. Monday last. Look, there are the Pyramids.

ADRIAN (*shouts*). Stop!

The taxi jerks to a halt. The next locale assembles: a group of Canadian Jugoslavs, very tough, fit and rugged. Jugoslav accents, tinged with North American. They defer to ADRIAN, *whom they like and admire. Meanwhile:*

ADRIAN. Sunrise Villas was, as the driver said, a knocking-shop pre-war, and it still has frilly lampshades on the chandeliers and peepholes in the doors. Last year they booted out the girls and put my charges in. Six have gone

for parachute-training, five are learning how to capture a
village, three have dysentery.

He introduces four volunteers:

These four are Petko, Luka, Bogdan and Josip.

PETER *shakes hands with them.*

Shall we be seated? Comrade Petko, take the minutes.

They settle as for a lecture.

PETKO (*reads his minutes*). 'The meeting welcomed Major
Crago' . . .

PETER *addresses the others.*

PETER. Thank you. First of all, I'd like to say . . . I'm sorry
there are only four of you here . . . how much we value your
support in the fight for freedom.

PETKO. 'Comrade Luka exposed the contradictions in the
Major's statement.'

LUKA. We are Jugoslavs who went to Canada to get away
from the King, the landlords and the Serbian Army. You
British are fighting to put them back in place. So why
should we help?

PETKO. 'Comrade Bogdan widened the perspective.'

BOGDAN. There is fighting there. There's maybe a lot of
fighting. This we know. Even if none of us knows exactly
where. What I can say, and this is for sure, is that it doesn't
involve the Chetniks.

PETKO. 'Comrade Josip struck a positive note.'

JOSIP. A successful army of resistance must ally itself with
popular aspirations. It must lock up the landlords, depose
the King and beat the Serbian Army.

Applause.

PETKO. 'Comrade Woolf summed up.'

ADRIAN *stands, lights a cigarette.*

ADRIAN. Britain is faced with a classic dilemma. As long as she allies herself with the forces of reaction, then there'll be no serious resistance in Jugoslavia or anyone else in Europe. But if she allies herself with the people's cause, what will that leave her dearly beloved kings? And all their right-wing governments in exile?

PETKO. 'The meeting was adjourned.'

Applause.

ADRIAN. Taxi!

A taxi is there. PETER and ADRIAN are about to get in. ADRIAN addresses the Canadians:

Town is out of bounds to all you comrades. There's a Chetnik spy, one Dr. Babic, if he knows we're training you up he'll blow his top.

Noisy protests.

Besides, we've only got room for two.

In the taxi. PETER, ADRIAN, LUKA, BOGDAN, all very squashed up. A bumpy ride over pits and potholes. LUKA is explaining to Crago:

LUKA. The anti-Nazi struggle cannot be won by a system in decay . . .

PAGAN. What system's that?

ADRIAN. Just listen.

LUKA. The ruling classes need the energies of the workers and the peasant strata . . .

BOGDAN. Don't forget the colonial oppressed, comrade.

ADRIAN. I vote we go to Groppi's.

LUKA. The war has progressed beyond its limited objective, see?

ADRIAN. Or perhaps the Kit-Kat?

PETER. Does anyone know you're training them up to be red-hot bolshies?

LUKA. It is a war against oppression of every kind. It is a war for people's liberation.

BOGDAN. National liberation.

LUKA. Popular liberation.

ADRIAN. Which means, you have to grasp the politics of the post-war era. Of an age of freedom. That's what the future needs!

LUKA. Here we are!

The taxi stops.

Groppi's. Music. Evening. Lots of customers: officers on leave, rich Levantines. Tables, umbrellas. PETER *and* ADRIAN *at a table with milk shakes.* LUKA *and* BOGDAN *explore.*

ADRIAN. Soggy cake, decayed umbrellas. Isn't it odd that Groppi's is so famous? The chaps in the desert dream about it. They imagine swaying palms and dancing fountains.

PETER. And exotic temptresses from far-flung places.

ADRIAN. Speaking of which.

MILA, *a very attractive Polish girl of 20, has arrived at their table.*

MILA. May I sit here? I wish to appear accompanied.

A waiter is there.

PETER. What would you like?

MILA. A raspberry ice. I'm starving.

PETER (*showing off his Arabic*). Ezma! Wahad ice-cream pink-one.

WAITER (*who used to wait at the Connaught Hotel*). One raspberry ice? Of course, sir.

He goes.

MILA. I have escaped from Poland. Warsaw. It is beautiful in the summer. See, I have a brooch.

She shows it to them.

It was given to me by my grandmother on her deathbed. Will you buy it? I am desperate. I have been robbed. Some damned Egyptian peasant.

ADRIAN. How did you get out of Poland?

MILA. Through Czechoslovakia, Hungary, Roumania and Bulgaria.

ADRIAN. All those countries are packed with Nazis.

MILA. So I noticed.

PETER. Weren't you afraid?

MILA (*with aplomb*). Of course!

LUKA *and* BOGDAN *come back.*

LUKA. We've done this dump.

BOGDAN. Let's try the Continental.

ADRIAN. Far too grand.

MILA. Let's go!

PETER. Taxi!

In the taxi. LUKA, BOGDAN, PETER, ADRIAN *and* MILA. MILA *is eating her ice-cream, waving the spoon for emphasis. The taxi bumps and swerves from side to side.*

MILA. I fled from Poland to find my husband. He is English.

PETER. Where is he now?

MILA. All I know is that he's in the British Army. We met in Warsaw. I was eating a raspberry ice. We called for another spoon and we fell in love. Domestic life was paradise. One weekend he was summoned back to London. Two days later, bang, the Germans begin bombardment. Come the tanks. No letters, telephone pfoo. One morning, I opened my bedroom window.

Out in the street there is an SS officer, he say to another, today we raid all the houses in this street. My papers are ready. I go. I travel one year. Tomorrow I will shout at the fools in the British Embassy. My husband is distinguished. He is obsessed by what is physical. He is contemptuous of the Polish men, he say they have no grasp of the romantic spirit. He dance on a table, he take me to a public place and touch my titties. I sell you this brooch for a thousand piastres.

PETER. I can't afford it.

ADRIAN. Neither can I.

PETER. If you've nowhere to stay, I could offer you a bed for the night.

MILA. You will jump on me, it will be too boring. (*To* ADRIAN.) I stay with you.

PETER. Why him?

MILA (*as to an idiot*). Because he is an obvious *pédéraste*!

LUKA/BOGDAN (*to the* TAXI-DRIVER). Stop! Hold it! Here we are!

The taxi stops.

ADRIAN. Not a minute too soon. Comrades, fan out.

In the Continental. Lots of customers: varied types as before. It's late. PETER and ADRIAN at a table. They've had quite a bit more to drink. The remains of MILA's ice on the table.

PETER. There's a war going on. A million miles away from stupid bloody things. My desk. The Hippo getting tidings of an elevatory nature. All the time, somewhere out there, it's real. It matters. However horrible it is, however mad and frightening. Imagine what she's been through. How old do you think she is, nineteen? Incredible. I think she's taken a shine to me. I do. I do. She's . . . Where's she got to?

ADRIAN. She's trying to flog the brooch..

PETER. Do you think it's real?

ADRIAN. You can get them for ten piastres down the road. Ask me another.

PETER. Here goes then. How can I send a mission when the Jugs won't fight?

ADRIAN. My Jugs will. It's only World War II that's stopping them.

PETER. Mihailovic won't fight.

ADRIAN. We've been through that. Resistance in Jugoslavia is being waged by a people's army.

PAGAN. How do you know?

ADRIAN. I have deduced it into being.

PETER. What do you know about the partisans?

ADRIAN. Nothing at all. Do tell.

PETER. There's a Soviet radio stunt keeps on about them.

ADRIAN. And?

PETER. Well, there's something else. The Hippo came into my office this morning and asked me, was I aware that there were twenty German divisions in Jugoslavia ?

ADRIAN. *Twenty?*

He whistles.

How would he know?

PETER. He has a private source. It comes on a motorbike every morning. My theory is that he can't admit he's got it. That's why he hoped I knew. So I could tell him. But I didn't. So I couldn't. But he knew it anyway.

ADRIAN. Hang on, hang on. This is important. Who is tying those twenty German divisions down?

PETER. The partisans. It must be.

ADRIAN *is moved, excited.*

ADRIAN. God, how thrilling. Theory becoming fact before one's eyes. A people's army. Proved. All that I've intuited from my team. My Jugs. My comrades. Real at last. Their hopes aren't wasted. All their energy, their zeal, is shared. A peasant-proletarian rising!

He stands on the table, completely carried away. PETER, by way of making light of this, applauds. The other customers join in. ADRIAN bows, climbs down and continues:

As I predicted. How I love those lads. My Volunteers. Can you imagine how my knees collapsed the day I met them. My first lecture. What I had decided, I would go for broke. Engels 'Peasant Revolt'. And they adored it. Missed their lunchbreak. Imagine undergraduates, if I chose that subject, how they'd rag me. And I'd done some talks in Bermondsey, anti-Mosley stuff, and they were no great shakes, I couldn't get the accent right. Oh thank you.

Their drinks have arrived. They drink.

What I have done, is fall in love with the human race. And if what one is, is a Jewish Hampstead swot who cannot kick a ball straight, then it's glorious when your affections are returned.

PETER. Are you really a queer?

ADRIAN. Do you want to know?

PETER. Not really.

ADRIAN (*taps his head*). It's here. (*Taps his heart.*) And here.

He laughs.

Oh yuk!

CRAGO (*with sympathy*). I'm awfully sorry.

ADRIAN. I'm fantastically happy, you fool!

PETER. Look out! It's Pagan.

PAGAN approaches. He looks drawn, pale and a bit tight.

PAGAN. Peter. Adrian. Drink?

He sits at their table.

PETER. There's only bogus whisky.

PAGAN. No, no, no, there's creme de menthe. (*To the WAITER.*) Same all round. (*To PETER and ADRIAN.*) Have you had a nice evening?

PETER. Yes sir.

ADRIAN. Fascinating.

PAGAN. Would you believe, it's midnight and I've only just left the Hippo's office. He's taken to calling me in for a chin-wag, as he puts it. Closes the shutters. No escape. The image comes to mind of some Edwardian masher about to pounce on a chorus-girl. And then he talks. And talks. Awash with whisky.

The waiter is there with their drinks. PAGAN *pays.*

I shouldn't be drinking this. I'm starving. What was that?

He sees the remains of MILA*'s ice-cream. Picks it up.*

ADRIAN. A raspberry ice.

PAGAN. How strange. I shouldn't bore you with my reminiscences. But there's a story attached. Shortly before the War broke out, the Bank had posted me to Warsaw, and I . . .

He looks up and sees MILA.

Good God!

PETER. What's is it, sir?

PAGAN. I've just seen my wife.

MILA *sees him.*

MILA. Tim?

PAGAN. Mila!

All watch as they embrace.

ADRIAN. Taxi!

End of scene.

Scene Four

THE HIPPO*'s office at* DOG. THE HIPPO *is about to give
dictation to* MILA. *He is wearing his jacket, unbuttoned. As
the scene progresses he takes it off, revealing a dirty vest. It is
night.*

He has a sheaf of papers: these are FERGUSON*'s signals.*

HIPPO. Memorandum: to Intelligence Committee, GHQ.
   Subject: Funds and facilities for Military Mission to
   Jugoslavia.

MILA (*writes*). G. H. Q.

HIPPO. Ssh!

   He points to his forehead.

   Grey cells at work. Military mission costs a fortune. Molto
   Moolah, get the picture? GHQ must be convinced that what
   we send will be deployed. Convinced in writing, dammit.

   He prowls around.

   Hate memoranda. Always have done. Brain goes haywire at
   the sight of paper. Holy Moses, what comes next? Here
   goes.

   Dictates:

   'Although our liaison officer has been confined to Chetnik
   HQ by . . . "Mm hm hm" . . . heavy snowfall . . . '

MILA (*writes*). 'liaison officer . . . '

HIPPO. ' . . . his opinion, Ferguson's, Captain's, Eddie's . . .
   Edward, Edwin, Figgis will know and something something
   spur to action.'

MILA. . . . Figgis . . .

HIPPO. Don't write that!

MILA. Don't shout! Never once in a thousand years has one of
   my family work for money. Tell me what you want to say, I
   write it.

A knock on the door and it opens. It's PETER, *breathless.*

PETER. I'm sorry sir. Good evening, Mrs. Pagan.

HIPPO. Enter, enter. (*To* MILA.) Find me whatsisname. Your husband. Tell him I want him pronto. PDQ. Now out!

MILA *leaves with style.*

Damn Polski nitwit. Shocking imposition on our hardpressed secretarial pool. Rule 23. 'Wives of officers may reside in Cairo only if engaged on vital work'. Tim Pagan knows this. He has swung her a job. He who never wangles. He has jeopardised internal admin for the sake of a poke. Almost makes you like the bastard. What do you want?

PETER. Eddie Ferguson's just been on the air, sir. It's pretty exciting news. There's been a guerrilla attack on the German airfield at Sarajevo.

HIPPO (*pleased*). Ah ha.

He consults a map. PETER *helps find the spot.*

PETER. It's here, sir. Sixty miles from the Chetnik HQ. Eddie said that from the mountain they could actually see the light in the sky and hear the explosions.

HIPPO. Hang on, hang on. What was Ferguson doing sixty miles away?

PETER. That's where they all were, sir. It wasn't a Chetnik action. The Chetniks didn't know a thing about it till it happened.

HIPPO. Then it's useless! Bloody useless! Ferguson has betrayed me! Thousands of pounds it cost to send that Antipodean bumpkin. Weeks of effort. Down the khazi. I want a war out there! I want a bloodbath!

MISS FIGGIS *comes in carrying files.*

FIGGIS. Here are your files. I'm sorry they took so long. 'Road maps.' 'Weather reports.'

She lays them out. THE HIPPO *spots another.*

HIPPO. I did not order the file on partisans!

FIGGIS. I know that, Colonel. But we felt it might be useful. After all, if they can pulverise a German airfield . . .

HIPPO. The partisans are scum! Filth! After the war we will shoot them in the streets like rats!

He tears the file up and jumps on it, while MISS FIGGIS *looks on in horror.*

Ferguson's signals are not to circulate in unedited form! Fatal for morale! I'll receive them! You will not! When's his next transmission?

PAGAN. Half past ten.

FIGGIS. He's coming up now.

THE HIPPO *dashes towards the door, seizing his pills, and saying:*

HIPPO. Don't let Pagan bunk off home. I need him.

He goes. MISS FIGGIS *picks up the ruined file. She starts to cry. The door opens and* ADRIAN *looks in.*

ADRIAN. How did it go? Your pincer action?

PETER *rolls his eyes and gestures towards* MISS FIGGIS.

PETER. Hopeless.

ADRIAN *sees* MISS FIGGIS *in tears.*

ADRIAN. Oh God. (*Whispers.*) Pat her on the back.

PETER (*whispers*). No, you.

ADRIAN. You first.

FIGGIS. Don't worry about me, please. I've had a difficult day.

She starts to clear up.

My files have been reorganised by Colonel Pagan. He says I was using a private system. It's a family system. My father's. A remarkable writer. He helped Mr. Churchill on all his most difficult books. You'd think it would suffice for a bogus colonel.

She has tidied up. Of the 'Partisans' file:

I'll take these out.

She goes to the door.

ADRIAN. Miss Figgis.

FIGGIS. Yes?

ADRIAN. Why is Pagan a bogus colonel?

FIGGIS. Didn't you know? The Hippo is working Army Rules. Rule 187, subclause 2, and a grand old favourite of the Hippos of this world.

She quotes from memory:

'An officer in command of three other officers of identical rank . . . ' the same as his own, that is, 'shall be promoted to whichever rank is next in seniority.' The Hippo swung a Colonel's rank for Major Dummett in Greece, a Colonel's rank for little Julian Pincher in Albania and the third was Pagan.

ADRIAN. And the Hippo went up to Brigadier.

FIGGIS. Exactly. It's like pressing a button.

ADRIAN. And the Hippo knows which buttons to press.

FIGGIS. He does, he does. He's . . . yes, I would say he's the best I've seen since my days at the BBC.

ADRIAN *leaps up, paces back and forth, thinking hard.*

ADRIAN. Let's think about this. If he wants to go up to Major-General . . .

FIGGIS. Which he does . . .

PETER. . . . three Brigadiers are needed.

ADRIAN. And where will they be? Greece is thick with missions, he could get a Brigadier tomorrow. Bulgaria, forget it. Hungary, don't be daft. Italy not for ages. Ah ha! Albania! Small country, small mission, but the size doesn't matter. That gives him two. And number three . . . ?

He picks up a file and waves it in triumph.

Us!

PAGAN. But he can't send a mission to Jugoslavia if the
Chetniks won't fight. Not even the Hippo can do that.

ADRIAN. He'll send a mission to the partisans.

FIGGIS. He can't! He'll have to persuade the Foreign Office,
Whitehall, GHQ . . .

ADRIAN. He will! He wants that third Brigadier. And
history's on his side. We've reached that point, which comes
in every British war, year three approximately, no listen
Peter, when so many officers have been shot or sacked or
led their regiments over cliffs, that there aren't enough left
to fill the important jobs. That's when we start to win.
Because the officers who take over are the Hippos. Sweaty
little thugs from third-class regiments. Counter-jumpers.
Opportunists. Men who've been snubbed and patronised for
years. Men who can hate. It is the time of the Hippo!
History is being moulded in their pachydermous paws. They
are a social movement. *He* is a social movement. And if
policy must be changed, he'll change it.

FIGGIS. I'm convinced.

PETER. You're right. My mission! Jugoslavia! Yoohoo!

He calls out and leaps for joy, hugs MISS FIGGIS.
ADRIAN *dances about.* PAGAN *comes in looking shifty.*

PAGAN. May I disturb the revels? I waited for the Hippo half
an hour and left, is that quite clear?

THE HIPPO *comes in after him.*

HIPPO. Ah, Colonel Pagan.

PAGAN (*under his breath*). Oh, God.

FIGGIS. Goodnight.

ADRIAN/PETER. Goodnight, sir.

PETER, ADRIAN *and* MISS FIGGIS *go.* THE HIPPO
closes the shutters and finds the whisky.

HIPPO. I've been trying to extract some sense from Ferguson's signals.

PAGAN. Are they not clear? The Chetniks haven't fought the Hun in living memory. Nobody wants a military mission more than I do, but I . . .

HIPPO. Somebody does. Yours truly. I am in love. I slaver. You'll have a snifter?

PAGAN. No, no whisky –

HIPPO (*who has already poured it*). Whoops! Too late, too late she cried!

Gives PAGAN *the glass.*

See the predicament, old boy, because I must request supplies. And I'd an excellent helper in my previous posting. Carp, young Carp, no tone to the boy, no background worth a mousefart, but I miss him 'cause I'm all on my owneo, frightfully tizzed and I cannot compose the blinking memorandum to GHQ.

PAGAN. Are you suggesting that I ghost it for you?

HIPPO. Asking. Jolly good practice.

PAGAN. No. I don't think so. No.

THE HIPPO *is sympathetic.*

HIPPO. You're probably wise. 'Cause GHQ might say it's balls. Might sling it back at me, then you'd be tarred with the brush of failure. Bastards hate me. Total and utter swine. I slaved like a nigger in their miserable employ, and that's what they treated me like, a wog. Who worked late while they were propping up the bar at Shepheards? Who had to work from last year's calendar? Who got the ink with lumps in it? Muggins. Good old Hippo. Well it's been a very pleasant chitchat and you've drunk my drink and I think we have the basis for an understanding. I want total and unshaken loyalty personally to me. You write that memo.

PAGAN. No.

HIPPO. Why not?

PAGAN. It won't be true.

THE HIPPO laughs.

HIPPO. Don't come it, Pagan. How's your wife? How's her typing? I hear Miss Figgis had to help her find the question-mark.

PAGAN. Are you implying corrupt behaviour?

HIPPO (*friendly*). Fine by me! It's good to know you're human.

He pours PAGAN another whisky.

I never married. Never say no to a poke, mind. But it doesn't impinge. I use the time to solve some niggling problem. Know the feeling?

PAGAN finishes his drink, moves it out of THE HIPPO's reach and rises to go.

PAGAN. I'll tell my wife you're satisfied with her work. She'll be . . .

HIPPO. Do you know how I joined the Army?

During the following he somehow fills PAGAN's glass. PAGAN sits down slowly.

My old dad was batman to an officer in the 2nd Wiltshires. Colonel Gore. I took the name in gratitude when he helped me into the regiment. Family name is Waters. I don't use it. Last time I saw my mum and dad, I hid behind a letterbox. Colonel Gore had no direct descendants. When he died, he left my dad the contents of his house. Carpets silver, furniture and paintings. Come the funeral, family Gore arrived. Oh what a flap. Had the old boy gone potty? Leaving these priceless objects to a dumb old clodhopping fool who couldn't appreciate them? They swiped the lot. They carried them down the stairs and into their waiting limousines. They gave my dad a cheque for fifty quid, which he thought was fair. And this is how I imagine that Sunday night. My dad in an empty house. Drinking his cup of tea. With not so much as a piece of brass to polish. Army gone. Master gone. As lost and uncomprehending as that dog, the late King George's dog, trotting behind the royal coffin. Never since then have I expected justice from my lords and masters. What have they done for me? I have been bilked and baulked and totally betrayed. By you and yours. Your fellow pointy bastards. Nothing personal,Tim. I like you. You're pig-ignorant, that's all. You live in a dreamworld. I could wipe that look off your face like a fucking rainbow.

He has a twinge of stomach pain. Suppresses it.

Do the words 'Uncle Harry' mean anything to you?

PAGAN. 'You must always believe what your Uncle Harry tells you.'

HIPPO. What's that?

PAGAN. It's a phrase from a book. *Three Men in a Boat.*

THE HIPPO *nods.*

HIPPO. Yes, that would fit.

He opens his briefcase, takes out a folder.

Uncle Harry is the deadliest secret of the war.

He takes out some sheets of blue paper.

These are enemy signals. Beastly Hun, desiring to send a message, uses an enciphering machine. We, the great and good, possess a de-enciphering machine in Bletchley, Hertfordshire. We intercept the signal, feed it in and all is revealed: their plots, their plans, what Hitler had for breakfast. An officer on the circulation-list of Uncle Harry will never see action. He will never be placed in any position where he might be captured by the enemy. He will live a life apart. He will long to tell the secret. It will gnaw his vitals. It will destroy his health.

He pats his stomach.

I *was* on the list in my previous post. Through fortune, or by hideous chance, nobody thought to take me off it when I came to DOG. Now Carp, my imp, my nemesis, brings me the latest on his motorbike every morning. Take a shufti.

He passes PAGAN *a sheet of blue paper.* PAGAN *reads:*

PAGAN. 'The 14th Panzer Division will reach Belgrade tomorrow'. When is tomorrow?

He looks at the date.

Today. This is a German signal.

He reads.

'We are calling up the Chetniks for assistance.' Are the Chetniks collaborating?

HIPPO. Perhaps. In war one can't always choose one's company. Read this.

He passes PAGAN *another intercept.* PAGAN *reads.*

PAGAN. 'Repeated attacks by partisans.'

THE HIPPO *passes him more intercepts.*

HIPPO. Read this. Read this. They're all the same. The partisans have overrun the country. They've tied down twenty German divisions. They've got the Chetniks on the run. Let's put it simply. The Reds are winning and our Chetnik allies are in dire distress. Where do you stand on that one, Colonel Pagan?

Pause.

PAGAN. You called me ignorant. Which I was. Till a personal crisis. Very low ebb in my life. Messy divorce. I begged the bank to post me anywhere, ends of the earth. Budapest, Prague, then Warsaw. And I returned to life. Falling in love was half the trick. And conversation. And the richness of people's minds. And then one met, from time to time, the hardline Communist. One saw their dogmatism. Their intolerance of beauty. And their longing to destroy it, if we let them.

HIPPO. So you'll write the memo?

PAGAN. I might help you with the phrasing. But my name must not appear.

He starts making notes. THE HIPPO *selects relevant files and papers, puts them within* PAGAN's *reach.* PAGAN *makes more notes, then writes a sentence. Professional look to this.*

THE HIPPO *watches.* PAGAN *goes on writing.* THE HIPPO *places the whisky within his grasp and goes out quietly.*

End of scene.

Scene Five

A conference-room at GHQ. A large table around which are seated a number of high-ranking officers from different branches of Intelligence. They include a Colonel VEATER, a Colonel PARROTT, THE HIPPO and PAGAN. A MR. LLOYD-LEIGHTON represents the Foreign Office. The meeting is being chaired by the Commander-in-Chief. His AIDE sits beside him.

COMMANDER-IN-CHIEF. DOG requests supplies for a mission to Jugoslavia. Has everyone read the memo?

Everyone has.

Frankly, Brigadier, I find it waffly. But the message is welcome. Captain Ferguson, you say, describes the Chetniks as a potent fighting force. Are there any comments?

PARROTT. Yes, sir.

AIDE (*murmurs to* COMMANDER-IN-CHIEF). Colonel Parrott, SIS.

PARROTT. Brigadier Gore suggests that the number of German divisions in Jugoslavia is five, or possibly six. Does he regard this estimate as complete? The figure accords with the Chetniks' modest efforts up till now, but if . . .

HIPPO. Are you, are you querying the estimate?

PARROTT. Yes.

HIPPO. Then I must ask, upon what basis?

PARROTT. I'd rather leave the basis out of it if I may.

COMMANDER-IN-CHIEF. Are there German divisions in Jugoslavia which he does not mention?

PARROTT (*lies*). I don't recall, sir.

COMMANDER-IN-CHIEF. Then your objection's futile.

PARROTT. I'm afraid it is.

THE HIPPO *is delighted. But:*

LLOYD-LEIGHTON. Might I say . . . ?

AIDE (*to the* COMMANDER-IN-CHIEF). Mr. Lloyd-Leighton, Foreign Office.

LLOYD-LEIGHTON The Balkans are traditionally a murky area. Ancient feuds abound which sometimes contradict the official lines of battle. Might the result be . . . how shall I put this? . . . that the Chetniks' response to the Hun invader is ambivalent?

COMMANDER-IN-CHIEF (*to* AIDE). What's he on about?

AIDE. No idea, sir.

LLOYD-LEIGHTON. Is Mihailovic collaborating with the Germans? We wouldn't be shocked if this were so, bearing in mind the historical context. But we wouldn't send him military aid any more than we would to the Vichy French.

COMMANDER-IN-CHIEF. What grounds have you for this suggestion?

LLOYD-LEIGHTON (*lies*). Well I can't say. One gets intelligence from so many sources these days.

COMMANDER-IN-CHIEF. Brigadier Gore? What is your answer?

HIPPO. Colonel Pagan?

PAGAN *is caught on the hop.*

COMMANDER-IN-CHIEF. There is no evidence of collaboration.

PARROTT, LLOYD-LEIGHTON and VEATER exchange glances.

Are there any more comments?

VEATER. I'll turn if I may . . .

AIDE. Colonel Veater.

COMMANDER-IN-CHIEF. What's his outfit?

The AIDE *replies with a tiny but eloquent gesture:* VEATER*'s outfit is too secret to spoken of.*

VEATER. . . . to the second page of Brigadier Gore's memorandum, where he quotes the attack on the German airfield at Sarajavo. A brilliant feat of arms. The question is, who did it?

HIPPO. We say the Chetniks and so did the BBC.

VEATER. I . . .

HIPPO. Did you not hear the broadcast?

VEATER. I wrote the broadcast. I delivered the script, in London, in my taxi to the BBC, and had a long and frankly dreadful conversation with Sir John Reith, who said it was self-evident nonsense. I pointed out that the Chetniks were being credited, as so often, for political reasons, and he bowed to pressure. Never did I think the broadcast was correct. Yet here we find the myth perpetuated. Why?

AIDE (*to the* COMMANDER-IN-CHIEF). The Yanks are waiting, sir.

COMMANDER-IN-CHIEF. Brigadier Gore, I can only authorise this mission with the full support of my Intelligence team. That support is lacking. Your request is therefore turned down. One final word. I suggest you note what Colonel Veater has implied, that some other crowd is doing the fighting. Surely these are the men you should be helping?

LLOYD-LEIGHTON. Are you suggesting a mission to Tito, General?

COMMANDER-IN-CHIEF. Who is Tito?

LLOYD-LEIGHTON. Happily I am authorised to answer this question. Sources close to the enemy suggest a partisan force. Its size and effectiveness are irrelevant to this discussion, for the following reason.

Tito is not a woman, as we thought at first, nor indeed a man, but a committee. T.I.T.O. is an acronym, like GHQ or DOG, and it stands for 'Tajna lnternationalna Teroristicka Organizacija'. International Terrorism. A ruthless Politburo with the aim of spreading Bolshevisation thoughout the Balkan area. We at the Foreign Office must consider the kind of Europe we want to see after the war. Enslaved or free? The question implies another. On whom can we depend to keep the flame of democracy alight? The answer is Mihailovic. No-one claims he's a very effective scourge of the Nazi horde. That's not his function. His function is to counter Russian influence, most especially once the war is over.

COMMANDER-IN-CHIEF. If we want to beat the Russians, we shall have to beat the Germans first.

LLOYD-LEIGHTON. Quite so, sir. Only not in Jugoslavia.

The COMMANDER-IN-CHIEF *rises, furious and frustrated.*

COMMANDER-IN-CHIEF. Thank you gentlemen.

As he leaves, to his AIDE*:*

I want to look at DOG in depth. Dreadful co-ordination.

He has gone. Everyone goes, except PAGAN *and* THE HIPPO. PAGAN *very upset.*

HIPPO. Send in Crago.

PAGAN *goes.*

They're conspiring. GHQ has stabbed me in the back. The BBC, the Foreign Office, up and up, as far as Anthony bloody Eden. Scheming, plotting, all of 'em in cahoots to hurl me into darkness, there to push a miserable pen, obscure, forgotten, stuck in the mud at *Brigadier!* No! Never! Now I defy you long, tall, pointy bastards! Arm yourselves! The Hippo's on the warpath!

PETER *comes in with his maps. So does* MISS FIGGIS, *carrying files.* THE HIPPO *opens his briefcase and produces a huge stack of Uncle Harry intercepts.*

Enemy traffic. Figgis, file it. Crago, analyse these. There's plenty more. Do maps. Do summaries. We shall send a military mission to the partisans. There's just one problem. British Foreign Policy's up the spout. We need an ally. Somebody highly placed. But loyal!

He thinks furiously.

Who do we know, who can contact Winston Churchill on a personal basis?

FIGGIS. Me, you silly fool. Yes me. I know him!

HIPPO. Magnificent creature!

He embraces her.

End of Act One.

ACT TWO

Scene One

PAGAN *and* MILA's *apartment. The bedroom, with a door leading to a bathroom. It's nearly dawn.* PAGAN *is in bed wearing silk pyjamas. The light is off but he is awake. The door to the hall opens.* MILA *comes in, in an evening dress, trying not to make any noise.*

PAGAN. I'm awake.

MILA. What happened to you?

PAGAN. I came home. I wasn't feeling up to scratch.

MILA. We waited for you.

PAGAN. Who is 'we'?

MILA. Oh, people from the office. Adrian. Peter Crago. Shall I come to bed?

PAGAN. It's quarter to five. It's hardly worth it.

She is sitting on the bed, She touches his shoulder, massages it gently.

You're making it worse.

She gets up. Goes into the bathroom. We hear the bath running. She comes in and out of the bathroom, getting undressed. Sits, undoes her suspenders and takes off her stockings. Meanwhile:

MILA. Did the Hippo bother you tonight?

PAGAN. Oh no. I'm very much out of tune with his present thinking. I'm the ancien regime, I'm tumbril fodder. He tells me nothing. Nobody does. Do you?

MILA *is in the bathroom. She calls out:*

MILA. What?

PAGAN. What do you know about the mission to Tito?

MILA comes back into the room.

MILA. I only know that it got the go-ahead.

PAGAN. Not from me.

MILA. Mr. Churchill passed through Cairo on his way to Casablanca. And Miss Figgis pulled a string, and the Hippo went to see him.

PAGAN. That's what you've heard?

MILA. Mm hm.

PAGAN. In the typing pool? Mr. Churchill squeezed the Hippo in between, let's say, General de Gaulle and Chiang Kai-Shek?

She doesn't answer. Pause.

Would you mind very much if I asked to be transferred?

MILA. What?

PAGAN. I'm being disloyal. Working for an officer I hate. A man whose every triumph makes me grit my teeth in anger. It rots the soul.

MILA. Tim, you're crazy. What about me? If you aren't working here, I'll get the chop. I'm hopeless. Where would I go? I'm Polish. I could be interned.

PAGAN. There's something I haven't told you. I attended a meeting at GHQ. I was asked a question, and I lied. One doesn't lie to men like that. It cuts across everything we're fighting for. And the Hippo's to blame. I really do think that if I stay I might do something violent.

MILA. Because you lied?

He nods.

When I was escaping through Europe, I lied a hundred times a day. In a city where I'd never been before, I'd lie with the way I walked. Confident, fast, as though I knew where I was going. I always arrived on market days, so I could lose myself in the crowd. Trying to remember which of my papers I was carrying. Was I Communist, Nazi, Austrian, Russian? All lies. Sometimes I wore a cushion in my dress so they'd think I was pregnant. I did it so often that my periods stopped. It's true! Once, at a station, the military policeman said, 'Your visa's lapsed, you're lucky, any other day of the year you'd be arrested.' I laughed as though I understood. Then I looked at the visa. Whoever it was, it was her birthday. One of my visas said I was the rabbi Shumsky, fortunately in Japanese. I loved that visa. It was such a ridiculous lie.

PAGAN *asks the question he's never dared ask before:*

PAGAN. What did you live on? How did you eat? Who did you get to help you? Were they men in uniform? *What* uniform?

MILA. I tell you one thing only. You've been honest all your life. It was a luxury you could afford. I had to give it up. Now you do the same till the end of the war. And don't ask questions.

She goes into the bathroom and turns off the taps.

PAGAN (*calls*). Mila.

MILA (*calls*). I'm having my bath.

PAGAN. Have it afterwards.

MILA *appears in the bathroom door, naked, with a towel wrapped round her.*

MILA. What?

PAGAN. Come here.

MILA. You'll keep the job?

PAGAN. Mm hm.

MILA. What about the Hippo?

PAGAN. I'll lie to him.

She gets on to the bed, puts a hand under the sheet.

PAGAN. It isn't the sort of thing I'm very good at.

MILA. What are you good at, Tim?

End of scene.

Scene Two

An empty space: it's the yard at the back of the DOG offices. Night. Darkness. PETER is seen above, at a first-floor window. He looks fit and trained, which he now is. He lowers a rope, glides down it, hits the ground, looks around, then moves stealthily to the centre of the yard.

From out of sight, someone is heard whistling a bird-call. PETER whistles in return. THE HIPPO appears out of the darkness.

HIPPO. Greetings, comrade. No sign of our task force?

PETER. No sir.

HIPPO. Any excuse?

PETER. The problem, sir, of getting them into town unrecognised . . .

HIPPO. Quite so, quite so. They will arrive by covert means!

He looks around him.

Magnificent night for the job, eh? Sliver of moon. Dark shadows. And the New Year beano in the map room should divert attention.

He produces a vehicle key from his pocket.

Key to the truck. Don't move.

He leaves stealthily. MILA, carrying a glass, comes out of the shadows.

MILA. Peter!

PETER. Ssh!

MILA. Come back to the party.

PETER. No!

MILA. I'm lonely. Talk to me, Peter. Make me laugh.

A whistle is heard out of the darkness.

What's that?

PETER. It's secret. Go away.

MILA. OK. I go.

As she goes:

I go.

She disappears into the darkness. ADRIAN *and the
Jugoslav volunteers appear from another direction. None
can be distinguished from the other, as they are all
disguised as Egyptian women in strict purdah.*

ADRIAN. Peter!

PETER. What?

ADRIAN. It's us. Look. Me. We got held up in the traffic.

THE HIPPO *appears.*

HIPPO. Ssh! Which of you is Captain Woolf?

ADRIAN *reveals himself.*

ADRIAN. I'm here, sir.

HIPPO. Taskforce will disrobe.

*They get out of their purdah. When they've done so, they
paint their faces with black shoe-polish.* THE HIPPO
continues meanwhile:

Final briefing. In the corner of the yard you will observe a
truck, DOG supplies for the use of. You will find inside a
number of boxes, marked by intended destination. Some say
Greece, the rest Albania. Our object is to capture the whole
bangshoot for Jugoslavia. You will bring them here. Major

Crago will be stationed in my office, first floor, and he will winch them up to safety. I shall remain in the centre of the yard and simulate normal behaviour. Ready?

They form themselves commando-style.

Count of five. Four. Three. Two. Good luck to you all. And one.

They fall to the ground and perform a very fast and efficient crawling exit into the surrounding darkness. PETER *leaves fast in another direction.* WOOLF *remains.*

HIPPO. Amazing!

ADRIAN. They've been waiting eighteen months for a chance like this.

HIPPO. Taste of action. Totally transforms the man. Look at me now. Gut pain vanished. Mind alert. I kip in a hammock. In my office. Cannot desert my post in the present ferment. Nap for an hour. Wake at dawn. And leap to the ground, imbued each morning with sheer zip, sheer blinding purpose. Brew up a cuppa. Good strong chai. And that's my ration foodwise for the rest of the day.

PAGAN *appears out of the darkness: he's been at the party.*

What do you want?

PAGAN. I was at the party. I was looking for my . . . What in the world is happening?

PETER *has appeared up above. As* THE HIPPO *continues, two Volunteers appear with a box. They attach it to* PETER*'s rope and he hauls it up.*

HIPPO. Mission to the partisans. They need supplies. Our Greek and Albanian missions do not need supplies. They have been utterly indulged.

PAGAN. Though Dummett and Pincher . . .

HIPPO. Bugger them both! I've made them brigadiers, what more do they want?

PAGAN. Oh I agree.

THE HIPPO *stares at him, suspicious.*

HIPPO. You do?

PAGAN. Oh, absolutely. And a mission to Tito. Just the job.
Have we permission?

THE HIPPO *is thoughtful for a moment, uncertain whether
or not* PAGAN *is to be trusted. As he continues, more crates
are delivered and hauled up:* ADRIAN *joins the exercise.*

HIPPO. Churchill, when I saw him, was in the bathtub.
Nursing a tumbler. 'Won't you sit down?' he said. I did.
Tap end. I'd written a memo. Three days work. Strenuous
mental effort. But he didn't read it. Laid it on the bathmat,
fixed me with his pale blue eyes and asked for a verbal
rundown. I thought, 'this is a wangle! Wangle away old
son!'. So I did. Military state of play. Chetnik perfidy.
Gallant partisans. A frank admission. 'Some, it appears, are
Bolshies.' The old man frowns. Soaps his hair, then asks
me: 'Are they killing Germans?' 'Yes,' say I, and vice-
versa.' 'What do you want me to do?', he asks. I'm ready
for this one. 'Have we permission, sir, to establish contact
with the partisans?' He looks at the Hippo sideways. Gives
the soles of his feet a scrub. And then he nodded.

PAGAN. Nodded?

HIPPO. Very slightly. *But I spotted it!* Mission accomplished!
Mission in the bag old boy! Our mission to Tito!

PAGAN. Have we nothing in writing?

HIPPO. Nothing exists which might alert the official channels!
That's the beauty of the nod, old boy. Tacit understanding
between two men of equal height. And us. (*himself and
Pagan*) And them. (*the Volunteers*) We few. Nobody else
must twig. Our lords and masters must be caught on the
hop. Crucial element of surprise. Once we've landed, once
we're thrashing the Hun on Balkan soil, let them scream
blue murder. I'll say 'Bollocks!' 'Cause I wangled a nod
from Churchill and deployed it.

PAGAN. Do we not tell the Chiefs of Staff?

HIPPO. There will be no collaboration!

PAGAN. When will the mission go?

HIPPO. Full moon. Friday week. The target area will be
Crnacko Polje, behind the lines of the German winter
offensive. It will be sixteen men in strength. The rank of
commanding officer will be Brigadier. And my luck's in,
old chum, because I've found one ready-made. An A.1
candidate, Malthouse, Bouncer Malthouse, dear old pal and
much maligned, he carried the can at Sidi Barrani for some
bloody almighty cockup.

A whistle is heard.

Ssh! Who's that?

ADRIAN is carried on by two Volunteers.

ADRIAN. Twisted my blasted ankle.

HIPPO. Next in command? I'll go!

He swiftly blacks his face. PAGAN *prepares to leave.*

PAGAN. Gentlemen, thank you. I'd better get back to the party
and find my wife.

HIPPO (*getting into the mood*). Hoo! Hah!

PAGAN. Sorry about the ankle, Adrian. Peter, are you up
there? No. Well. Good night.

He goes.

HIPPO. Woo! Woah!

*He throws himself to the ground and commando-crawls into
the darkness.* PETER *appears on ground level.* ADRIAN
sees him.

ADRIAN. Isn't he stunning? I was walking past the lavatories
this afternoon and he came leaping out like a cuckoo-clock
and pulled me in and said security was on my tail, and not
to worry, he'd protect me. Truly grateful for the way I'd
trained the lads up. And my organisational skills. I said I'm
loving every minute. And I meant it. Gosh, I meant it. Why
aren't you at your post?

PAGAN's *voice is heard calling 'Mila!'.* PETER *comes closer to* ADRIAN.

PETER. She's up there.

ADRIAN. Who?

PETER. Mila. She's up in the Hippo's office. She's been helping me pull the crates up. She's incredibly strong. What am I going to do? Tim's so bloody decent. Look how nice he was about your ankle.

ADRIAN. Know what I think? You should. Go to bed, I mean, with whoever it is you happen to be in love with. I see it as a totally unalienated human action. Well, that's my theory. All it lacks is some empirical proof. That's your department.

A whistle is heard from out of sight. ADRIAN *gestures up to the window.*

Duty calls.

PETER *climbs up the rope and out of sight.* ADRIAN *sits alone for a moment. From the direction of the offices, the sounds of 'Auld Acquaintance' are heard.* ADRIAN *murmurs to himself:*

Happy New Year.

THE HIPPO *reappears with the Volunteers. He's carrying a crate. At the same time,* MISS FIGGIS *appears.*

FIGGIS. It's after midnight. Such a shame to let it pass unnoticed. I've saved up this.

She produces a bottle of whisky.

HIPPO. Most welcome!

FIGGIS (*to* THE HIPPO). And this signal has arrived from London.

HIPPO. Let me see.

He opens it. MISS FIGGIS *and* WOOLF *watch. The others go on working.*

Oh Crikey.

FIGGIS. What?

HIPPO. It's making me jumpy.

FIGGIS. What does it say?

THE HIPPO *reads.*

HIPPO. Mm hm. (*Reads.*) Mm hm. (*Reads.*) I think it's good. The mission to Tito has official sanction, thanks to, and I quote, 'the personal interest of Mr. Churchill.'

FIGGIS. But that's splendid!

HIPPO. Hold your horses. 'Personal interest'. Not sure I like that. Smacks of meddling. (*Reads more.*) No, I don't think so. 'Cause he's presented us with a commanding officer!

ADRIAN. Who?

HIPPO. Not Bouncer Malthouse. Back to the knacker's yard for Bouncer. This is somebody else. A captain. But he won't be a captain long.

ADRIAN. His name?

HIPPO. Don't rush me. (*Reads.*) Bothwell.

FIGGIS. Francis Bothwell?

HIPPO. Have you heard of him?

FIGGIS. His father's Hamish Bothwell, Chairman of the Bank of Scotland.

HIPPO. That isn't his fault.

FIGGIS. Oh, quite.

HIPPO. I'm trying to like the bastard. Height?

FIGGIS. One couldn't exactly tell from the photos.

HIPPO. Photos where?

FIGGIS. The Times, I think, and the Daily Mail.

HIPPO. What was he doing in the blasted papers?

FIGGIS. It started with the plot to abduct the Kaiser.

HIPPO. Kaiser Bill?

FIGGIS. Why, yes. As you will know, until last year the Kaiser was living in exile near the Hague. So when the Nazis invaded Holland, somebody had the bright idea of getting him to London and putting him in charge of a German Government-in-exile.

HIPPO. What's all this got to do with . . . ?

FIGGIS. I'm trying to tell you. Captain Bothwell was in command. He got the Kaiser as far as Amsterdam, and they were just about to board a fishing smack when they were challenged by the harbour police. There's a rather silly story doing the rounds at Bush House that they'd mistaken the Kaiser for the Duke of Gloucester. Be that as it may, they raised the alarm, the Kaiser died of a heart attack and it was all hushed up.

HIPPO. And Bothwell got away?

FIGGIS. He escaped from Colditz, twelve months later. That's what got him in the papers.

HIPPO (*disgusted*). If Winston Churchill had scoured the earth, he could hardly have found an officer more designed to send my monkey up the pole.

ADRIAN. Still, he's prime promotion-fodder, wouldn't you say, sir?

HIPPO. True! I'll give him a chance.

The Volunteers have finished: they line up.

LUKA. Mission accomplished, Comrade Brigadier.

HIPPO (*to* FIGGIS). Pass the goblet!

MISS FIGGIS *circulates the whisky.* THE HIPPO *addresses the assembly:*

A new year's dawning! Hope! Horizons! Woolf, for starters: what do you want from the war in the months to come?

ADRIAN. I'm sorry, sir. I was never any good at games.

The Volunteers encourage him.

All right. I hope that history will take its course. And that our mission gets there safely.

HIPPO. Figgis?

FIGGIS. Is this a personality test of some kind? Then I won't say 'victory'. Far too obvious. Peace, of course. I hope the Reading Room at the British Museum survives the war. I hope, some day, that I can work there. Next?

HIPPO (*to the Volunteers*). You! The proletariat! Speak! No, while you're thinking. What I hope . . .

He stops, choked with emotion.

Don't laugh. I've a lot in here, and it's all bunged up.

He thumps his heart.

Dignity for all. And men walk proud. Respect. And justice. Yes, it could be like that. It's up to us.

FIGGIS (*quietly to* ADRIAN). Personally I blame the pills.

HIPPO. Now what we should do, for luck and making it all come true, is somebody tall and dark, a stranger, enter. In a perfect world he'd carry a lump of coal. Who's game?

FRANCIS BOTHWELL *appears above, at the window of* THE HIPPO*'s office. He is tall, dark, aristocratic and very handsome. He wears the uniform of a Brigadier. He is 26.*

BOTHWELL. Is Brigadier Gore down there?

HIPPO (*stares*). Who's that?

BOTHWELL. I'm Francis Bothwell.

HIPPO (*to the others*). Scarper!

Everyone goes. BOTHWELL *slithers down to ground level with amazing grace and speed.* THE HIPPO *pumps his hand.*

BOTHWELL. I tried your office . . .

HIPPO. Empty!

BOTHWELL. No . . .

HIPPO (*not listening*). I burst the bars! To roam the glorious wide and open. I'm the Hippo!

PAGAN *is heard, out of sight, calling 'Mila'. BOTHWELL stares at THE HIPPO's face, which is still stained black with shoe-polish.*

Something the matter?

BOTHWELL. Nothing important.

HIPPO. Good, good, because I thought for a moment you were looking at me in a funny way. Ah, Pagan.

PAGAN *has appeared.*

Distinguished visitor. Francis Bothwell. Who's for the amber fluid?

He looks for the whisky.

PAGAN (*to* BOTHWELL). You must excuse our informality. Festive season.

BOTHWELL. It seems to be catching.

PAGAN (*polite interest*). Is it indeed?

He finds the whisky.

BOTHWELL. It certainly is. I've just barged in on two of your staff who were seeing the New Year in with rather a bang in the Brigadier's hammock.

PAGAN. Oh God!

THE HIPPO *spots the whisky. Grabs it.*

HIPPO. Ah ha! The culprit! Thank you, vicar. (*To* BOTHWELL.) A wee libation?

He holds out the bottle. PAGAN *wanders away in obvious distress, adding to the general impression of mental imbalance. Meanwhile:*

Quite a turnup for the books, your popping up, old chap, and I'm glad to have had the chance to assess your character. And I like the cut of your jib. Heard lots about you. And I didn't like it. So I shall expunge it from the slate of memory. I bring you tidings of an elevatory nature. You will be . . .

He stares at BOTHWELL's *uniform.*

BOTHWELL. What?

HIPPO. Why are you dressed as a Brigadier?

BOTHWELL. I am one.

HIPPO. I have not yet promoted you.

BOTHWELL. I saw the PM at Chequers last weekend, and *he* promoted me.

HIPPO. Oh, thank the Lord!

He whoops with delight.

He told you about our little chinwag, did he?

BOTHWELL. Yes he did.

HIPPO. Because I laid with a trowel about the Tito boys.

BOTHWELL. He told me.

HIPPO. Excellent, excellent.

BOTHWELL. He wants you to know that the mission will have the highest possible status.

HIPPO. Couldn't be better.

BOTHWELL. I shall be the PM's personal emissary to the partisans.

HIPPO. Ah ha.

BOTHWELL. I shall report to Number 10.

HIPPO. And Cairo.

BOTHWELL. Oh indeed. To the Commander-in-Chief himself. DOG will supply and brief me. GHQ will give you every assistance.

HIPPO. Hold it one moment. Are you not on DOG establishment?

BOTHWELL. I am on GHQ establishment.

HIPPO. But you are, are you not, under my command?

BOTHWELL. I am not. Not technically. Not in practice. After
    tonight, I'm tempted to add: not even in fun.

THE HIPPO *recoils.*

HIPPO. You will take that back, before I sing a different tune.

BOTHWELL. 'Swanee River' perhaps?

THE HIPPO *stops in his tracks. A terrible thought strikes
him. He puts his hand up to his face, touches it, sees the
black on his fingers. Looks hard at* BOTHWELL, *makes a
decision.*

HIPPO. You are unsuitable for the post. You will never go to
    Jugoslavia. Nobody at DOG will brief you. You will receive
    no maps, no summaries, no supplies, no men, no transport.
    Get the picture?

BOTHWELL. Yes.

He laughs.

Fascinating. Wouldn't have missed it for the world. Good
night.

To PAGAN:

Rum do, Colonel. Good night to you.

He goes, whistling 'Way down upon the Swanee River'.
THE HIPPO's *stomach gives him a twinge. He clutches it.
Drinks again to knock out the pain. It doesn't work.*

PAGAN. Don't hog it, old boy.

THE HIPPO *gives him the bottle.* PAGAN *drinks.*

HIPPO. Can I trust you, Pagan? What are you thinking? What
    do you want from the war in the months to come?

PAGAN. To destroy the enemy.

HIPPO. You're coming on. I'll tell you a secret. If we want to
    beat the Germans, it is imperative that we beat the British

first. Starting with him. How would it be if we briefed him for the Tito mission, flew him out and dropped him to the Chetniks?

PAGAN. Would we not get a slapdash reputation?

HIPPO. True.

He thinks.

I've got it. Nobble his parachute. Out of the hatch and down he sails and splat. No, as you were. He's sly. Whichever parachute we give the bugger, he'll choose another one. We can't have the whole damn mission going splat. Or can we?

PAGAN. I have a better idea. Do you know Whiteworks?

HIPPO. Rumour-spreading outfit?

PAGAN. That's the fellow. Whiteworks is run by a very dear friend of mine from happier days. One Toby Jenifer. Highly connected. Friend of the CiC. Toby and I have a long-outstanding lunch appointment.

HIPPO. Well?

PAGAN. I shall revive it. You will meet him. You will ask him to spread a rumour concerning Francis Bothwell. Something which would make him unemployable. Make it up.

HIPPO. One snag.

PAGAN. What's that?

HIPPO. He won't believe a vulgar toad like me.

PAGAN. We'll soon fix that. Toby and I were fellow-bankers. I'll make up a third at lunch, and you will follow my lead precisely. He'll believe you then.

HIPPO. Let battle commence!

End of scene.

Scene Three

*Out of the end of the previous scene, a hotel dining table
becomes visible, beautifully laid for lunch. Waiters bring
chairs.* PAGAN *and* THE HIPPO *converge at the table and
take their places.* PAGAN *is ill and drunk, but lucid.* TOBY
JENIFER *is seated between them. Smartly dressed waiters
hover in attendance.*

A pause. JENIFER *and* PAGAN *have already given their
orders.* THE HIPPO *is puzzling over the menu and its
unfamiliar terminology.*

JENIFER. Try the asparagus.

HIPPO. Where's that?

> PAGAN *points it out on the menu.*

> No, I don't think so. Shoot my gut to buggery, sad to say.
> Normally I would be munching a double whisky in the
> Long Bar, would I not, Colonel Pagan?

PAGAN. Oh, indeed.

JENIFER (*with irony*). Indeed.

PAGAN (*to* JENIFER). How is Patricia?

> JENIFER *is riveted by* THE HIPPO *who, hot and ill at
> ease, is unbuttoning his tunic down the front.*

> Isn't she called Patricia?

JENIFER. She's, ah, helping out at a works canteen in Peckham.

PAGAN. Bloody good show.

> *He continues, while* THE HIPPO *reveals his dirty vest.*

Now Margaret, as Patricia might have told you, married her
airline pilot. Cleaned me out, except for some shares she
didn't know about and the house in Suffolk. Went through
hell, old boy, and then my luck went zing, I landed not
precisely on my feet, let's say on more erotic parts of my
anatomy.

JENIFER. How's the work, Tim?

PAGAN *casts an eloquent glance at* THE HIPPO.

PAGAN. See for yourself, eh? (*To* THE HIPPO.) How're we doing?

THE HIPPO *is still studying the menu.*

HIPPO. I'm cogitating. Don't mind me.

PAGAN. How is the rumour factory?

JENIFER (*this is his party piece*). Well it's rather like training ferrets, I imagine. One selects the rumour, mucky little creature, and one strokes its fur, and then one whacks it on the tail and off it shoots, and if it's a good 'un, it'll have made it around the town by sunset.

HIPPO. That reminds me, doesn't it, Colonel Pagan . . . ?

PAGAN. Order your lunch.

HIPPO. I will. In time. This is urgent business. Highly confidential, so we shall not need the monkey-suit brigade.

The waiters take the hint and melt away. To JENIFER:

Francis Bothwell. Know him?

PAGAN (*to* JENIFER). Hamish's eldest.

JENIFER. Yes, I know him well. I understand he's bound for the Balkans.

HIPPO. No, no, no, wrong end of the stick entirely. Bloody almighty cockup and it cannot happen.

JENIFER. Why?

PAGAN. The Brigadier feels he has a character defect.

JENIFER. Has he?

HIPPO. Yes he has, and I want it put about.

JENIFER. May I ask your authority?

HIPPO. No.

JENIFER (*annoyed*). Well, you'd better tell me what this character defect is.

HIPPO. He's arrogant. Looks at people in a sarky fashion.

JENIFER. Bothwells have been pleased with themselves since the battle of Bannockburn. With ample reason.

HIPPO. You'll spread it about then?

JENIFER. I could try. I hardly think it will cut much ice.

HIPPO. You don't?

JENIFER. Why should it?

PAGAN (*to* THE HIPPO). Perhaps you ought to explain the cause of his behaviour.

JENIFER. Well?

HIPPO. Glug trouble. Jekyll and Hyde. Civil enough when he's sober, then the drink starts talking. Daily occurrence. In my office. Puking, legless, half-delirious. Imagine the effect on our courageous allies when he's poured out over the snows in that condition.

JENIFER *is relieved.*

JENIFER. Paratroopers aren't selected for their sobriety. I for one would find it worrying if they were. The test is courage, wouldn't you say, Tim?

PAGAN (*neutral*). Quite.

HIPPO. Oh very much quite.

JENIFER (*to* THE HIPPO). Are you trying to tell me something?

THE HIPPO *looks at* PAGAN *for support.* PAGAN *nods in encouragement and whistles a phrase of 'Swanee River'.*

HIPPO. Well, this is the nub, old boy. And it goes against the grain to talk about a brother-officer behind his back. But facts are facts. He's yellow. That Kaiser caper. Bothwell panicked. Ran like a rabbit. Buggered the whole damn enterprise.

JENIFER (*with distaste*). Are you listening, Tim?

PAGAN. Hung on each word, old bean. It's no use gawping. Do as he says or tell him you don't believe a word.

JENIFER. Whether I believe it isn't the point. It hadn't crossed my mind that I was *meant* to believe it. I imagined Colonel Gore was cooking up some necessary fiction. My reservation was a practical one, the fact that nobody else would believe it either. Am I honestly meant to think that this extraordinary farrago is the truth?

HIPPO. Every word.

JENIFER. Then I'm appalled. And I must tell you, Brigadier, I saw Francis Bothwell eighteen months ago on his father's estate, when he was sober and of splendid character. Can you explain the paradox?

HIPPO. Brain deterioration.

JENIFER. What?

HIPPO. Worse each year. By the time he's thirty, they'll have written him off entirely. He'll be gibbering. Drooling idiot.

He taps his nose.

Syph. And that is *fact*.

JENIFER (*convinced*). Good God!

HIPPO. Pitiful.

JENIFER. Tragic. Utterly tragic.

HIPPO. So you'll put it about, eh?

JENIFER. Certainly not!

HIPPO. Now look here, Colonel Whiteworks . . .

JENIFER. Jenifer.

HIPPO. Jenifer Whiteworks . . .

JENIFER. Whatever the stern demands of war, there are some elementary decencies one must observe. In my opinion. Stuffy and unfashionable though that may sound. And I cannot repeat that story unless you order me to.

HIPPO. That's what I'm doing.

JENIFER *resigns himself to this awful task.*

JENIFER. Very well. Nothing to eat, I think.

He prepares to go.

We shall meet no doubt. Tim, I think you should see a doctor.

He stops. Reflects.

Poor, poor Francis. What a terrible trick of fate. To face disease and a premature death for a natural indiscretion which we've all committed.

HIPPO. Speak for yourself.

JENIFER. Let's not be sanctimonious. All of us, at one time or another, have been . . .

HIPPO. Not with a bloke!

JENIFER. What did you say?

HIPPO. Feller's a bender.

JENIFER. *What?*

HIPPO. You heard me. He caught it off some big buck nigger with a twelve-inch cock.

> JENIFER *doesn't believe this for a moment. He casts his mind back over everything else he's been told. He doesn't believe that either. He's ice-cold angry.* THE HIPPO *continues, oblivious.*

Do you get the picture?

JENIFER. I believe I do.

HIPPO. Makes one ashamed to be an Englishman.

JENIFER. I should think it might.

HIPPO. And you'll . . .

JENIFER. Put it about? You may rest assured I shall report this conversation to the highest quarters. Good day to you both.

He goes.

HIPPO. Funny. He seemed a bit miffed.

PAGAN. You're rumbled.

HIPPO. Eh?

PAGAN. You're finished.

HIPPO. How?

PAGAN. You cannot lie to a man like that about a man like
that. Not if you're not a man like that yourself. Not if you're
you.

THE HIPPO *rises in panic. Looks around for* JENIFER,
who has gone.

HIPPO. You led me on. I trusted you. And you betrayed me.

PAGAN. Everything I believe in is betrayed. Honour. Rank.
My colonel's flash of course was a mere convenience. How
do I know, quite simple, it's like any office, one must sleep
with a secretary. That's the other thing. My marriage. Quite
destroyed, except for the bed thing. Cannot explain this
blooming of desire and, yes, ability. I'm forty-three for
God's sake, what can I do except to welcome it and hope it
lasts, but as for the rest, a nightmare. How can I love a
woman I cannot trust? She only has to move a saucer and I
shudder. I cannot sit at a table with my wife!

He shouts at THE HIPPO.

Do you see what I'm trying to say? I lied to men I respect
because of you. At GHQ. Funds for the Chetnik mission.

HIPPO. You muggins. Call yourself a liar? Not in their league,
old boy. They knew. Except for the CiC. 'Cause they
believe what their Uncle Harry tells them.

PAGAN. You're saying they knew the real resistance and
ignored it?

HIPPO. That's what they're like.

MILA *approaches the table.*

MILA. Tim.

PAGAN *sees her.*

Have you finished your lunch?

PAGAN. Not yet.

MILA *looks at them both. Sits.*

MILA. I was worried about you. We went for a drive, and the car broke down. I can't stay long.

PAGAN. Would you like a raspberry ice?

MILA. You're mad.

PAGAN. I am. I love you.

MILA. Tim, I . . .

PAGAN. Don't say anything.

Pause. After a moment, PAGAN *turns to* THE HIPPO:

Of course, you're right.

End of scene.

Scene Four

England. 1948. A table laid for breakfast. MISS FIGGIS *is drinking a cup of tea. She has the Observer spread in front of her and is doing the crossword.*

ADRIAN *comes in. He's just got up.*

ADRIAN. Morning.

FIGGIS. Hello, Adrian. Do I wish you a happy Easter?

ADRIAN. If you like. Where are our hosts?

FIGGIS. Oh, they're up and about. Do you want the paper?

ADRIAN. Not if you're reading it.

FIGGIS. Take it. I can finish the crossword later.

She gives him the paper. He reads.

Did you sleep well?

ADRIAN. Somebody came in very late last night.

FIGGIS. That was me. I'd been to midnight mass in the village. A nice little Suffolk church. They had a very good turnout. But I missed the gate on the way back. I had to splash my way through a field.

Pause.

I remember Tim showing me a photo once in Cairo, taken, oh, I don't know when, exactly. The house was set in grazing land in those days. But it's sugar beet now, and sprouts.

MILA *comes in with a small basket. She is pregnant. She and* MISS FIGGIS *have seen each other already this morning.*

MILA. Happy Easter.

ADRIAN. Hello, Mila.

MILA (*to* MISS FIGGIS). See what I made.

MISS FIGGIS *looks in the basket.*

FIGGIS. What are they?

MILA. Eggs!

MISS FIGGIS *takes one out of the basket. It has a pattern painted on it.*

FIGGIS. That's very pretty. Are they purely decorative? Or do we eat them?

MILA. If we were in Poland, first we'd roll them down a hill. Adrian, look!

ADRIAN. I've seen them.

MILA *lays out the eggs: one for each.* PETER *comes in. He has been working in the garden. Muddy Wellingtons. To* ADRIAN:

PETER. Good morning.

ADRIAN. 'Morning. You're looking very agricultural.

PETER. Well I am.

He puts his arms round MILA.

We're living off the land, aren't we, my darling?

ADRIAN. I'm going back to bed in a minute.

MILA. You're meant to be writing a book.

PETER. He slept all yesterday.

MILA. He slept all Friday.

FIGGIS. He falls asleep in the Reading Room. Well, only sometimes.

MILA. Eat!

They pick the shells off their decorated eggs and eat. After a while:

PETER. Adrian wants to pick my brains.

ADRIAN. I'm researching the Cairo chapter.

FIGGIS. It's no use asking us. We were cogs. All we saw was what we were working on. None of us knew the overall picture. So we forget what the war was like. We remember the stories we were told by a friend of a friend, and we think they happened.

PETER. Like Kaiser Bill in Amsterdam.

FIGGIS. Oh, very much Kaiser Bill..

PETER. And the invisible tank.

FIGGIS. Yes, that was classic.

MILA. One of those stories was true.

FIGGIS. Oh, which was that?

MILA. The one about how Tim died.

Pause. She goes on eating her egg.

PETER. I can't say I've heard that one.

MILA. It was after you went to Jugoslavia. Tim was ill. He used to sit and cry at his desk. We used to say to men who came for interviews, 'If there's anything strange that Colonel Pagan does, pay no attention.' They asked, 'Why?' We said, 'It's his way of testing how you will react in difficult circumstances.' Once he saw a man for a job in Greece, and half-way through the interview, Tim went white as a sheet and he fell on the floor. The man thought, 'Oh this is an easy one.' He sat and watched. After a bit, he thought, 'Oh, maybe I call for help.' But Tim was dead.

Pause.

ADRIAN. Do you dine out on that?

PETER. She's never mentioned it.

FIGGIS. Surely the Hippo was involved? What I heard, was that he'd called in Whiteworks, and told the most terrible lies about Brigadier Dummett.

ADRIAN. No it was Bothwell. And it all links up. Because when poor old Tim got wind of it, he had an apoplectic fit. I mean, quite literally. And that's what killed him. That's what *I* heard.

MILA. Tim was killed because he knew too much.

FIGGIS. By whom?

MILA. The Russians.

ADRIAN. Oh phooey!

MILA (*angry*). Tim was a hero! A hero!

ADRIAN. The greatest fantasy, of course was Peter's, about the partisans.

PETER. I know what I saw. The heroism of the men and women there. And what they were fighting against was evil. So the war was right. It was a total moral certainty, which I hadn't felt in Cairo to put it mildly. I supported them then, and I support their government now.

ADRIAN. Unreservedly?

PETER. Yes, when you're around.

ADRIAN. Never confuse the leadership with the rank and file.
We all love sturdy peasants. What's foolish of you, Peter, is
to expend that love on a petty-nationalistic oligarchy like
the Tito regime. If the Soviet Union chucked it out
tomorrow and set up a workers' state, it would be utterly
right to do so.

MILA. I'm not happy Peter helped the Reds.

Pause. PETER *is so annoyed he can't think of anything to
say. Pushes his egg away.* MISS FIGGIS *changes the subject.*

FIGGIS. Does anyone know what happened to the Hippo?

It seems that nobody does.

ADRIAN. Do you?

FIGGIS. I know what I *heard.*

End of scene.

Scene Five

Cairo, 1942. THE HIPPO *alone with a suitcase. Lightning,
thunder.*

HIPPO. I've made a vital discovery.

*He puts down his luggage. Takes out his canister of pills,
takes a pill. Reads the label:*

'Take in moderation'. Bollocks. Nothing puts me out. Not
gas. Not chloroform.

*Another concatenation of lightning and thunder, which he
takes as a tedious reminder of some kind.*

Yes, yes, yes, I've got it. Who's that?

*A young officer rides on, driving a Royal Enfield Flying
Flea motorbike. This is* CARP: *he's young, plain, Midlands.*

Major Carp! What do you want? Where am I?

CARP. Cairo airfield.

HIPPO. Am I?

He shakes his head as though awakening from sleep.

So I am.

He is indeed at the airfield. Lights twinkle and aeroplanes are heard revving up. His attention settles on CARP.

What are you doing here, Major?

CARP. I'm not Major any longer. GSO (2) Intelligence Planning (Planning). Rank of Lieutenant-Colonel, goes with the job.

HIPPO. Well done. Well done. I like you, Carp. You're clever but it's not offensive. Scholarship boy. I spotted you when they posted you out as miserable Captain. Raised you up, when not a bugger in the bar would bum a round off you, not with that accent. I've had a quite astounding insight. Struck me today in the course of a fearful meeting. Audience with the CiC. One Colonel Jenifer in attendance. Cutting things were said about me. Guttersnipe. A petty gangster. Morals of a chimpanzee. It didn't surprise me. All my life I've thought those bastards are against me. And they *are* against me. That's the insight. Shattering. After years of patient service. Mute devotion. Grovelling. One exception. New Year's Eve. Young Bothwell. Could have got him if I'd wanted. Could have wangled him under my command, there are ways and means. I'd have had my third Brigadier. Promotion. Fame and glory. And an army of one million partisans. What a fantastic prize! But I looked at Bothwell. Tall, blueblooded, pointy hero. And I couldn't abide him. So I picked a fight and lost. A proud defeat. Because I'm sick to death of being their Little Lord Fauntleroy. I tell you what I am, eh, Carp, I am a damned rebellious stumpy, booted down to the rank of Major, out of a job, sitting on my only suitcase on the tarmac at the airfield while my future is decided.

CARP. That's what I've come to tell you.

HIPPO. Eh?

CARP. Your future.

HIPPO. Yes, I'm listening. Fire away.

CARP. We need a volunteer.

HIPPO. Don't look at me, old boy. Never volunteered for
anything in my life. Staunch principle. Unless it were
extremely attractive but I hae ma doots. What is it? Might
one cop it? What's the danger ratio?

CARP. Hundred per cent.

HIPPO. Ah. Well, then I might just reconsider. Thought for
a moment you were saying it might be hazardous. But if
it's . . .

Thinks again.

What? You don't mean . . . ? Blimey.

CARP. Plans are in place for a major assault on Europe. The
landings will take place in Sicily. It is vital that the enemy
is deceived. A senior officer is required to drive a jeep along
the German lines near Tripoli, where at a prearranged signal
it will explode. Amongst the officer's remains will be found
the plans for a supposed invasion of Sardinia.

HIPPO. When you say 'volunteer' . . . ?

CARP. Oh, it's totally pukka, bona fide, you can spit in my eye
if you like. They simply . . .

HIPPO. . . . thought I might be interested?

CARP. That's right.

HIPPO. Because it's not as though you're selling it very hard.

CARP. There is a positive side. In order to give the maximum
credibility to the plans, the officer concerned will have been
. . . I'm sorry, will be . . . a general.

THE HIPPO *is silent.*

The pay is excellent and I believe the perks include . . .

HIPPO. I'm thinking.

PETER's voice is heard:

PETER. Sir!

PETER appears out of the darkness. He is in full battledress and kitted out for a drop.

PETER. It's good to see you, sir. We heard you'd got the . . .

HIPPO. No no no, it's quite the contrary. I'm being heavily wooed. The mission's going tonight, eh?

PETER. In a few minutes. I'm just escaping from the Wing-Commander's hospitality.

HIPPO. There's Captain Woolf.

ADRIAN appears from another direction, dressed as usual.

Over here! (*To* PETER.) He's looking glum. (*To* ADRIAN.) How are your Jugs?

ADRIAN. It would have been nice if they'd been allowed to drink with the sahibs. But they're fine. Thrilled to be going back home. For ever, hopefully.

He's on the verge of tears.

I'm sorry. Pig of a cold.

BOTHWELL is there at a distance, dressed for the drop.

HIPPO. And there's young Lochinvar!

BOTHWELL. Major Crago! We're leaving pronto.

He disappears into the darkness.

ADRIAN (*to* PETER). Historic moment.

PETER. Yes, isn't it just. Look after yourself. I'm sorry you . . .

ADRIAN. No, no, it's fine. I'm terribly pleased. So very happy for you all. Take care.

ADRIAN and PETER embrace, then part in different directions. No-one there except for CARP and THE HIPPO.

CARP. Have you decided?

HIPPO. Tell them, thanks for thinking of me but I have to refuse. It isn't just the rank. It never was. It's being remembered. Who, in years to come, will remember a clumsy clod of a general whose only achievement was to leave this world in a bang and a puff of smoke?

CARP. They'll remember you for winning the war in Jugoslavia.

HIPPO. Will they? *Did* I?

CARP. Policy was wrong. Everyone knew. But you were the only man with the guts to change it.

HIPPO. Me and Winston. Perfectly true.

CARP. The only question is whether you'll be remembered as a miserable Major? Or a General?

HIPPO. If you put it like that, old chap . . . the sky's the limit.

He shakes CARP*'s hand in agreement.*

Done.

Stirring music. Out of sight, a Liberator aircraft throbs into life. An RAF NCO comes into sight saying 'Come along, lads.' The mission follows him into sight en route to the 'plane: a crowd of men and officers, in full battledress and parachute harness. The Jugoslav Volunteers are among them. So are PETER *and* BOTHWELL. *Different emotions from them all, some joking and larking about, some checking some last-minute detail, some grave.*

At the sight of THE HIPPO, *several peel off to salute and shake his hand with warmth. Others join them: for a few moments, he's surrounded. Meanwhile:*

HIPPO. Bothwell! No hard feelings. Bloody good luck to you. Peter! Give them hell eh? Up and at 'em! (*To another.*) Yes it's me! They booted me out an' I came bounding back. (*To others.*) Know what they are? Up there? Top floor? A bunch of bastards. Hate me. Always have done. But they cannot do without me. Back they crawled. And I said 'yes'. 'Cause

I'm the Hippo! I'm their British backbone!

Everyone else has gone. Image: apotheosis of THE HIPPO, *alone, triumphant.*

End of play.

MRS. KLEIN

Mrs. Klein was first staged in the Cottesloe auditorium of the National Theatre of Great Britain. First preview was 5 August 1988; press night was 10 August 1988. The cast was as follows:

MRS. KLEIN   Gillian Barge
PAULA   Zoë Wanamaker
MELITTA   Francesca Annis

Director Peter Gill
Set designed by John Gunter
Costumes by Stephen Brimson-Lewis
Music by Terry Davies

Characters

MRS. KLEIN, *fifty-two*
PAULA, *early thirties*
MELITTA, *early thirties*

Place: London

Time: Spring 1934

Nicholas Wright gratefully acknowledges the use of Phyllis Grosskurth's biography *Melanie Klein*, published by Hodder and Stoughton, 1985.

ACT ONE

MRS. KLEIN *is sorting through old papers.* PAULA *is listening.*

MRS. KLEIN. It's quite incredible what one keeps.

Tears up a photograph. Finds a piece of paper.

This is a poem he wrote.

Reads it.

Excuse me.

She cries. Holds her hand out. PAULA *takes it. She slowly stops crying.*

I think that's it till next time. So: our coffee should be ready. You'll have some?

PAULA. Thank you.

MRS. KLEIN. Now what's this?

PAULA. I've brought you something.

It's a cake-box.

MRS. KLEIN. But my dear you shouldn't have spent your money. No don't tell me.

Opens it.

Paula, this is fantastic of you. Poppy-seed cake, no reason you should believe this, was my mother's speciality.

Gives PAULA *the poem.*

You can read this.

She goes out. PAULA *reads.* MRS. KLEIN *comes back with coffee. Pours.*

MRS. KLEIN. I'm in a very adequate state, all things considered. I cough a lot but then I'm smoking more. I sleep enough, not much. I have my knock-out drops if I should need them but I'm holding off so far. No dreams, which is unusual for me. Normally I'm an active, colourful dreamer. Now each night the show is cancelled. Most annoying. Milk?

PAULA. No thank you.

MRS. KLEIN. Then I'll need another cup.

PAULA. It doesn't matter.

MRS. KLEIN. Sure?

PAULA. Quite sure.

MRS. KLEIN *gives her the cup.*

MRS. KLEIN. You're welcome. Chiefly what I feel is numbness. Here inside. As though some vital part of me had been removed. The tears don't help. All they do is make a thorough nuisance of themselves. And then they stop and leave me feeling exactly as I did before. Remote. Closed up. And dead. You'll have some cake?

PAULA. Yes thank you.

MRS. KLEIN. So: my work goes on. I read, I write, I entertain a few old friends, I see my patients. Clear a space. I'm on my own today. My cleaning woman has a family crisis in Southend. Or so she says. The truth is that she needs a break from my unnatural calm. And so do I. But there we are, I may not like it but I'm stuck with it. I don't know why. I don't have insight into my emotions, not just now. Some other time. So: eat.

They do.

But why no dreams? No, that's enough about me. The poem, you read it?

PAULA. Yes.

MRS. KLEIN. So tell me.

PAULA. It was written when he was young – .

MRS. KLEIN. He was. He was a boy, he was fifteen.

PAULA. It's a love-poem. Though the woman seems older than him. Who was she?

MRS. KLEIN. I doubt she ever existed. Not in life. Though to my son, of course, she breathed, she moved, she comforted. She was the mother.

PAULA. Yes I see.

MRS. KLEIN. She was myself. I would like you to do some work for me.

PAULA. What kind of work?

MRS. KLEIN. You're not too busy?

PAULA. No.

MRS. KLEIN. Thank God, thank God. Have some more cake.

PAULA. No thank you.

MRS. KLEIN *has some more.*

MRS. KLEIN. I'm famished. I've been eating scraps. Cheese on toast, sardines on toast, ridiculous. And so this morning up I got and cooked myself a hearty British breakfast. Then I looked at it. And then I gave it to the pekinese. He's not here now. He'll be living the life of Riley for the next ten days, in kennels, up by Primrose Hill. He won't be bothering you. His name is Nanki-Poo. A wandering minstrel he. You know your Gilbert and Sullivan?

PAULA. When you say he won't be bothering me – ?

MRS. KLEIN. Quite so. Let me explain.

A set of keys.

These are my spare keys to the front door. My cleaning woman has her own. Keys to the rooms upstairs, my bedroom, my consulting room, I'm putting somewhere safe, she'll tell you if you ask, but for emergencies. She says she'll water the plants. If you could watch the window-boxes. Let me see.

Her notebook.

I made a list. I felt compelled to. And this in itself is strange, because my memory's good. I woke at four o'clock this morning, wondering, 'What am I making lists for, is there perhaps some paranoiac aspect to it?', but I couldn't think it through at that hour. I've stopped the milk. I've stopped The Times, I've stopped the Daily Mail. The central heating has instructions pinned above it. Sunny is with my daughter. Sunny is the car, the Sunbeam. Make of it what you will. Food is in the fridge, and when you leave at night please check the windows and of course the door. Now is there anything else domestic? Good.

PAULA. I'm sorry – . Do you want – ?

MRS. KLEIN. If I could do my list? And questions after.

At the desk.

Letters here. Periodicals here. Messages on this pad.

Letters.

These I would appreciate your posting for me.

A pin-box.

I've left some money here for odd expenses and your travel. I won't feel happy otherwise. I'll worry that you're feeling in some way imposed upon. So spend it freely. Here. Five shillings. Good, that's settled.

Another letter.

This I don't know what to do with. It arrived this morning. Marked: 'To await return'. It comes from Dr. Schmideberg. I don't like it. I don't even like the envelope. It looks as though it's about to burst with hostile matter. This is what professional enemies are like. They're vampires. They're dependent. They want love. And so they nag and pester. Should I read it? Should I leave it? Should I burn it? If I burn it, can I blame the post? I'll – . No I can't decide.

She puts it down.

At such a time I don't deserve to be so persecuted. Next. The proofs.

PAULA. The proofs?

MRS. KLEIN. You know the system?

PAULA. If you tell me what it is you want I'll – .

MRS. KLEIN. Fine, come look.

Proofs on the desk.

You've read the book?

PAULA. Of course, I – .

MRS. KLEIN. I thought so. This will be the second German-language edition.

A book.

This is the first. There are some misprints which I've put a ring round. So you must check both. I've marked in pencil where I want revisions.

Notes.

These are they. This arrow goes back, then skip, then on, yes?

Another book.

Some revisions, though not all, are in the second English edition, here.

A dictionary.

English-German, German-English.

Manuscript.

Here's the new chapter. So you must watch the numbering.

Another manuscript.

This is the foreword. Do you type?

PAULA. Two fingers.

MRS. KLEIN. Likewise. Three copies. Carbon here. You understand?

PAULA. Yes.

MRS. KLEIN. Sure?

PAULA. Quite sure? When is the copy date?

MRS. KLEIN. Forget the copy date, it's weeks ago, I want them posted to Vienna first post Wednesday at the latest.

PAULA. Fine. I'll show you what I've done on Tuesday.

MRS. KLEIN. I won't be here.

PAULA. You won't – ?

MRS. KLEIN. I have a funeral to attend.

PAULA. I'm sorry, yes, I see, so will you –

MRS. KLEIN. I shall be back the following weekend.

PAULA. Then you won't have seen them.

MRS. KLEIN. Plainly not.

PAULA. So if there's anything I get wrong – .

MRS. KLEIN. They'll print it wrong and I'll look stupid. But I'm not expecting that to happen.

PAULA. Why?

MRS. KLEIN. Because I trust you.

PAULA. But we've never met.

MRS. KLEIN. I've seen you at the Institute, you're highly thought of. Will you do it?

PAULA. Yes.

MRS. KLEIN. You're a good girl. I didn't ask you if you'd like a glass of sherry.

PAULA. No.

MRS. KLEIN. Too early? Likewise.

Pause.

You like my flowers? I shan't be looking at them, take some home.

PAULA. I haven't room.

MRS. KLEIN (*dry*) . No room for a bunch of flowers? You're
not by any chance exaggerating?

PAULA. Perhaps a little.

MRS. KLEIN. Just a little.

Pause. Relaxed. They are both accustomed to long pauses.

Besides I liked your comments after Edward Glover read
his paper on suggestion. At that Scientific Meeting. You
were very acute. You shut him up for weeks, that's no mean
tribute. When was it now? At Christmas. Yes, the
seminar-room was full of shopping-bags. That was you?

PAULA. It was.

MRS. KLEIN. I knew it. Tell me, who is worse in your
professional estimation, Glover or Schmideberg? No I
mustn't compromise you. Glover's not a dunce exactly but
he's too dogmatic. Like some mid-Victorian,
mutton-chop-whiskered tyrant of the breakfast table,
ghastly.

Laughs, then stops.

Dr. Schmideberg needs help.

Pause.

The heck with it.

She goes to the drinks cabinet and pours two sherries.

So we've never met? I felt I knew you.

PAULA. We've been introduced. But never – .

MRS. KLEIN. Never sat and talked. It's very pleasant. And
I'm glad you arrived a fraction late. I was with a patient.
Nine years old last week. So, not my youngest but my most
demanding. He wouldn't stay in the consulting-room today,
he felt it pressing in on him, he took against it. So we came
down here. There, that's his train, his Daddy-train he calls
it. He played, I played. If you'd been on time I wouldn't
have let you in. Because my patients cannot be disturbed.
The world must wait. I'm sure you feel the same. Now this
is a Manzanilla which I'm rather proud of.

They sit and drink their sherry. Pause.

MRS. KLEIN. You have family back at home?

PAULA. I do.

MRS. KLEIN. You hear from them?

PAULA. My mother writes. My brothers.

MRS. KLEIN. Have you sisters?

PAULA. No.

MRS. KLEIN. That's not a simple 'no'.

PAULA. I had an older sister.

MRS. KLEIN. Were you close in age?

PAULA. She died before I was born.

MRS. KLEIN. So you're important to your mother.

PAULA. Yes.

MRS. KLEIN. To comfort her. Or so you see it. And you're married?

PAULA. Yes.

MRS. KLEIN. He's not an analyst?

PAULA. He's a doctor.

MRS. KLEIN. That isn't what I asked.

PAULA. He's not an analyst.

MRS. KLEIN. He doesn't approve?

PAULA. He doesn't approve.

MRS. KLEIN. And where've you put him?

PAULA. Where – ?

MRS. KLEIN. He's not in England?

PAULA. No. In Zurich.

MRS. KLEIN. Ah. So did he – ?

PAULA. He left Germany first. I stayed on. Because there wasn't so much pressure on me.

MRS. KLEIN. Though I heard you'd been arrested.

PAULA. It wasn't serious. Just a small misunderstanding. They searched the house and took some books and dropped the charge.

Pause.

MRS. KLEIN. It frightened you.

PAULA. Yes.

MRS. KLEIN. You're Jewish.

PAULA. Yes. But it was worse for my husband. He was more political than I am.

MRS. KLEIN. When you say your husband was political, do you mean he isn't now or that he's no longer your husband?

PAULA. We're divorced.

MRS. KLEIN. And how do you find it?

PAULA. Lonely.

MRS. KLEIN. Likewise.

Gives PAULA *her glass, marks a place on it with her finger.*

MRS. KLEIN. I can manage that much more. And help yourself.

PAULA *pours sherry.*

MRS. KLEIN. My son was fond of politics when he was younger. And his friends. Just like in any other intellectual family. But I've never been political myself. Although I've had good cause to. I've been spat at in the street. My children too. And now I hear each week from friends at home, the windows smashed, the star of Judah painted on the doors, the papers scattered, the maid hysterical, the children in tears. I know about it, thank you, and it won't get better. I can't stop it. You can't. Can your husband? In these terrible times we live in? And it doesn't interest me to try. That's not my style.

She sees her sherry, drinks.

Somebody said you had a daughter.

PAULA. What?

MRS. KLEIN. Your daughter.

PAULA. I'm sorry I didn't hear you. I've a daughter, yes. She's nine. She's in Berlin. She's with some Catholic friends.

MRS. KLEIN. And will she join you?

PAULA. Soon.

MRS. KLEIN. So what is your problem?

PAULA. I'll need a decent place to live.

MRS. KLEIN. Where are you now?

PAULA. In Bethnal Green.

MRS. KLEIN. I've never been there, what's it like?

PAULA. It's horrible. It's a slum.

MRS. KLEIN. And do you practise there?

PAULA. I try to.

MRS. KLEIN. It must be hard.

PAULA. It's impossible. Either my patients can't afford to pay me or they leave.

MRS. KLEIN. It's early days.

PAULA. I'm thirty-four. I don't have a proper coat. I've never lived like this.

MRS. KLEIN. You're angry.

PAULA. Yes.

MRS. KLEIN. You should apply to change your visa.

PAULA. I have.

MRS. KLEIN. Then you must ask again. I'll put a word in for you. No, don't thank me. I do little enough for you these days. Pass me that box.

It's the box with Hans's letters in it.

I feel that Hans would like his poem to go to you.

She gives PAULA *the scrap of paper.*

PAULA. I can't accept it.

MRS. KLEIN. No strings. It's his.

PAULA. Thank you.

She takes it.

MRS. KLEIN. But there's something on your mind.

PAULA. I don't know why you're doing this. Why you're letting me help you. Isn't there someone else who – ?

MRS. KLEIN. Who?

PAULA. You have your English friends.

MRS. KLEIN. I was holidaying in St. Ives last week and a very good English friend came with me. Mrs. Riviere. I like her, she's a loyal colleague and an adequate clinician, not outstanding. We stayed a week, then motored back and stopped in Salisbury. A bed and breakfast place, no heating, didn't like dogs and Mrs. Riviere discovered that she'd left her fox-fur back in Cornwall. This is a woman who takes a fox-fur on a walking holiday. So she rang the hotel, and suddenly it's the manager's wife. 'Is that Mrs. Klein?' 'No, it's her friend, I think I left my fox-fur on the terrace – '. But it's me the woman wants to talk to. There's been a telephone-call for me, from Budapest, a foreign lady, Mrs. Vago. 'Yes', I say, 'My sister-in-law. And what was so important that she telephones?' I'd left the number here, so – . 'Is it bad news?' I ask. The woman says: 'It is my duty – '. She was trying to be considerate. I say, don't go around the houses, I'm a grown-up woman, I'm sitting down. She says, it's about my son. He's had a climbing accident. I'm sitting in the hallway looking at a green baize board with postcards on it. Stonehenge. I was looking at it, thinking, 'What does that mean?' She was talking. 'Are you there?' She thought I'd fainted. I said: 'Tell me please: this accident my son had: was it fatal?' She replied: 'I'm sorry,

Mrs. Klein, you won't believe this but I can't remember.' I said, 'Don't worry, I believe you, but I can't explain it to you, not right now, just tell me: have you written it down?' She says: 'I'll find it'. I waited. In a state of some suspense. I heard her shuffling papers, banging drawers. Then it struck me: how, without appearing callous, would I raise the subject of my friend's fox-fur? And I was worried about her fur because I didn't *really*, *absolutely* think she'd sympathise. Although she did. And she was admirable. But yet I didn't trust her. Why? Because I don't trust any of them. Not with this. Not now. They don't feel homelike. I want my home around me. I want the good things close and safe. I want to hear the German language. You speak German and you bring me poppy-seed cake. Also I like you.

She passes the box to PAULA.

MRS. KLEIN. Put it beneath the stairs and bring my coat and hat. And my umbrella. And my bags, no, leave them there but count them, there are two and a hatbox.

PAULA. Are you leaving now?

MRS. KLEIN. Yes now, the taxi's due in – . Check the gloves are in the pockets.

PAULA *gets her coat, etc. while* MRS. KLEIN *writes down a telephone number.* PAULA *comes back with coat, etc.*

MRS. KLEIN. You can reach me at this number. Budapest is not that far, my sister-in-law speaks perfect German. Now do I need to spend a penny. No.

She dresses.

I won't suggest you see me to the station. You'd be better advised to start the work at once.

Checks in her notebook.

Scissors. Needles. Who needs needles.

Doorbell rings.

Ticket. Passport. Money. Glasses.

Doorbell.

MRS. KLEIN. Glasses. Glasses. Say I'm ready. Take the bags
out.

PAULA *goes out.* MRS. KLEIN *finds her glasses.*

Keys.

*She takes a large bunch of keys out of her handbag. Locks
the drinks cabinet. Finds Dr. Schmideberg's letter; puts it in
the filing cabinet. At some point the taxi driver hoots his
horn.* MRS. KLEIN *puts the keys in the bookshelf and
selects a book to hide them behind. One last look round.
She goes out.*

PAULA *comes back. Puts on a light, draws the curtains.
Sits at the desk, moves things round to find a working order.
Starts work.*

Music.

Time passes.

Some hours later. PAULA *is still working. Front door heard
opening and closing.*

PAULA. Hello?

MELITTA *comes in.*

MELITTA. What the bloody hell are you doing here?

PAULA. I'm reading proofs.

MELITTA. What for?

PAULA. She asked me to.

MELITTA. When?

PAULA. This afternoon.

MELITTA. She wasn't here this afternoon.

PAULA. I saw her.

MELITTA. Here?

PAULA. Yes here.

MELITTA. Oh Jesus Christ.

PAULA. What is it?

MELITTA. Nothing.

PAULA. Would you like some coffee?

MELITTA. No. I need a drink. And you?

PAULA. I'm not thirsty.

MELITTA. Never stopped *me*.

Tries the drinks cupboard.

It's locked.

PAULA. Let me try it.

Does.

That's strange.

Tries again.

It is. I'm sorry.

MELITTA. Darling it's not your fault. You carry on.

PAULA. I will. Did that sound rude? She wants them done by
   Wednesday and it's taken me four hours to do one chapter.

Pause. MELITTA moves around the room.

MELITTA. Aren't you freezing?

PAULA. No.

MELITTA. Why don't you put the heating on?

PAULA. I tried. It didn't light and I was worried I might break
   it so I left it. Let me finish.

*Pause. MELITTA looks over PAULA's shoulder at her
work.*

MELITTA. I'm in this.

PAULA. I know, I've just been doing the footnote.

MELITTA. And that's not an ashtray.

PAULA. No?

MELITTA. It's part of a coffee-set.

Replaces saucer with ashtray.

Here.

Empties stubs, moves around, stacks sherry glasses and generally tidies up.

PAULA. Are you here for something special?

MELITTA. No, I happened to be driving past and saw the light on. Someone's moved a book.

PAULA. Not me.

MELITTA. So let me get this straight, you saw her here this afternoon.

PAULA. That's right.

MELITTA. Because she should have left on Tuesday.

PAULA. No, she left as planned. I'm sure of that. Because when Walter rang me – .

MELITTA. *Walter* rang you?

PAULA. Yes, he – .

MELITTA. Why?

PAULA. He had a message. That she wanted me to call on her. She'd got my letter and she – .

MELITTA. Letter?

PAULA. Yes. I wrote a letter. Everyone else was writing to her. I assumed you wouldn't mind.

MELITTA. Why should I mind?

PAULA. I mean, I didn't think *she'd* mind.

MELITTA. And so the sequence was: you wrote a letter to my mother and she sent an invitation via my husband. That's what happened.

PAULA. That's what happened.

MELITTA. And?

PAULA. She asked me if I'd – .

MELITTA. No not you.

PAULA. Your mother?

MELITTA. Yes my mother. How did she seem?

PAULA tidies her papers for an orderly start next day.

PAULA. Her dreams have stopped, I don't know if she told you. And she cries from time to time but the tears don't help. She's still denying the loss. Is this what you want to know, I don't – ?

MELITTA. Go on.

PAULA. She's trying to re-instate the lost loved object: keeping Hans's letters in a place of safety. Tearing other papers up, because she sees them perhaps as hostile. She has periods of elation. And of deep depression. She's in mourning.

MELITTA. Did she mention me?

PAULA. She said you had the car.

MELITTA. What else?

PAULA. I don't remember.

MELITTA. You're a liar.

PAULA. That may be. I can't discuss it, not at this time of night. I'm sorry Melitta.

She goes out. MELITTA *tries to open top drawer of filing cabinet. Locked. Goes to desk, rummages round in top drawers. Finds only pins, elastic bands, etc. Moves away.* PAULA *comes back wearing a hat and coat.*

MELITTA. You've got your coat on.

PAULA. Yes. It's late, I'll miss my Underground.

MELITTA. I'll drive you home.

PAULA. What for?

MELITTA. Oh don't you want me to?

PAULA. I'd love you to. I hate the tube. It's full of drunks and madmen. But it just so happens that through no decision of my own I live the other end of London.

MELITTA. But I've got the car.

PAULA. I'll pay for the petrol.

MELITTA. Rubbish, you can't afford it.

PAULA. Fine. Let's go.

MELITTA. Let's stay for a moment.

PAULA. Not too long. I'm tired. (*Her eyes are strained.*) I have to check each word. Although she's changing nothing essential. Misprints. Extra foot-notes. Foreword. Brand new chapter. (*Laughs.*) Quite a lot in fact but nothing essential.

MELITTA. So you're doing her secretarial work?

PAULA. Not really.

MELITTA. And her letters, will you file her letters?

PAULA. No.

MELITTA. Although they're streaming in in sackfuls, so it seems.

PAULA. They won't need filing.

MELITTA. So you'll put them where?

PAULA. In here. (*Basket.*) The filing cabinet's locked.

MELITTA. Well that's a bore. She asked me to collect some papers. But I don't know where the keys are.

PAULA. I don't know.

MELITTA. Well somebody must.

PAULA. The cleaning woman knows. They had an arrangement, hide them – somewhere in the house, I don't know where, it's not my business.

Pause.

Most of the house is locked. She's locked the cellar door, she's locked the rooms upstairs. It's symbolic. The house is her.

Pause. PAULA *smiles.*

Let's go.

MELITTA. When I was briefly – fairly briefly – couple of months – or less – prevailed upon to be her private secretary – I threw a vase and hit that bit of wall behind you.

PAULA. I'm reading proofs. Which suits me fine. I don't like weekends at the best of times, they're lonely and depressing so I don't mind helping. But I'm not her secretary, I'm not her anything else, let's make that clear.

MELITTA *looks up a number in her address book.*

MELITTA. There's a fascinating paper by Ferenczi on neurotic weekends. He says that during the week our work routine soaks up aggressive feelings. Here we are.

Finds number. Dials.

But then at weekends they let fly. You follow? That's why Sunday is the day we dread the most. Pandora's box stuffed full of nameless hatreds. And the lid not properly closed. (*To telephone:*) Oh bloody answer. Stupid savages. Hello. Oh thank you, can I speak to Mrs. P? (*To herself:*) Oh Bugger. Pow. Pownall. (*Into telephone:*) Mrs. Pountney. Phew. Yes this is Dr. Schmideberg speaking. S.C.H – . Doctor, that's right. No, no-one's ill, I simply – . (*To* PAULA *in comic cockney:*) 'Gawn to fetch 'er 'usband.' Hello. This is – . No, there's nothing wrong, I have your name down here in my address-book as an avenue to Mrs. Pountney, I believe she lives on the floor above you. Yes I do, it's twenty to eleven.

PAULA. Melitta.

MELITTA *in fury bangs the telephone on the desk.*

MELITTA. I'm sorry, I dropped the phone. That's very kind, if you could have a look, that's right. Tell her it's Melitta. She knows me, yes, she very kindly cleans my mother's house

for her. Tell her I'm there, I'm here, and everything's locked
up and ask her where the keys are. No there isn't any need
to – . (*To* PAULA:) Now he's putting his wife back on.

PAULA. Melitta.

MELITTA. What.

PAULA. She's gone away for the weekend.

MELITTA. Mrs. Pountney?

PAULA *nods.*

MELITTA (*to telephone*). One moment please. (*To* PAULA:)
Has she gone far?

PAULA. To South – . South something.

MELITTA. Southport? Southsea?

PAULA. No, it's something anal.

MELITTA. Southend.

PAULA. That sounds right.

MELITTA (*to telephone*). Thank you, I've just found out.
Good night.

Rings off.

Damn that woman. Damn her. God rot her to hell. Vile
crone. I've begged my mother a thousand times to sack her.
But she won't. She can't. She sees the cleaning-woman as
her mother. Wouldn't you say?

PAULA. It crossed my mind, Melitta, but I didn't like to call
attention to it. Can we go now?

MELITTA. Did she get my letter?

PAULA. Yes.

MELITTA. And did she read it?

PAULA. Not while I was there. She said you'd marked it to
await return. No, let's be frank. She felt attacked by it. So
she was hostile to the letter and to you. But not you, her
daughter. No. To Dr. Schmideberg. She only spoke of you

as Dr. Schmideberg. The daughter's good, she loves her, but the doctor's bad, it's casebook stuff. It won't last. She'll read your letter soon. In fact she probably took it with her.

MELITTA. Jesus Christ.

PAULA. What now?

MELITTA. I'm feeling sick.

PAULA. Do you want a glass of water?

MELITTA. No.

PAULA. Try putting your head between your knees.

MELITTA. I need a drink.

PAULA. Let's see what we can do.

Goes to the drinks cabinet. Examines it. Takes out the top drawer.

I thought so.

Reaches down inside.

One can always find a way in somehow, as my professor would say.

Gets bottles and glasses out.

Whisky? There's two kinds. Oh this is Irish. Irish Scotch, that's rather amusing.

MELITTA. Pour it.

PAULA. Yes I am doing.

MELITTA. One for you.

PAULA. I have.

They drink.

PAULA. I bought a whisky once in a public house. In Bethnal Green. But it was such a noisy and disgusting place I couldn't enjoy it. This is different. This is homelike.

Pause.

MELITTA. Do you have those dreams where something absolutely vital has been hidden away? In some familiar place? You search and search. But the handles keep on coming off the doors. Or empty rooms are suddenly crowded. Or the railway-ticket's missing from your handbag, or the platform's vanished. And you can't admit whatever it is you're doing. Because it's shameful. Do you?

PAULA. They're anxiety dreams. Everyone has them.

MELITTA. I feel I'm in one all the time.

PAULA. I dream I've killed a child. I told my analyst. She interpreted that I'd felt deserted by her over the Easter break. I said I doubted that was much to do with it, I'd been having this dream for thirty years. She said, 'Ah ha, and my consulting-room is number 30.'

MELITTA. Are we like that?

PAULA. I hope not. What about yours?

MELITTA. She wasn't giving satisfaction so I sacked her.

PAULA. What went wrong?

MELITTA. I thought she was my mother. And I couldn't work through it. Couldn't stop thinking, 'damn the bitch', or 'does she love me?'. So she thought, and I agreed, that I was stuck in the transference. I'm a sucker for transference. Can't resist it. Do it to anyone. Dentist. Window-cleaner. Nanki Poo. So on we slogged. For years and years. And nothing changed. Except that bit by bit I realised that to all intents and purposes she *was* my mother. It was my mother put me on to her. She reads my mother's books, she quotes them word for word and once a month she meets her for tea at Whiteleys. And I couldn't bear it, darling.

PAULA. Who've you gone to now?

MELITTA. Never you mind.

PAULA. I'd like to change my analyst.

MELITTA. Who do you have your eye on?

PAULA. Well it's more a question would she take me.

MELITTA *spills her whisky. Composes herself. Marks a level on the glass with one finger.*

MELITTA. Be a good girl and fill it up to *here* this time.

PAULA *does. She looks at the bottle.*

PAULA. It's seven years old. She must be quite a connoisseur.

MELITTA. She is. We drove through France two years ago and just as we were getting on quite well she went in for a claret tasting competition and won first prize. They'd never had a woman champion. Now the mayor sends her a postcard every Christmas. She's a local hero.

PAULA *smiles.*

It isn't funny, being her daughter. Try it. Perhaps you have.

PAULA. I don't know what you mean.

MELITTA. You've changed.

PAULA. How's that?

MELITTA. You're like some stubborn, slow amoeba making its gains by stealth.

PAULA *goes to the pin-box and rummages for her five shillings.*

Just what do you think you're doing?

PAULA. I'm getting a taxi.

MELITTA. Put that back.

PAULA. It's my expenses.

MELITTA. Well you might have told me you had taxi-money.

PAULA. I forgot.

MELITTA. Forgot. You didn't want to leave. You're burrowing in.

PAULA *throws the box on the ground . It opens and the money falls out.*

PAULA. I have a mother of my own. I don't need yours. If that's the undercurrent. Why do you think I'd want to hurt

you? Why? You're like a sister to me. You've been kind
and good and generous to me. Nobody else from home
has helped me. Not till now. Until your mother, true. Who
seems neurotically attached to me for some strange reason.
I can't help it. And I don't care tuppence for your boring
little Oedipal tangles. I have other problems thank you.
I've a daughter in Berlin, I have consulting-rooms in
Bethnal Green.

MELITTA. Who put you there?

PAULA. Not her.

MELITTA. They all did. At the Institute. Committee level.
Refugees not wanted. Not in Hampstead. Too much healthy
competition. That's why they've dumped you all in these
extraordinary places.

PAULA. You don't surprise me. Analysts are only human.
If you threaten our professional livelihoods you'll get some
very primitive responses. That was grubby of you.

MELITTA. Did she tell you how he died?

PAULA. She said a climbing accident.

MELITTA. He killed himself.

Pause.

PAULA. How do you know?

MELITTA. I rang my aunt. Auntie Jolan. Mrs. Vago. Talks for
ever, cost a fortune. I could tell at once that she was hiding
something. So I asked her very obliquely. Where he went
that morning. What he wore. All the little details that I
needed to complete the picture. She resisted. Started
howling. Then she banged the phone down. But I'd got my
answers. I've got good material. And I've worked it
through. I've reached the only possible interpretation.

PAULA. Does your mother know?

MELITTA. Well that depends on whether or not she read my
letter.

PAULA. Oh Melitta. She'll be – .

MELITTA. Yes I know.

PAULA. You told her?

MELITTA. Yes!

PAULA. It's horrible.

MELITTA. Yes I know.

PAULA. How could you?

MELITTA. Well I think I must be barmy.

Another drink for both.

MELITTA. When you saw it, where was it left exactly?

PAULA.There. (*The desk.*) It's gone now.

MELITTA. Yes I looked.

Pause.

PAULA. I'm starving.

MELITTA. Likewise.

Pause.

PAULA. Was the letter very – ?

MELITTA. Very detailed. Very convincing. Very persecutorily sadistic.

PAULA. Oh my God.

MELITTA. Exactly.

Pause.

MELITTA. I was sitting in the Wigmore Hall tonight. And they were playing Schubert. So divine. And all that horrible hatred seeped away. I felt that I was looking at it from high up. From somewhere in the ceiling. It was like a pile of rotting clothes. Far distant. From my dizzy height of rational thinking. I felt utterly sane. So I came round here to get my letter back. It seemed so simple. Now all I can imagine is my mother in her first class Pullman, looking for some further reading, putting down her copy of the Psychoanalytic Quarterly – .

She laughs.

PAULA. No, Melitta –

MELITTA. No. Or maybe her Country Life –

PAULA. Or Vogue!

They both giggle.

MELITTA. Or Lilliput!

Both giggle hysterically.

MELITTA. She'll climb into bed –

PAULA. No, berth!

MELITTA. What?

PAULA. Berth, you know, the – .

MELITTA. Berth, that's right, she'll take her corsets off –

Both giggle furiously.

– then up she climbs and –

PAULA. – does her nightie up to her chin –

Both collapse with laughter.

MELITTA. And then she reads – she reads –

PAULA. 'You cow, you murderess – '

MELITTA. No no no – it's worse that that – .

PAULA. 'Bitch, you killed him – !'

They slowly stop giggling. Then one of them starts giggling again, and both collapse with laughter but this time with a sense of guilt. They stop.

Pause. They share a handkerchief, wipe their eyes.

Maybe she won't believe it.

MELITTA. She's not stupid.

PAULA. No.

MELITTA. It'll kill her.

PAULA. Yes it very likely will.

MELITTA. Except she could have left it here. It could be in this room.

They gaze round the room.

PAULA. What was the book you thought I'd moved?

MELITTA. 'The Interpretation of Dreams'.

PAULA *stands up.*

PAULA. That seems significant.

Goes to the bookshelf. Removes the book and takes the keys out.

I thought so. Catch.

She throws them across the room. MELITTA *catches them.*

PAULA. Have a look.

MELITTA *opens the filing cabinet.*

MELITTA. You keep watch.

PAULA. Who for?

MELITTA. Parental super-egos, darling. Do it.

She unlocks the filing cabinet.

PAULA (*whispers*). Go on.

MELITTA *opens the top drawer to its fullest extent. The cabinet topples forwards into her arms. She struggles to push it back.* PAULA *runs to help her.*

MRS. KLEIN *comes in, dressed for travel as last seen.*

MRS. KLEIN. Melitta?

MELITTA. Mother?

MRS. KLEIN. Paula, you're a big strong girl, if you could help the taxi fellow.

PAULA *goes out.*

MRS. KLEIN. So: I'm back.

MELITTA. What happened?

MRS. KLEIN. Aren't you pleased to see me? Give your
mother a kiss.

They kiss.

MRS. KLEIN. Look in your handbag, I've no money, only
marks and travellers' cheques.

MELITTA *does.*

It's wonderful you're here my darling. Stay the night. Your
room's the same. I've kept it as it was. Some books are new,
some boxes, half a billiard-table, as a matter of fact it's
packed with rubbish. Stay.

PAULA *comes in with luggage.*

PAULA. One more bag to come. He wants his fare.

MRS. KLEIN. I'm not surprised, he's just got married. To a
nice Irish girl, he tells me, and they have some minor sexual
problems but I think I've helped him. (*To* MELITTA.)
How're we doing?

MELITTA. I've got a shilling.

MRS. KLEIN. That's no good, the fare is four and ninepence.

MELITTA. Paula's got some money, haven't you Paula?

MRS. KLEIN. Thank you Paula.

PAULA *crouches and looks round the floor for the money
from the pinbox.*

PAULA. Sorry it must have rolled.

MRS. KLEIN (*to* MELITTA). What's she up to?

PAULA. Got it.

MRS. KLEIN. Quite a party you've been having.

PAULA *gives her the two half-crowns.* MRS. KLEIN *takes
more money off* MELITTA.

MRS. KLEIN. Sixpence for the tip, that's five and thruppence. Off you go now.

PAULA *goes.*

MELITTA. Did you get my letter?

MRS. KLEIN. Later. What's she doing here?

MELITTA. Working late.

MRS. KLEIN. I wish she'd go. She found the keys I notice. And the whisky. Make me a cup of tea. I need to make a note of something, personal, not unpleasant. Turn the heating on.

MELITTA *goes out.* MRS. KLEIN *gets her notebook. Loosens her shoes. Takes hat off.* MRS. KLEIN *puts a record on. Slow movement, Haydn, Quartet in C, Op. 54 No. 2.*

Interlude

Not very long but marks a pause longer than a usual dip in the action. MRS. KLEIN *makes notes. Listens to the music, cries. Wipes her eyes, shakes her head . Makes more notes. At some point* PAULA *comes in with a suitcase.*

MRS. KLEIN. I'm working.

PAULA *puts it down quietly and goes out.*

MELITTA *comes in with a tray of tea-things.*

End of Interlude.

MELITTA. Paula's sitting in the hall.

MRS. KLEIN. At least she's quiet.

MELITTA. Be nice to her.

MRS. KLEIN *goes to the door and calls through it.*

MRS. KLEIN. Paula, we've got an extra cup. Come in for a moment.

PAULA *does. They all sit.*

MRS. KLEIN. Now who is to be mother?

MELITTA. That's your job.

MRS. KLEIN. Do it! Paula has an Underground to catch.

MELITTA. She missed it hours ago.

MRS. KLEIN. So how's she getting home?

MELITTA. I'm driving her.

MRS. KLEIN. You can't, you're sozzled.

MELITTA. I am not!

MRS. KLEIN. I'm teasing you, my darling. Pour the tea.

MELITTA *pours tea.*

MRS. KLEIN. That's my girl. I've earned my rest. I am exhausted. But euphoric. Something wonderful has happened. Dover station. In the buffet, where I ate a cheese and pickle sandwich, quite disgusting, first I dozed and then I fell asleep. A wooden bench. A lucky bench because I dreamt on it.

She pauses, takes MELITTA*'s hand.*

I know this tea, it's kitchen tea, it comes from Mrs. Pountney's caddy, it's the nicest cup of tea I've ever tasted.

I saw a mother and her son. The son had either died or was about to die. The mother was dressed in black, her collar was white. I didn't feel sad to see them. I felt slightly hostile. So: I woke. And saw the boat-train just about to leave for London so I took it.

MELITTA. What about the boat?

MRS. KLEIN. The boat had left.

MELITTA. You missed it?

MRS. KLEIN. I decided not to take it.

PAULA. You resisted it?

MRS. KLEIN. Paula, look in the fridge, you'll find some nice salami.

PAULA *goes.*

MRS. KLEIN. I didn't like to say while she was here. It struck me just in time that I could not attend the funeral for an obvious reason.

MELITTA. What?

MRS. KLEIN. I might have met your father.

MELITTA. And?

MRS. KLEIN. He might have propositioned me.

MELITTA *breaks into surprised laughter.*

MRS. KLEIN. No good?

MELITTA. No good. Besides he's married.

MRS. KLEIN. Not that *that* would – . No you're right. There's something deeper. Deep resistance. Do me a favour, don't tell her. How long's she staying?

MELITTA. As long as I do.

PAULA *comes in with salami, plates and a knife.*

MRS. KLEIN. Paula you're staying the night. (*To* MELITTA.) Now where's she sleeping?

MELITTA. Sofa.

MRS. KLEIN (*to* PAULA) . Sofa.

MELITTA (*this is a routine they used to do in the past*) . So: this mother.

MRS. KLEIN. So this mother. Mother and son. A dying son.

MELITTA. Or dead.

MRS. KLEIN. Who told you dead?

MELITTA. Look at your notes.

MRS. KLEIN. No I believe you. But he wasn't Hans. Because the mother wasn't me. Because I felt hostility towards her. So I – .

PAULA. What about the dress?

MRS. KLEIN. Too much prompting. Find the salami. Dress, a dress, quite right, black dress white collar which I – . Which I'm wearing at this moment. So: a hint of my unconscious knowledge that it's I who is bereaved. So my denial is weakened. Only slightly. Quite a long way to go. (*Sees the salami.*) You found it, thank you.

Starts cutting it up.

In my childhood, in the summer, we would go on picnics. All the family. And my father used to sit on a stump and say to me: 'Melchen, darling, here's a nice thin piece of salami'. And he'd cut it.

She gives a thin piece to PAULA.

MRS. KLEIN. And he'd give it to me. Then he'd turn to my older sister, and he'd say: 'And now a nice thick slice of salami for my favourite daughter'.

She gives a thick piece to MELITTA. *Cuts more salami and gives it all to* MELITTA.

Now this, Melitta, was a learned man, a student of the Talmud, what was called a *bocher*, spoke in German, English, Slovak, French, he learned from some old chap who fought at the battle of Waterloo. And yet, unthinkingly, he stirred up envy in me.

PAULA (*wanting another piece of salami*) . Could I – .

MRS. KLEIN. – have a bath, of course.

MELITTA. It won't be hot yet.

MRS. KLEIN. True, it will be cool and healthy. (*To* MELITTA.) Run the taps.

PAULA. I'd rather – .

MRS. KLEIN. Fine, you do it yourself.

PAULA. I wonder if you'd mind if – .

MRS. KLEIN. Bathtime.

Goes out, leaving MRS. KLEIN *and* MELITTA *eating salami.*

MELITTA. Did you take my – ?

MRS. KLEIN. Have children.

MELITTA. Mother.

MRS. KLEIN. I'm broody. I want to be a nice warm bobba. I want to smell of cooking-oil and make-up. I want enormous corseted hips for little boys to throw their arms round.

MELITTA. Did you read my letter?

MRS. KLEIN. No.

MELITTA. I guessed you hadn't.

MRS. KLEIN. I'm sorry.

MELITTA. If you give it back I'll write you an up-to-date one.

MRS. KLEIN *gives* MELITTA *the keys and indicates the filing cabinet.*

MRS. KLEIN. Bottom drawer.

MELITTA *looks for her letter and finds it.*

MRS. KLEIN. The middle drawer contains my dealings with the world. It is my ego drawer. The top drawer is my super-ego drawer, it's full of tax reminders, bills for the rates, all those harsh commands which come from up on high. The bottom drawer is dark and filled with menace.

MELITTA. You put my letter in your id drawer!

MRS. KLEIN. Yes, who cares. Don't stand there like an idiot, darling, sit beside me.

MELITTA. Shouldn't I make the beds up?

MRS. KLEIN. They can wait.

MELITTA. She'll need a towel.

MRS. KLEIN. She'll find one. No, I locked them up. I locked the soap up. You should have seen me more these last few days. You missed some fine old symptoms. Sit.

MELITTA *does.*

MRS. KLEIN. That's better.

Pause.

MRS. KLEIN. In a moment, in the fridge, you'll find some nice Gewürztraminer.

MELITTA. Fine.

MRS. KLEIN (*of the letter*). What's in that letter?

MELITTA. Paula tells me you were hostile towards it.

MRS. KLEIN. I thought you were attacking my criminality paper. Quite absurd. I saw the address and – . Let me see it.

MELITTA *hands it to her.*

MRS. KLEIN. Yes, it was the way you'd underlined the 'Mrs'. *Mrs.* Klein. Like you're the learned doctor, I'm the uppity layman.

MELITTA. Show me.

MRS. KLEIN *gives it to her.*

MELITTA. That's a smudge.

MRS. KLEIN *takes it back. Looks.*

MRS. KLEIN. So who did this?

MELITTA. The postman probably.

MRS. KLEIN *puts glasses on, looks harder.*

MRS. KLEIN. There you are, I had a persecutory delusion. I felt my little torch of knowledge was being crapped on yet again, you'll pardon me, that's what it feels like when it happens. Though it isn't you I blame, my darling. Glover's the worst.

She slices off a piece of salami.

MELITTA. You mean the wurst.

MRS. KLEIN. The wurst, that's right. Yes, Glover's the wurst.

Playfully stabs the salami. Laughs.

Somebody told me Edward Glover took his Easter holiday inside a cloud. Right in one. With his wife and little backward daughter, whom he loves and takes wherever he goes, despite, or possibly because of her condition. So. They went to Scotland. Up a mountain. Right to the top. Set up camp and then the mist descended. So they couldn't leave their tent. But Edward Glover stuck to plan and stayed there for a fortnight, while his wife and daughter begged for mercy. Finally he upped their pegs and down the slope they walked and not a quarter of a mile below are sunny fields and rippling brooks and people in their bathing costumes. The weather was fine, there was a tiny cloud up there, that's all, and in his boring daddy's dogmatism he had spent his holiday inside it.

MELITTA *laughs.*

MRS. KLEIN. Perhaps you see less of him these days?

MELITTA. Rather more.

Pause.

MRS. KLEIN. You *will* attack my criminality paper.

MELITTA. Probably. Yes.

MRS. KLEIN. In the Journal?

MELITTA. Probably in the Journal. In the Journal.

MRS. KLEIN (*suddenly angry*). Why do you do this?

Pause.

What I write, I've learned and proved in twenty years of clinical practice. And you've seen the results.

MELITTA. I have. You're a great clinician. But Mother, you can't write rubbish and expect me not to say it's rubbish.

MRS. KLEIN. No I don't, because I know you see the so-called rubbish, 'dreck' you called it once, the *poisonous faeces*, aimed at you in person. I can see it, everyone else can see it. It's an embarrassment. Why exhibit your sores in public, darling?

MELITTA. Sores?

MRS. KLEIN. Yes sores, emotional sores. If I fought back you'd see some dreck all right. I could finish your career. Only I won't attack my daughter.

MELITTA (*suddenly angry, shouts*). No, you get your little toadies to attack your daughter.

MRS. KLEIN. I don't write papers for my fellow thinkers.

MELITTA. You'll do anything to win. You'll pack committees, you'll fiddle agendas, you'll steal other people's patients.

MRS. KLEIN. When did I steal a patient? Whose damn patient?

MELITTA. Mine last month.

MRS. KLEIN. He begged for refuge. You'd confused him. You're a bad clinician.

MELITTA. Why?

MRS. KLEIN. You want the truth? Good, fine. You reassure your patients. When they cry you hug them. And you say their clouds have silver linings and you give them tips on life. What can they learn from that about themselves? All they learn is that you're nice to them, which as a matter of fact you aren't, you're bloody destructive.

Take that patient. All his life, like everyone else, like you, like me, like all the world, he has projected his infant experiences on to the people around him. But it's only now, with me, he starts to see them. Now, in that powerful, terrifying thing we call the transference. Because, unlike his wife or child or you, I am detached. So the *screen*, as it were, is blank. And he projects and sees, *on me*, those images from his cradle. You obscured that screen with your emotions. You felt pity. And you felt protective. Rubbish.

Dreck, dreck, dreck. If you want to be an analyst of any worth you have to trust your patients with the truth. However harsh. They're strong. They'll take it.

MELITTA *gives her her letter.*

MRS. KLEIN. What is it?

MELITTA. It's the truth about Hans.

Goes out.

End of Act One.

ACT TWO

Later.

MRS. KLEIN *and* PAULA. PAULA *is on the sofa.*

MELITTA*'s letter, unopened. A bottle of wine.*

Pause.

MRS. KLEIN. Where's Paula?

PAULA. I'm Paula. Melitta's upstairs. She's having a bath.

MRS. KLEIN *pours wine for them both.*

MRS. KLEIN. I've had two great depressions in my life. One when I was an angry housewife. One in Berlin when nobody paid enough attention to me. Now number three is looming. I can see it. Like a thick black line just over my field of vision.

She opens MELITTA*'s letter. Glances at a page.*

Should I read Melitta's letter?

PAULA. Perhaps not now.

MRS. KLEIN. Quite right.

She tears it up. Throws the bits of paper in the waste-paper-basket.

Pause.

Deep depression.

Pause.

MRS. KLEIN. So. my dream.

PAULA. Your mother and son.

MRS. KLEIN. *This* mother and son. And the associations ran as follows. Picnic, father, sibling envy, Battle of Waterloo. That's hopeless. Battle of – .

Pause.

Homework. I think I'm getting somewhere. Brother's homework.

Pause.

There is a nasty woman comes to mind who brought her equally nasty son to help my brother with his homework. I was twelve. It seems to me that mother and son was them.

PAULA. Why dream about them now?

MRS. KLEIN. Because I never forgot that evening. It was horrible, frightful. Everybody was upset. My mother was in tears, my brother rushed into his room and slammed the door, I could have killed them both.

PAULA. For being upset?

MRS. KLEIN. Because they – . No, not *them*. This woman and – .

She registers the misunderstanding.

I'm feeling worse now. Like the ceiling's getting lower. Say something, anything.

PAULA. I have a dream in which the ceiling's getting lower.

MRS. KLEIN. Tell me, it can't be worse than what's going on up here.

PAULA. There's a small girl. But she's older than me. She's moving her dolls round the floor. She makes me feel uneasy. And the roof keeps sinking. Suddenly a little door flies open and she – .

MRS. KLEIN. Ssh. She's coming down.

MELITTA *comes in carrying bed clothes.*

MELITTA. I've come to say good night. If we're still talking to each other.

MRS. KLEIN. We're still talking.

MELITTA. Did you open it this time?

MRS. KLEIN. Yes I did.

MELITTA. And how do you feel?

MRS. KLEIN. I feel severe depression coming on, but I'll survive it.

MELITTA. Good. I mean, that you'll survive it.

MRS. KLEIN. I'll survive it.

MELITTA. No hard feelings?

MRS. KLEIN. Not on a conscious level.

MELITTA. I was sitting in the Wigmore Hall tonight and thought about it and I – .

MRS. KLEIN. Let's not talk about it now. All right?

MELITTA. All right.

MRS. KLEIN. And so.

MELITTA. And so. Did you really mean to get there?

MRS. KLEIN. Where?

MELITTA. To Budapest.

MRS. KLEIN. It seems unlikely.

MELITTA. But you would have done. If I'd gone with you. If I'd dragged you.

MRS. KLEIN. If you'd dragged me, yes I might have.

MELITTA (*to* PAULA) . We used to live in a flat quite near the castle. Big tall shutters. Always dark inside. (*To her mother.*) We could have gone to see it. We could have gone to the Hotel Gellert for coffee and cakes. I could have cheered you up.

MRS. KLEIN. That's not your metier.

Pause.

MELITTA (*to* PAULA). Two sheets. Three blankets. Say if you want an extra pillow. Would you rather sleep upstairs?

PAULA. The couch is fine.

MELITTA. The sofa.

PAULA. What?

MELITTA. The couch comes next week. Or haven't you asked her yet?

MRS. KLEIN. If you mean that Paula wants to be my patient, I had guessed as much. She'll ask me in her own good time and I'll consider it then. Good night.

MELITTA. Good night.

PAULA. Good night.

MRS. KLEIN. Melitta.

MELITTA. Yes?

MRS. KLEIN. Don't turn the heating off.

MELITTA. I wasn't going to. 'Night.

She goes.

PAULA. That was tactless of her.

MRS. KLEIN. She'll be back.

MELITTA *comes back in.*

MELITTA. What about my letter?

MRS. KLEIN. It's the middle of the night for God's sake. I've been travelling. I'm depressed. I'm in mourning.

MELITTA. So am I.

MRS. KLEIN. So what do you want, to bully me about it? Give me time.

MELITTA. We'll talk about it over breakfast.

MRS. KLEIN. Maybe.

PAULA. If she doesn't want to read it then she shouldn't have to.

MELITTA. If she – .

MRS. KLEIN. *That* was tactless.

MELITTA. But she said she had. She said – .

MRS. KLEIN. If I may clarify? I opened it and Paula told me not to read it so l tore it up. Something's being resisted.

MELITTA. Yes it is!

MRS. KLEIN. But what?

MELITTA. I'll tell you.

MRS. KLEIN. Good, you tell me. Well?

PAULA. I'll go upstairs.

MRS. KLEIN. I want you here.

MELITTA. Why can't we talk about it just we two?

MRS. KLEIN. Because there's no such thing as just we two. There's always a third. At least a third. The mother. Perhaps the father, perhaps a rival sibling. Always the room fills up. Start with two, why not with three? Either way we'll end up throwing a party. Good, let's start.

MELITTA. Last Friday Hans was – .

MRS. KLEIN. In your opinion Hans's death was not what it appeared. I read that far.

MELITTA. He left the – .

MRS. KLEIN. Then the ceiling started moving so I stopped.

MELITTA. Mother, listen.

MRS. KLEIN. Yes? Go on. Go on.

MELITTA. Last Friday Hans left the boarding-house where he was staying in Rosenberg.

MRS. KLEIN. Not Rosenberg my dear. You're stuck in the past. It was Rosenberg when you and he lived there as children. After the war the name was changed. It's called Ruzomberok. Which means the same. One moment please.

She pauses and puts her hand over her eyes.

Well?

MELITTA. He left the boarding-house – .

MRS. KLEIN. You think of it as Rosenberg because the name evokes a time of primitive content. Before all this. My presence gave you warmth and comfort.

MELITTA. You were hardly ever there.

MRS. KLEIN. I wasn't well. And so the doctor did what doctors do, prescribed a holiday and then another, then a rest-cure and they all joined up.

MELITTA *laughs.*

And you were cared for by your bobba. Who was God's own housewife. She was a saint on earth as long as she was not one's mother. That was my little problem and I failed to solve it and I got depressed.

MELITTA. You could have written.

MRS. KLEIN. The way I felt I'd have depressed you too.

MELITTA. You missed my birthday.

MRS. KLEIN. Oh, so now we're get to the momentous crisis. I missed your birthday and you're scarred for life.

MELITTA. I am. Not just –

MRS. KLEIN. And maybe the cat jumped on your cradle so now you can't drink milk. Melitta that is popular psychiatry, it's rubbish, it's for chambermaids. So you had a bad experience, rise above it. Take it to your analyst, she's good, I like her. Where'd we got to. Yes: he left the boarding-house and – . Let me tell you something. I would walk you to the square. And find a bench. When you were five or six, a difficult age, and Hans was three. I'd buy you ice-creams and I'd introduce you to the pigeons. And I'd watch the fountain. And I'd sit and wait to go back home where Mother would have staked her claim to Jewish motherhood by cooking a five-course dinner. And I'd feel despair. That this was it. My life. My waste of life. So I escaped. And don't think you've got cause to feel resentful. You've a doctorship, a fine career and if you choose to throw it away

that's your decision. Now: he travelled to the mountains.
How?

MELITTA. He took the bus. He bought a single ticket.

MRS. KLEIN. No that doesn't make sense. To get the special
rate you buy two tickets, one to get there, one to – . Has the
system changed?

MELITTA. He wasn't coming back.

MRS. KLEIN. I'm confused. Paula, explain.

PAULA. He – .

MELITTA. Mother, what do you think I'm trying to tell you?

MRS. KLEIN. What?

Pause.

You mean he – ?

Pause.

And this is how you spring it on me?

MELITTA. Mother – .

MRS. KLEIN. Let me say: his recent letters gave no cause for
worry. He was well and happy. Two weeks ago he wrote to
tell me all about a Cossack costume which he'd put together
for a party. Boots from somebody at work, the hat from – .
Two whole pages. Quite a tedious letter. But it doesn't seem
a likely one from someone who's about to kill himself.

MELITTA. He was – .

MRS. KLEIN. Wait, wait, wait. How do you know he only
bought a single ticket?

MELITTA. The return half wasn't in his pockets.

MRS. KLEIN. How do you know?

MELITTA. Aunt Jolan searched them.

MRS. KLEIN. And you rang her up? That says something.

MELITTA. Can I go on?

MRS. KLEIN. I'm here, I have no patients waiting.

MELITTA. Only Paula.

MRS. KLEIN. Paula's listening, Paula's fine. Continue.

MELITTA. He was wearing ordinary weekday shoes, not climbing boots.

MRS. KLEIN. I hear you.

MELITTA. He'd taken nothing to read.

PAULA. This is ridiculous.

MRS. KLEIN. Let her go on. She needs it. Well?

MELITTA. He took nothing to eat.

MRS. KLEIN. So there's a restaurant in the mountains.

MELITTA. He ate breakfast there. He left a tip. He gave the waiter all his change. He'd nothing left.

MRS. KLEIN. No banknotes?

MELITTA. No.

MRS. KLEIN. His wallet?

MELITTA. Empty.

PAULA. They could have robbed the body.

MRS. KLEIN. I hadn't visualised him as a – . It might be better if you keep your comments to yourself. (*To* MELITTA:) Go on.

MELITTA. They found him at the foot of the cliff which looks back over Ruzomberok.

MRS. KLEIN. Ah.

MELITTA. Do you know it?

MRS. KLEIN. No, I – . No.

MELITTA. It's a beauty-spot. Sunday trippers stop to use the telescope. We went there often, he and I, as children. There's a river-bed below. We used to stand on the edge when bobba wasn't looking. Trying to make our stomachs churn. He knew it well. He'd seen it a hundred times. So why go back?

PAULA. Why not? A favourite place, why not go back? He didn't feel like climbing. That's why the shoes were wrong. No book. Was he a student?

MRS. KLEIN. He was a chemist in a paper-mill.

MELITTA. Hans went nowhere on his own without a book. That's what he was like. Except when he was fourteen, when you stopped him.

MRS. KLEIN. Stopped my son from reading books, darling that would be unique in Central Europe.

MELITTA. Mother you did.

MRS. KLEIN. I don't recall it and I don't believe it.

MELITTA. You told him the books were symptomatic of his hero-worship for his father. So he stopped.

MRS. KLEIN. He stopped himself.

MELITTA. You stopped his music lessons.

MRS. KLEIN. I did not, he stopped attending them. I went on paying for weeks since nobody told me.

MELITTA. He stopped because you told him that wanting to play the violin was a repressed masturbation fantasy.

MRS. KLEIN. It sounds extreme because you've isolated it.

MELITTA. You even stopped him being in love.

MRS. KLEIN. This is cheap.

MELITTA. He loved a boy at school. You broke them up.

MRS. KLEIN. If Hans were truly homosexual I'd have accepted it. Although I might not like it. But he isn't, wasn't. And that boy was miles beneath him.

MELITTA. Then that actress, and you said she was a mother-figure with a penis.

MRS. KLEIN. Did you see her?

MELITTA. Then that very decent Polish girl. You stopped that too, you said she interfered with the analysis.

MRS. KLEIN. She did. That summer we were getting nowhere, then her father was transferred, she left town and we made good progress.

PAULA. Who was 'we'?

MRS. KLEIN (*to* MELITTA). So, tell her.

MELITTA. My mother analysed Hans for three hundred and seventy hours from the time he was thirteen to the age of sixteen and a half. She analysed us both. We were her first patients. She wrote us up. I'm Lisa in 'The Role of School in Libidinal Development'. Remember? How does it go? 'She has so far (she is now fifteen) shown only an average intelligence'. That was me. That's what's she wrote about me.

MRS. KLEIN (*to* PAULA). It seemed important to remain detached.

MELITTA. But Mother.

Pause.

MRS. KLEIN. Yes I know.

PAULA. She was your daughter.

MRS. KLEIN. Yes.

Pause.

MELITTA. I'd lie there trying to think up what to say to her. Trying to think of something so banal, so ordinary that she couldn't interpret it. My history lesson. 'What's history about?' she'd ask me. In her clinical voice. My mother in her clinical voice, imagine. I'd say: 'Oh, history lessons, that's what people did in ancient times, battles and so on.' She'd say: 'What happened in ancient times is you, the infant, seeing your father and me having sexual intercourse. That's the battle.' It sounds absurd. It wasn't. That was the worst of it: she's so damn good. I felt that slotting into place, the snap, the 'Yes, that's right'. And I'd be stuck

with a horrible truth about myself I couldn't deal with.
She used to light her cigarette, her special way, the match
pushed forward so the sparks shot into my lap. That was
my hatred flying back. The carved brown cabinet stood
there waiting my command to fall and crush her. Or the
mat to trip her up. She spilled the ashtray. Muck on the
varnished floor. My vengeful shit. All that was good,
destroyed. My mother destroyed. My fault. My guilt.

MRS. KLEIN. I did good work.

MELITTA. And the results?

MRS. KLEIN. You're not so bad. It's Dr. Schmideberg I'm not
too fond of.

MELITTA. I'm Dr. Schmideberg. Can't you understand?

MRS. KLEIN. I'm Melanie Klein.

Pause.

Is there more about Hans?

MELITTA. Yes. Somebody saw him.

MRS. KLEIN. When he – ?

MELITTA. No. Before. The Lutheran pastor in Ruzomberok.
Jolan told me. They're old friends. She trusts him.

MRS. KLEIN. Well?

MELITTA. He was waiting for a train first thing that morning.
He was on the platform at the station. And he noticed Hans.

MRS. KLEIN. The railway station?

MELITTA. Yes. The pastor asked him where he was going.
Hans said, to Budapest. The pastor said, good, we'll travel
together. Hans said no. He said he wanted to smoke. He
seemed nervous. The pastor said, is something wrong? Hans
said no. The pastor didn't believe him.

MRS. KLEIN. Why was Hans going to Budapest?

MELITTA. To see Aunt Jolan. So he said.

MRS. KLEIN. Go on.

MELITTA. He asked the pastor to forgive him.

MRS. KLEIN. Is there more?

MELITTA. He hoped the pastor wouldn't be shocked by
something he might hear about him. He said he was sure
that what he was doing was right.

MRS. KLEIN. That's all?

MELITTA. That's all.

MRS. KLEIN. So he planned to go to Jolan perhaps to find
some comfort in her.

MELITTA. But he changed his mind. He never caught the
train.

MRS. KLEIN. He went to the square and caught the bus. Yes,
that feels right. I see it.

Pause.

Will it affect the place of burial?

MELITTA. No.

MRS. KLEIN. Because they – ?

MELITTA. Nobody knows what happened.

MRS. KLEIN. Just us. That's good.

About to pour herself another glass. To MELITTA.

You'll have some now?

Pours a glass. MELITTA *accepts it.*

MRS. KLEIN. What none of us cares to ask is why a healthy,
reasonably happy man of twenty-seven should – . Paula,
you're too polite to ask. (*To* MELITTA.) You're too
defensive. I'm too frightened. No I'm damn well not.

PAULA. None of us knows he – .

MRS. KLEIN. We know.

PAULA. He didn't leave a message.

MRS. KLEIN. He did. Though it was probably unconscious. It was meant for me. He chose a place which looks across the valley towards Ruzomberok. Rosenberg. Rose mountain. The breast. Now that's indicative. When Hans was an infant, what was the first pre-occupation of his ego?

PAULA. The breast.

MRS. KLEIN. The breast. The breast on to which the child projects the warmth and goodness which he feels. The good breast.

And its opposite. When the child is angry, envious. When the child's anticipation turns from love for the good-but-yet-to-come, to hate for the good which seems so miserly with its goodness. This is the breast the infant, in its primitive mind, attacks. Tramples, kicks, annihilates. Pinches, mangles, gnaws, tears apart. Devours. Pierces. Poisons with imagined faeces. And in short, destroys by all the means which infant sadism can devise. This is the breast on to which the child projects – projects – his murderous hatred. So that the breast itself seems hateful. Vengeful. Mercilessly cruel. The bad breast. And the prototype for adult fear and dread.

You'll have some more?

Pours wine.

No wish to boss you about my dear, but you'll be very little help to your neurotic patients till you lead them by the hand back to that primitive jungle. Which is wild and strange as only a jungle can be. And *illimitably* rich. You can do it. You've had a child. (*Of* MELITTA:) She has problems in this area, no, she knows my feelings, I can say this.

MELITTA, *unnoticed by her mother, starts to cry.*

It's when the infant recognises you that something new occurs. He starts the greatest struggle in human life. He sees his mother as a person. Good and bad together. She, whom he's been torturing in his mind, is the one he loves. This is the dawn of guilt. It leads to fathomless depression. It is out of that depression he must climb in order to become a healthy adult. And it's hard. It hurts. To see what we've

done to the one we love, it hurts, it hurts. (*To* MELITTA:)
Don't drink.

She removes something from MELITTA*'s glass with the tip
of her finger.*

Piece of cork. It's gone. Now you're in tears. You wanted to
hurt the wicked mother. Now you find she's also the good
and loving mother. Hurt the one, you hurt them both,
darling I am one and the same. You cry. That's good. If I
could cry like that I'd be a happy woman.

MELITTA. It isn't true. There are bad mothers. Mothers who
are totally bad. You're one. We never felt you loved us. You
were interested in us, that's all. But we loved you. He loved
you terribly, terribly. And you could never accept his love.
You always changed it. Made it yours. Everything had to be
yours. Whatever we did, whatever we had, whatever we
wanted. You'd make us think it wasn't really happening, or
we didn't like it. Or you'd choose it for us. Anything. A
dress in a shop, a train-set, my degree.

MRS. KLEIN. I chose your husband?

MELITTA. I was compensating.

MRS. KLEIN. Quite.

MELITTA. I was neurotically dependent on you.

MRS. KLEIN. So you made a break for freedom.

MELITTA. Yes I bloody well did.

MRS. KLEIN. What's interesting is that you chose a man my
age. A mother-substitute. And what a disaster he turned out
to be. A drunk, a fool. You fled from bondage into bondage.
And you always will as long as you are crippled by your
unresolved ambivalence towards me. So, resolve it. I can't.
Nobody can but you. It's your job. Do it.

Pause.

The alternative is suicide. Either actual, as in Hans's case.
Or else, symbolic, which is how you're going at present.
And I can't lose any more children. Help me, darling.

Forget the Institute. Forget the rows, the meetings. That's for weekdays. Tonight you are in my house. We're mother and daughter. And I'm saying, Melitta, Melchen, dearest, sweetheart, what must we do to have a sensible, adult, mother-and-daughter friendship?

MELITTA. You don't want one.

MRS. KLEIN. How am I stopping it? What do you want? Or don't you trust me?

MELITTA. No.

MRS. KLEIN. Good, so now there's something solid we can start with. Set me a challenge. Try me.

MELITTA. I can't think what to say.

MRS. KLEIN. No rush. Make yourself comfortable, free-associate.

MELITTA *sits up straight.*

So do it your own way.

MELITTA. I'm driving down to Glyndebourne next week.

MRS. KLEIN. I'm listening.

MELITTA. It's 'Cosi'. I got the last two tickets. I was planning to go with Walter. Now you're back I still intend to go with Walter.

MRS. KLEIN. Good, he should enjoy it.

MELITTA. There are six teaspoons in the kitchen drawer, they used to –

MRS. KLEIN. Take them. Paula dear, this must be dull for you, I'm sorry.

MELITTA. I've bought a dinner-service. I chose it myself. It's Susie Cooper, polka-dots, I know you'll hate it.

MRS. KLEIN. This is superficial. When did either of us have our emotional homes in crockery departments. You're resisting something. Tell me.

MELITTA. There's a blanket in the boot of the car. It's mine. I want it.

MRS. KLEIN. You say the blanket but it's not the blanket.

MELITTA. I want the car. I want Sunny.

MRS. KLEIN. You *have* Sunny.

MELITTA. I have half of Sunny.

MRS. KLEIN. But you only paid for half.

MELITTA. I'll buy you out.

MRS. KLEIN. Though as things stand you have the use of Sunny whenever you ask.

MELITTA. I don't like asking.

MRS. KLEIN. So you want him to yourself.

MELITTA. That's right.

MRS. KLEIN (*thoughtful*). You think I can't be trusted not to damage the father's penis?

MELITTA. Mother, I do promise you, it isn't a penis. It's a 1927 Sunbeam. You say you let me use it. And you nearly always do. But when you can't, I feel irrationally resentful. And I think it would remove a source of tension between us if we did what adults mostly do, have cars of our own.

MRS. KLEIN. Good, fine.

MELITTA. I'll write you a cheque.

MRS. KLEIN. Not now, not now – .

MELITTA *writes a cheque.*

Well, as it suits you.

MELITTA *gives her the cheque.*

MELITTA. Two hundred and thirty-seven pounds ten shillings. That's half the cost less depreciation plus the licence.

MRS. KLEIN. Thank you.

MELITTA. As you see, I plan to stay in London.

MRS. KLEIN. That will be nice for me.

MELITTA. So you can stop persuading your eminent friends to buttonhole me at the Institute and tell me how much easier I might find it if I practised in New York.

MRS. KLEIN. They don't need my persuasion. People worry about you. New York is beautiful, the people are kind, demand is high, the fees are monstrous. I know the money-racket doesn't interest you but think of Walter. So we hoped you would consider it. Which you have. You choose to stay in London. As your mother I'm delighted. As your colleague I must warn you, I shall give no quarter. If your activities are inconsistent with your membership of the Society, I shall say so, so will others, you'll be forced to resign. You'll have to become some kind of therapist nonsense, thumping cushions with your patients. This may sound harsh, but it's the truth. Let's have things open and honest between us. As I know you want.

MELITTA. There's something else.

MRS. KLEIN. What?

MELITTA. I've changed my analyst.

Pause.

I said I –

MRS. KLEIN. I heard you.

Pause.

MRS. KLEIN. Just as you were getting somewhere. May I say, I think you're making a big mistake?

MELITTA. It's fine so far.

MRS. KLEIN. So far? So when did you start?

MELITTA. Three weeks ago.

MRS. KLEIN. I see. Of course I'm disappointed that you never thought to share your problem with me.

MELITTA. I discussed it with my analyst and decided not to.

MRS. KLEIN. You've rehearsed this conversation.

MELITTA. Yes.

MRS. KLEIN. I – . Yes quite right. Although it puts me in a strange position.

MELITTA. Me too.

MRS. KLEIN. What do I say to get her to take you back?

MELITTA *laughs.*

Is something funny?

MELITTA. Mother, I'm not going back.

MRS. KLEIN. Why not? You've made your gesture.

MELITTA. No.

MRS. KLEIN. You're adamant.

MELITTA. Yes.

MRS. KLEIN. And who've you gone to?

MELITTA. Edward Glover.

MRS. KLEIN *throws her wine at her.*

MRS. KLEIN. Drink that.

She grabs scraps of MELITTA's *letter out of the waste-paper-basket.*

Eat these. Eat these. I'll stuff them down your throat. Poisoner. Eat. Eat.

She hits and attacks MELITTA, *rubbing bits of paper into her face and hair.* MELITTA *doesn't resist.* PAULA *pulls her off.* MRS. KLEIN *sits, surprised by her actions.* MELITTA *sits.* PAULA *watches. Each of them ends up in a different part of the room from before.*

PAULA (*to* MELITTA): Melitta?

MELITTA. Leave me alone, the pair of you.

MRS. KLEIN. Why don't we all sit quietly for a moment. Just we three.

Pause.

I say we three. Though as a matter of fact we've quite a crowd collecting. (*To* MELITTA:) If you end up staying with Glover – . Which I don't advise. But if you do – .

MELITTA. Mother.

MRS. KLEIN. Listen. If you do. You'll need to watch the counter transference. Remember his backward daughter. Glover sees you as the brilliant child he's always wanted.

MELITTA. I'd thought of that.

MRS. KLEIN. Of course, of course.

Pause.

And you should ask yourself who he is.

MELITTA. Glover?

MRS. KLEIN. Yes, to you. Just think about it.

MELITTA. I can tell you now. It's been a good three weeks. I see him as the father you betrayed.

MRS. KLEIN. That's your perspective. Now I'll tell you why he hates my work. He sees me as the wanton mother casting aside the wonderful father Freud.

MELITTA. He could be right.

PAULA. Melitta is my dead sister.

MRS. KLEIN. Well we all knew that. She's also you: the unloved daughter.

PAULA (*to* MRS. KLEIN). Who was she to you, when you were trying to drown her in symbolic urine?

MRS. KLEIN (*with irony*). Well I can't imagine.

MELITTA. When she rubbed symbolic faeces in my hair. (*With irony.*) Yes that's a tough one.

MRS. KLEIN. Really, Paula.

Pause.

MRS. KLEIN (*to* MELITTA) . Though as a matter of fact I loved your bobba. I don't know why I got so nasty about her. All she was, was a typical bossy Central European Jewish mother. There are worse things. I hope. I see I can't amuse you.

MELITTA. Who was Hans?

MRS. KLEIN. My dream suggests as follows: that my envious triumph when my brother failed in something, just for once, was carried over into my feelings towards my son. I loved my son, but felt ambivalent towards him.

MELITTA. And you wished to harm him.

MRS. KLEIN. Wished it on some primitive level.

MELITTA. Primitive but effective.

MRS. KLEIN. So you think I killed him.

MELITTA. He killed you. He killed the you in him.

MRS. KLEIN. And why?

MELITTA. To punish it.

MRS. KLEIN. No this I can't go along with. He wished to save the me he loved from his sadistic onslaughts. So he killed them. And in doing so, killed himself. Now don't look blank, Melitta. Just because you never tried it. When did you save me from your sadistic onslaughts?

MELITTA. Mother, that's why I'm here. Hans died because he couldn't bring himself to hate you.

MRS. KLEIN. What about you, you can?

MELITTA. I can. I do.

MRS. KLEIN. Although there must be some ambivalence.

MELITTA. No. Not now.

MRS. KLEIN. You're saying you hate me pure and simple. Speak: I'm curious.

MELITTA. Yes.

MRS. KLEIN. Although we – sit and talk.

MELITTA. Never again.

She takes her key-ring out of her bag. Disentangles a single key.

MRS. KLEIN. No don't do that.

MELITTA (*holds them out*). My key.

MRS. KLEIN *looks at her cases.*

MRS. KLEIN. I shan't unpack tonight. Paula dear, you'll find a tiny bottle somewhere.

PAULA *looks in a case.*

And I'll need my nightdress.

MELITTA. I hung your blue one over the heater.

MRS. KLEIN. That was kind.

MELITTA. That's all it was.

MRS. KLEIN. I know.

Pause.

(*To* PAULA:) She was late, you know. Then finally I felt her pushing. In I went. And nothing. Nothing. Off you get, they said, we want the table. No, I cried, he' s – . He. She was my first-born. I said, I feel him coming. But they heaved me off and I went waddling towards the door. And out she dropped. Just dropped. While I was standing up. And how they laughed. They said – in a nice way – that's how cows have babies. You should call your baby Buttercup. I said: I'll call her little Melanie. Melitta.

She looks at her watch.

Half-past-six.

PAULA *gives her the little bottle.*

MRS. KLEIN. Thank you. My knockout drops.

PAULA *has also taken out an alarm-clock.*

MRS. KLEIN. Leave the alarm. I'll sleep in in the morning. Please don't wake me.

PAULA is about to help her with her coat.

MRS. KLEIN. I can manage.

She goes out.

PAULA. How do you feel?

MELITTA. The same. I'd love a slotting into place, or snap or something. Get some sleep. I'll dress and go. Ssh!

PAULA. What?

MELITTA. She hasn't closed her door yet.

They listen. They hear a very slight noise.

PAULA. There.

MELITTA. No that's the bathroom.

They listen.

When will you start? With her, I mean.

PAULA. She hasn't agreed.

MELITTA. She will.

PAULA. I need her.

MELITTA. Yes.

PAULA. I need her in all kinds of ways.

MELITTA. I know. I always knew it. In my cynical soul. I knew it the moment I saw you working at that desk.

She holds up a hand to stop PAULA replying. Listens, then goes out and upstairs.

PAULA finds the telephone number MRS. KLEIN gave her before leaving. Picks up the telephone, dials the operator.

PAULA. Hello. I want – . I'm sorry, I can't speak any louder. I want to make a call to Budapest. 92435. No, personal. Mrs. Jolan Vago. V.A. – . Yes, I'll wait.

Rings off. Picks up a book. MELITTA *comes in, dressed.*

MELITTA. You're up.

PAULA. You left your door-key.

MELITTA. I gave it back.

PAULA. She left it here.

MELITTA. She always does. I always take it. But it's different now.

Pause.

Except I always say it's different now. I tell you what. I'll wait till morning. And I'll see how it feels without.

PAULA. Without the key?

MELITTA. Without my mother. If it's fine, or not too bad or can be done without recourse to razors in the bath I'll – .

PAULA. What?

MELITTA. I'll write a book. And leave my husband. Have a child and go to China. In that order. But if not: I'll grovel down from Hampstead Garden Suburb in the morning at about eleven.

PAULA. Take the key.

MELITTA. I have my pride. I think I have my pride.

She picks the key up, then puts it down.

I have my pride. You do keep looking at the phone.

PAULA. I don't. Good night.

MELITTA. Good night.

MELITTA *goes out.* PAULA *starts making up her bed. The telephone rings. She answers quickly.*

PAULA. Mrs. Vago? ( ) Hello. I hope I haven't – . ( ) I'm calling from London, I'm a friend of Mrs. Klein's, I'm – . ( ) No I know she's not. She asked me to ring and tell you that she's very sorry but she won't be coming. ( ) Physically well but – . ( ) Yes she's very distressed. ( ) I will, Mrs.

Vago, there was something I wanted to – . ( ) Yes, a family
friend. ( ) Berlin. ( ) It is, yes, Mrs. Vago, there's a very
important question I must ask you.It's about Hans. ( )
I know she did, I – . ( ) I think you know. I think there's
something which you haven't told us. And I think you ought
to. ( ) She's upset already.

The alarm-clock goes off. PAULA *tries to turn it off while
still continuing the conversation. Can't find the switch.*

( ) No it's different here. ( ) It's just an alarm-clock, go on. ( )
I knew it. ( ) Yes. ( ) I see, and tell me about the wallet. ( )
And?

She turns the alarm-clock off.

She, won't she'll be relieved. You see, she thought he'd – .
No, it doesn't matter. ( ) Very expensive, yes. ( ) I'm sure
she will, perhaps later today, she's sleeping now. ( )
Likewise. ( ) God bless you too. Good-bye.

*She rings off. Sits and thinks for a moment or two. Turns off
the lights. She lies down on the sofa, covers herself with
blankets, still thoughtful. Closes her eyes.*

Music.

Time passes.

It is some hours later.

Cracks of daylight through the curtains.

PAULA *is still asleep.*

MRS. KLEIN *comes in. She wears a new dress. She goes
quietly and without turning lights on to the filing-cabinet.*

PAULA *wakes.*

PAULA. What time is it?

MRS. KLEIN. It's not eleven o'clock yet. Go back to sleep.

She rummages in the filing cabinet.

PAULA. I can't.

MRS. KLEIN. So: maybe it won't disturb you if I draw the curtains.

PAULA shakes her head. MRS. KLEIN draws the curtains. Bright spring day outside.

MRS. KLEIN. In my garden I have pigeons, blackbirds, finches, swifts and robins. And I sometimes hear an owl. I find this very reassuring for a London garden. Now you'll have some coffee?

PAULA. Thank you.

MRS. KLEIN. Don't get up.

MRS. KLEIN goes out. PAULA lights a cigarette. MRS. KLEIN comes back in with coffee. Gives it to PAULA, goes back to her files.

MRS. KLEIN. I'm hunting out my criminality paper. Since I fear it's in the firing-line. Now where've you got to, naughty fellow. Here.

Finds it.

There's something you could do. If you could stay till supper. Six o'clock. It's Hans's service then. We'll say a prayer in Hebrew. You remember any Hebrew?

PAULA. No.

MRS. KLEIN. Likewise. Too bad, we'll drink a glass of sherry maybe. What I must do before is make a difficult call to Jolan to explain my absence.

PAULA. I've told her.

MRS. KLEIN. What?

PAULA. I rang her up last night. I didn't wake you?

MRS. KLEIN. No you didn't but I'm wondering why you took it on yourself to trouble her?

PAULA. I did it for you. For you and Hans. I had to. Something didn't feel right. That letter about his Cossack costume. I recognised it. I've a mother and I write to her every week. She wants two pages or she'll think there's

something wrong. And so she gets them. But I can't exactly
tell her the truth about my life. It's too – .

MRS. KLEIN. Too what?

PAULA. It's mine. And so I fill it up with trivia. Just like he
did. He was hiding something. So I moved the material
round and found a different interpretation. And I felt that
snap, that 'yes'. And rang Mrs. Vago.

MRS. KLEIN. So, I'm listening.

PAULA. Hans had fallen in love.

MRS. KLEIN. In love?

PAULA. The woman's older – . Older than he was.

MRS. KLEIN. How much older?

PAULA. In her thirties. She's a singer. Jolan likes her. She
lives in Budapest. She has a husband there and children.
Two: a boy and a girl.

MRS. KLEIN. Surprise me. And?

PAULA. I understood it all. It's simple. Hans was meeting her
at the station. They planned to spend the Easter holiday
together. He was waiting on the platform and he saw the
pastor. He felt nervous.

So he lied: he said that he was going to Budapest, to see
Aunt Jolan, knowing the pastor knew her. He warned him
there'd be gossip. He asked him to forgive him. But he
wasn't ashamed: he knew that what he was doing was right.
The train came in. They took the bus. She put the tickets in
her handbag. He didn't bring a book or climbing boots.
Why should he? They breakfasted together and he left an
enormous tip; he wanted to impress her.

MRS. KLEIN. Why the mountains?

PAULA. They'd booked a room in the tourist hotel. He left his
money there. She took it back to Budapest and gave it to
Mrs. Vago. She said he'd gone for a walk. While she was
getting dressed. Mid-afternoon. She waited. Then she went

to find him, and she – . That was the first she knew. It seems he'd tried to find a path that isn't there now. And the ground had fallen away. That's all. That's all.

Pause.

MRS. KLEIN. What's interesting is that I feel intense resentment. Not of you, so much, you meant well. But this *woman*, who the hell was she, what's her name?

PAULA. I don't know.

MRS. KLEIN. A singer?

PAULA. Yes.

MRS. KLEIN. Opera? Cabaret?

PAULA. Mrs. Vago didn't tell me.

MRS. KLEIN. Had they – ? Yes, that afternoon you say.

Pause.

I cannot adjust to this. I can't accept it. (*Angry.*) What the hell are you trying to tell me, that he died by chance?

Pause. PAULA shocked and upset.

MRS. KLEIN. He never mentioned her. Not once, not once. Who are her parents?

PAULA. I didn't ask. Where she comes from, where they met. It's nothing to do with – .

Suddenly angry, shouts.

Don't you see? It's nothing to do with you, you stupid bloody woman. He was free.

MRS. KLEIN. No no. The facts remain the same – .

Pause. She crumples.

Oh God, I've lost him.

She starts to cry. Cries for a long time. After a bit she holds her hand out.

Come.

PAULA *holds her hand. After a bit* MRS. KLEIN *stops crying.*

MRS. KLEIN. Real tears. So my denial is *greatly* weakened. Yes, I'm starting to recover.

Pause.

I said the facts remained the same. Well, *certain* facts. My guilt remains. So does my wish to make amends. Now my appointment book is somewhere.

She finds it. Opens it.

MRS. KLEIN. This is what you want?

PAULA. It is.

MRS. KLEIN. Because you must be sure.

PAULA. I'm sure.

MRS. KLEIN *looks through her appointment-book.*

MRS. KLEIN. Where are we.

Looks upwards.

And the ceiling's moving upwards. I feel open. Easier. Tears, you know, are very much equated with excreta in the unconscious mind. Through tears the mourner eases tension, casts bad objects into the outside world. You know my fees?

PAULA. I do.

MRS. KLEIN. They're what's expected. You must decide to place that value on my time. And yours.

PAULA. I'll manage.

MRS. KLEIN. I can offer you Mondays, Wednesdays, Fridays, Saturdays. At eleven a.m. Now must I put these in my book, you tell me.

PAULA. Eleven o'clock is fine.

MRS. KLEIN *writes times in her book.*

PAULA. In fact we're late.

MRS. KLEIN. I beg your pardon?

PAULA. It's Saturday now. And look at the clock. We've lost five minutes.

MRS. KLEIN. My consulting-room is locked. And there's the stairs.

PAULA. Let's stay down here.

MRS. KLEIN. It's all too much, I'm utterly exhausted, not this morning. No.

PAULA. Please, Mrs. Klein.

MRS. KLEIN. I see. Very well. But from Monday we must be more formal.

PAULA lies on the sofa, pulls a blanket over her feet. MRS. KLEIN moves a chair into position.

MRS. KLEIN. And not the coffee please.

She removes the cup.

Pause. MRS. KLEIN sits.

MRS. KLEIN. Whenever you want.

She waits with a singular expression of alertness: her professional manner. Different from the way she's looked at any previous point in the play.

Pause.

PAULA. I'm worried about the doorbell.

MRS. KLEIN. You worry that if it rings I might abandon you.

PAULA. I know you won't. You told me yesterday. You said the world must wait.

Pause.

I know this isn't helpful, but I can't help thinking as an analyst. You feel guilty about your children.

MRS. KLEIN. Mm hm.

PAULA. You see the harm you've done.

MRS. KLEIN. Go on.

PAULA. You want to pay them reparation. But for one of them it's too late.

MRS. KLEIN. Mm hm.

PAULA. You want to pay Melitta reparation.

Pause.

You're doing so now.

Pause.

I terribly want you to reply to that.

MRS. KLEIN. You were afraid I'd left you.

PAULA. No. I felt content.

MRS. KLEIN. You felt – .

The doorbell rings. MRS. KLEIN *does not react to it.*

MRS. KLEIN. You feel perhaps that you've replaced Melitta as my daughter.

Doorbell.

PAULA. I have.

Doorbell.

MRS. KLEIN. Mm hm.

PAULA. I feel –.

MRS. KLEIN. I'm listening.

Doorbell.

End of Play.